Library of
Davidson College

Public Law and Public Policy

edited by
John A. Gardiner

The Praeger Special Studies program—utilizing the most modern and efficient book production techniques and a selective worldwide distribution network—makes available to the academic, government, and business communities significant, timely research in U.S. and international economic, social, and political development.

Public Law and Public Policy

PRAEGER SPECIAL STUDIES IN U.S. ECONOMIC, SOCIAL, AND POLITICAL ISSUES

Praeger Publishers New York London

Library of Congress Cataloging in Publication Data

Main entry under title:

Public law and public policy.

   (Praeger special studies in U.S. economic, social, and political issues)
   Includes bibliographical references.
   1. Public law—United States—Addresses, essays, lectures. 2. Public policy (Law)—United States—Addresses, essays, lectures. I. Gardiner, John A., 1937-
KF384.P8   342'.73   76-12851
ISBN 0-275-23320-0
ISBN 0-275-85750-6 student ed.

PRAEGER PUBLISHERS
200 Park Avenue, New York, N.Y. 10017, U.S.A.

Published in the United States of America in 1977
by Praeger Publishers, Inc.

789 038 987654321

All rights reserved

© 1977 by Praeger Publishers, Inc.

Printed in the United States of America

ACKNOWLEDGMENTS

This volume is an outgrowth of a series of panels presented at the 1976 annual meeting of the Midwest Political Science Association. In addition to the persons whose papers are included in this volume, I would like to thank those who, as panel chairpersons, presenters, and discussants, helped to focus the issues and ideas contained herein: Burton Atkins, Janice Bullens, Gillian Dean, Jerry Goldman, Stephen Halpern, Herbert Jacob, William Jenkins, William McLauchlin, Elinor Ostrom, Robert Roper, John A. Stookey, Susette Talarico, Edmond J. True, Stephen L. Wasby, Lettie M. Wenner, and Gordon Whitaker.

Chapter 9, "School Desegregation: A Cost/Benefit Longitudinal Analysis," previously appeared in the *American Politics Quarterly* and is reprinted by permission of the authors and Sage Publications, Inc.

Finally, I would like to thank Valerie G. Connor for her assistance in the preparation of the manuscript.

CONTENTS

	Page
ACKNOWLEDGMENTS	v
LIST OF TABLES AND FIGURES	xii
INTRODUCTION: THE ANALYSIS OF PUBLIC LAW POLICIES John A. Gardiner	xv

Chapter

1 PUBLIC POLICY AND THE FEAR OF CRIME IN LARGE AMERICAN CITIES
Wesley G. Skogan   1

    The Impact of Public Policies on Crime   3
    Sources of the Fear of Crime   6
    Implications for Crime-Control Policy   12
    Some Recommendations   15
    Notes   17

2 THE IMPACT OF DEFENDANT RACE IN TRIAL-COURT SANCTIONING DECISIONS
Thomas M. Uhlman   19

    The Metro City Criminal Court   20
    Alternative Explanations for Interracial Sentencing Disparities   27
        Criminality Component   27
        Class/Status Component   28
        Racism Component   30
    A Path Analysis of Metro City Data   31
    A Reduced Model   37
    Conclusions   40
    Notes   42
    References   48

Chapter		Page
3	ETHNOGRAPHY AND THE STUDY OF TRIAL COURTS Lynn M. Mather	52
	The Ethnography of Law	53
	Courts in the Wider Context of Dispute Resolution	57
	The Court Process	60
	Conclusion	62
	Notes	62
	References	63
✓ 4	ECONOMIC ANALYSIS OF CRIME AND THE CRIMINAL-JUSTICE SYSTEM Nicholas Elliott	68
	Theories of the Etiology of Crime	69
	The Economic Theory of Crime	71
	Methodological Implications	73
	The Economic Theory and Irrational Behavior	74
	The Impact of the Criminal-Justice System	78
	Empirical Tests of the Theory	79
	Problems with the Economic Theory of Crime	80
	The Assumption of Diminishing Returns	80
	Measuring Crime	81
	Future Applications	83
	Notes	85
✓ 5	DETERMINING THE IMPACT OF LEGAL POLICY CHANGES BEFORE THE CHANGES OCCUR Stuart Nagel Marian Neef	90
	Post-Impact Analysis versus Pre-Impact Analysis	90
	The Impact of Judicial-Process Changes on Plea-Bargaining Settlements	92
	Plea Bargaining as a Buying and Selling Transaction	92
	Relevant Judicial-Process Changes	93
	Implications for Improving Plea Bargaining and the Judicial Process	95
	The Impact of Jury Size on the Probability of Conviction	97
	Empirical Comparisons	97
	Deductive Comparisons	98

Chapter		Page
	Significance of the Analysis	100
	Additional Applications	102
	Other Examples	102
	Deduction and Induction Combined	103
	Notes	104
6	THE IMPLEMENTATION AND IMPACT OF JUDICIAL POLICIES: A HEURISTIC MODEL	
	Charles A. Johnson	107
	A Heuristic Model of Impact Phenomena	108
	A Review of Existing Research	114
	Theory and Impact Phenomena	122
	Notes	124
	References	124
7	JUDICIAL IMPACT AS A FORM OF POLICY IMPLEMENTATION	
	Lawrence Baum	127
	Judicial Impact and the Implementation Model	127
	The Study of Policy Implementation	130
	The Judicial-Impact Literature	131
	Empirical Research: Describing the Impact Process	132
	Theory-Building: Explaining the Implementation Process	133
	Future Directions in the Study of Judicial Impact	134
	Notes	136
✓8	WHEN COURTS SHOULD MAKE POLICY: AN INSTITUTIONAL APPROACH	
	Lief H. Carter	141
	Four Types of Questions about Judicial Policymaking	142
	Indicators of Institutional Policy Effectiveness	145
	Judicial Policy Effectiveness	148
	Further Illustrations: Five Easy Cases and Three Difficult Choices	149
	Conclusion	154
	Table of Cases	155
	Notes	156

Chapter		Page
9	SCHOOL DESEGREGATION: A COST/BENEFIT LONGITUDINAL ANALYSIS Harrell R. Rodgers, Jr. Charles S. Bullock, III	158

    Research Design for the Measurement and Explanation of Change   159
        Measuring Change—The Dependent Variable   159
        Theoretical Framework   161
        Independent Variables   164
    Research Findings   168
        Coercion   168
        Black Activity   168
        White Opposition   170
        Private Schools   171
        Superintendent Change   171
        Multivariate Analysis   172
    Summary and Conclusions   172
    Notes   173

| 10 | THE POLITICS AND ECONOMICS OF PHARMACEUTICAL REGULATION
David Seidman | 177 |

    The Regulatory Context   178
        The Market for Pharmaceuticals   178
        Pre-1962 Regulation   179
        Thalidomide   180
        Post-1962 Regulation   181
    Protection and Overprotection: The Dilemmas of Regulation   182
    Four Alternative Approaches   184
        Economics   184
        Medicine and the Drug Lag   186
        Pressures and Disasters   187
        Structure   189
    Reactions and Interactions   190
        The Nelson Hearings   190
        Reactions to Wardell   195
    Conclusions   197
        On Congress and Policy Analysis   197

Chapter		Page
	On FDA and Policy Analysis	199
	On the Potential Impact of Policy Analysis	200
	On Pharmaceutical Regulation	200
	References	201
✓11	THE ROLE OF STATE PLANNING IN THE DEVELOPMENT OF CRIMINAL-JUSTICE FEDERALISM Malcolm M. Feeley Austin Sarat Susan O. White	204
	The Provisions of the Safe Streets Act	206
	Understanding the Act	208
	Strategies of Implementation	216
	Revenue-Sharing Strategy	217
	The Cutting-Edge Strategy	218
	Centralized-Planning Strategy	220
	Conclusions	222
	References	223
12	THE POLICY IMPACT OF POLICY EVALUATION: SOME IMPLICATIONS OF THE KANSAS CITY PATROL EXPERIMENT Jeffrey Henig Robert L. Lineberry Neal A. Milner	225
	Notes toward a Theory of Experimental Impact	227
	On the Imponderability of Impact	230
	Why Impact is Imponderable	231
	Policy Content and Communication	231
	The Organizational Context	233
	The Political and Structural Context	234
	After the Experiment: The Case of Kansas City	235
	Avoiding the Confrontation of Unpleasant Findings	236
	Conclusion: On Evaluating Evaluations	238
	Notes	239
ABOUT THE EDITOR AND THE CONTRIBUTORS		243

LIST OF TABLES AND FIGURES

Table		Page
1.1	The Deterrability of Common Crimes	4
1.2	Victimization and the Fear of Crime	7
1.3	Personal Victimization and Perceptions of Safety	9
2.1	Independent Variables Included in the Metro City Data	21
2.2	Percent by Race of Defendants Convicted in Selected Crime Categories	23
2.3	Percent by Race of Defendants Jailed in Selected Crime Categories	25
2.4	Mean-Sentence Severity by Race in Selected Crime Categories	26
2.5	Variables Included in Race-Sentencing Path Model	35
2.6	A Reduced Race-Sentencing Model: Significant Pathways of Influence	39
2.7	An Operational Race-Sentencing Path Model: Simple Correlations	41
5.1	The Impact of Jury Size on the Probability of Conviction	101
9.1	Desegregation Changes: Indexes of Dissimilarity	162
9.2	Correlates of Desegregation Change: 1967-68 to 1970-71	169

Figure		Page
1.1	Determinants of the Fear of Crime	2
1.2	Robbery Rates and the Fear of Crime	14
2.1	Criminality Component	28
2.2	Class/Status Component	29
2.3	Racism Component	30
2.4	General Race-Sanctioning Model	31

Figure		Page
2.5	Race-Sanctioning Model, Including SES and Prior Record	32
2.6	Race-Sanctioning Model Where SES and Prior Record Remain Unmeasured	33
2.7	A Fully Defined Race-Sentencing Path Model	34
2.8	A Reduced Race-Sentencing Path Model	38
2.9	Criminality and Class/Status Linkages	46
2.10	Three-Variable Path Model	46
2.11	Time Sequences in the General Race-Sanctioning Model	47
4.1	Hypothetical Crime and Sanction Data	74
4.2	Data as the Result of the Interaction of Supply-and-Demand Functions	75
4.3	The Behavioral Impact of Increasing the Costs of Engaging in Illegal Activities under Differing Decision-Making Rules	76
4.4	The Impact of the Underrecording of Crime on Measuring the Relationship between Police Outputs and Crime	82
5.1	The Impact of Judicial Process Changes on Plea-Bargaining Settlements	94
6.1	A Heuristic Model of the Implementation and Impact Process	109
12.1	A Rough Diagrammatic Scheme of the Process of Experimental Impact	229

INTRODUCTION:
THE ANALYSIS OF
PUBLIC LAW POLICIES
John A. Gardiner

Since the late nineteenth century, U.S. scholars have maintained a strong interest in the field of public law. This interest is illustrated by the continuing popularity of courses covering legal theory and jurisprudence, the institutions of the legal system and the development of major constitutional doctrines, law and society, the legal profession, and so on. In recent years, research in public law has been supplemented by studies of the state and lower federal appellate courts, trial courts, and the myriad agencies, organizations, and individuals—police, prosecutors, lawyers, litigants, legislators, and interest groups—that interact with the courts. The doctrinal and institutional analysis perspectives of early research have been augmented by the tools of ethnography, sociology, psychology, economics, mathematics, and so on, generating a truly multidisciplinary body of literature describing and explaining the operations of our legal institutions.

The past few years have also seen the growth of a second body of literature, variously described as public policy, policy analysis, and policy evaluation. Supplementing prior research on the behavior of political actors and the processes by which political decisions are made, the public policy literature has emphasized two issues, each with long histories in social science research. The first goal of the public policy studies has been explanatory, to identify the sources of public policy in the inputs to and processes of various policymaking systems. The second goal is evaluative and prescriptive in nature, measuring the consequences of public policies and processes, and assessing those consequences against various stated or unstated policy goals and objectives. Furthering these goals, a large number of works have emerged focusing on the policymaking roles of various law-related institutions and on the impact of public programs in various law policy areas.

The chapters in this book bring together these two lines of research through analysis of a series of policy issues concerned with the field of law. Many assess existing literature in emerging research areas, identifying promising topics for future exploration. Others present original research illustrating the wide range of opportunities available to examine law policy issues. As is inevitable in new areas of research, these essays intermingle issues of research methodology and research findings, and readers are encouraged to consider additional applications of the approaches taken by these authors. Finally, because these 12 chapters are intended to illustrate a new, broad research area rather than focusing on precisely intermeshing segments of a discrete topic, they necessarily differ in their perspectives and consider a number of common issues. They are often provocative rather than definitive; it is hoped that they will serve to stimulate the interest of others concerned with related issues.

In Chapter 1, Wesley G. Skogan analyzes a matter of intense concern throughout the 1970s: crime in U.S. cities. Skogan distinguishes between actual rates of crime, public fear of crime (for example, leading to changing behavioral patterns to avoid victimization), and crime as an issue on various political agendas. He then analyzes recent survey data to assess the extent to which public policies can reduce crime rates and/or fear rates, and concludes that some more precisely targeted programs offer more promise of impact for the public than the scatter-gun programs and promises now generated by criminal-justice agencies. Skogan emphasizes that different crimes in fact threaten different populations and are responsive to (or immune from) different public policies; even where agencies can do nothing to affect the occurrence of crime, Skogan feels that much can be done to ameliorate unwarranted fears of crimes, focusing available citizen and agency activities on those crimes that in fact can be reduced and using other resources to assist those who have already suffered victimization.

In Chapter 2, Thomas M. Uhlman analyzes an issue that has been widely debated but seldom satisfactorily documented, the degree to which minorities are treated differently than whites in urban trial courts. Using data on convictions, proportions sentenced to jail, and length of prison sentences in "Metro City," he argues that defendant race is significantly related to sanctioning outcomes. The explanatory value of race vis-a-vis other components in a detailed path-analytic model differs, however, between conviction decisions and sentence decisions. Uhlman concludes that variations in prior criminal record are a significant source of variations in sanctioning, but that institutional racism nevertheless plays an independent role in criminal-justice decisions.

As indicated earlier, recent social science research related to public law has moved beyond the doctrinal and institutional approaches that characterized early studies. In Chapter 3, Lynn M. Mather reviews the ethnographic literature, illustrating the utility of ethnomethodology in understanding the various participants and processes in trial courts. Nicholas Elliott surveys developments in economic analysis of crime and criminal justice issues in Chapter 4. The hypothesis that offenders and potential offenders react to the perceived risks and benefits of criminal behavior, Elliott argues, is a useful basis for the analysis of criminal justice system policy issues. Stuart Nagel and Marian Neef, authors of Chapter 5, give several examples of opportunities for deductive analysis of legal policy issues, arguing that in many situations the impact of a potential policy change can be predicted prior to its adoption by the application of empirical premises derived from related policies. After summarizing the deductive approach, they apply it to the issues of plea bargaining and jury size.

The next three chapters address the role of courts in the development and implementation of public policy in the United States. In Chapter 6, Charles A. Johnson reviews the expanding literature on the impact of judicial decisions. Working toward a heuristic model of judicial impact, Johnson articulates an interrelated set of concepts, distinguishing the reactions of various populations directly or indirectly affected by court actions. In Chapter 7, Lawrence Baum reconceptualizes the problem of judicial impact in terms of a set of theories dealing with policy implementation; the similarities between administrative and judicial policy processes suggest the feasibility of developing general theories of policy development and implementation that will also facilitate identification of the unique characteristics of different types of decision makers. In Chapter 8, Lief H. Carter undertakes the task of asking what role courts should play in policymaking. With a focus on the constitutional-interpretation functions of the U.S. Supreme Court, Carter argues that the Court as an institution possesses particular capacities and incapacities that render some policy issues more appropriate for its attention than others. An understanding of the political, informational, and technological attributes of various policy problems, he concludes, will assist judges in deciding when and where they can effectively participate in the policymaking process.*

The final four essays in this volume focus directly on the politics of policy development in various law issues. Harrell R. Rodgers, Jr., and Charles S. Bullock, III look at school desegregation in Chapter 9. Applying a number of the theoretical arguments introduced in Chapters 6 through 8, they seek to identify the factors that have influenced local acceptance or rejection of Supreme Court decisions. Conceptualizing the decision to comply with desegregation mandates in terms of a calculation of the relative utilities of compliance and noncompliance (comparable to the crime analyses of Elliott in Chapter 4), Rodgers and Bullock conclude that compliance most frequently followed sustained federal coercion, producing fears among local officials that outweighed local segregationist sentiment. Chapter 10 shifts the scene to administrative policymaking, for example, the regulation of pharmaceuticals by the Food and Drug Administration (FDA). David Seidman traces the dilemmas that are inherent in this area of legal policy, since any policy necessarily represents an uncertain trade-off between the risks of injury to some drug-takers and the benefits of better health for others. The arguments as to where the line should be drawn between protection and overprotection unfold repeatedly within the FDA, before congressional committees, and among various segments of the research community.

Chapter 11 continues the emphasis on policy implementation with an analysis of state response to the Safe Streets Act of 1968, which provides federal funding for state and local crime and criminal-justice programs. Malcolm Feeley, Austin Sarat, and Susan O. White describe the various interpretations that state planning agencies have put on their Law Enforcement Assistance Administration (LEAA) roles and the conflicts that emerge between local perspectives (LEAA is simply to provide funds that will be used wherever localities choose) and national goals (the LEAA program is designed to reduce crime and improve criminal justice, therefore funds must be committed to the most innovative and

---

*The Supreme Court's cautious approach in cases decided during the summer of 1976, in prescribing legitimate conditions for imposition of the death penalty, is consistent with Carter's analysis.

effective programs available). Finally, in Chapter 12, Jeffrey Henig, Robert L. Lineberry, and Neal Milner confront one of the most perplexing issues in applied social research: When will policymakers make use of the information provided for them? Chapters 9, 10, and 11 illustrate the varying definitions that policymakers give to their agencies' "goals," recognizing the multiplicity of personal, organizational, and political motivations underlying policy decisions; Chapter 12 studies the reactions of local police departments to a research project that came to the disconcerting conclusion that preventive patrol, the primary activity of most street policemen, had no identifiable impact. Utilizing the judicial impact and policy implementation perspectives that appear elsewhere in this volume, Henig, Lineberry, and Milner conclude that the impact of policy evaluations must always be regarded as problematic because local policymakers may not in fact make decisions on the basis of the rational goals that evaluators ascribe to them. In this, as in the other law policy areas discussed in this volume, one must be constantly alert to interactions among policymaking organizations, the political systems within which they operate, and the policies with which they deal.

Public Law and Public Policy

CHAPTER 1

PUBLIC POLICY AND THE FEAR OF CRIME IN LARGE AMERICAN CITIES
Wesley G. Skogan

Soundings of public opinion indicate that crime is the number one concern of a plurality of Americans.[1] Gallup informs us that the residents of large cities place it ahead of even unemployment and the cost of living, and the New York *Times* headlined "More New Yorkers Turning to the Right, Despite City's Reputation as Liberal" when it saw the results of its own poll on the problem.[2] The issue is a recent one: a Gallup poll of big-city residents commissioned in 1949 found that only 4 percent regarded crime as their community's worst problem.[3] Crime emerged as an important issue on the public agenda about 1965. It has remained high on the list for over a decade, however, thus showing more staying power than most political, economic, or social ills.

Although it is a constant concern, the sources of discontent over crime are not always clear and neither are the appropriate prescriptions for politicians or administrators who could profit by reducing it. This chapter reviews some new data that speak to the efficacy of policies that have been employed to reduce or ameliorate the impact of the fear of crime in large cities. Most traditional policies attack the problem by attempting to reduce the frequency of victimization. In this category are included efforts to reduce police-response time, increase police manpower, and apprehend criminals. Others attempt to limit the seriousness of consequences of the most frightening offenses. Victim compensation

---

This chapter was written while the author was a Visiting Fellow (Grant 76 NI-99-0032) at the National Institute of Law Enforcement and Criminal Justice, Law Enforcement Assistance Administration, U.S. Department of Justice. Points of view or opinions stated in this chapter are those of the author and do not represent the official position or policies of the U.S. Department of Justice.

FIGURE 1.1

Determinants of the Fear of Crime

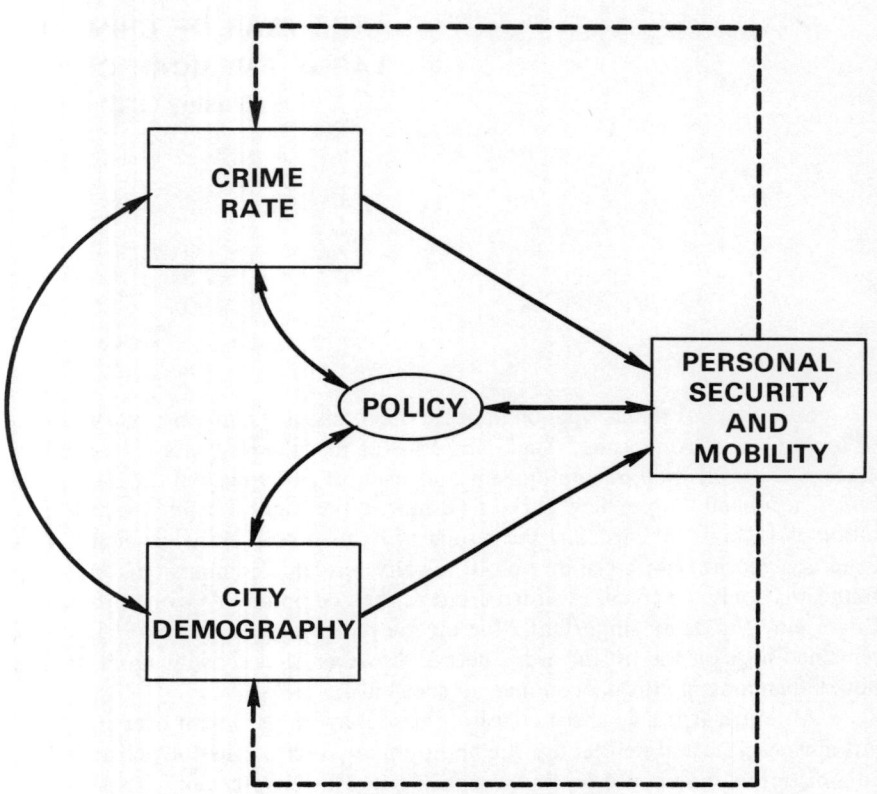

Source: Compiled by the author.

schemes and improved facilities for treating the victims of rape are included here. Some address the fundamental causes of crime and personal insecurity, including environmental-design projects and community crime-prevention programs. The remainder get at fear and its consequences directly, providing symbolic bases for feelings of safety and security. This is perhaps the major payoff of investments in intensive uniformed patroling and streetlighting. These relationships are sketched in Figure 1.1. The data on crimes and victims—which primarily were collected in the federal government's victimization surveys—are organized around six working hypotheses that must be confronted by prospective social engineers in the criminal-justice system:

(1) Policies have different effects on different types of crime, and often that effect is negligible.
(2) Different types of crime have different effects on the fear of crime, and that effect varies from group to group.
(3) The fear of crime is usually generated vicariously and not by direct victimization.
(4) The fear of crime is affected by many social factors that have little to do with victimization, directly or indirectly.
(5) The relationship between expressed fear and actual behavior is problematic.
(6) The causal system underlying the fear of crime is characterized by positive feedback and accelerating rates of change.

After mobilizing evidence supporting these propositions, the chapter concludes with a few modest recommendations that seem congruent with the argument developed here.

THE IMPACT OF PUBLIC POLICIES ON CRIME

Policies have different effects on different types of crime, and often that effect is negligible. The relationship between criminal-justice policy making and the crime rate is at best uncertain. Field experiments and statistical exercises designed to tease out the deterrent effect of increments of man and material or the effects of new crime-control strategies typically uncover only small effects.[4] One reason for this is that many crimes simply are not deterrable by the criminal-justice system. Many are furtive in nature, and not even their victims are clear about what has happened, when, or by whom. Many take place in private rather than in public places, and thus are not much affected by variations in patrol density or tactics. A substantial number of crimes of violence involve parties who know, love, or are related to one another; motivated by passion, they are not preventable even by programs aimed at the presumed root causes of crime. Finally, many or most crimes are not even reported to the police in the first

TABLE 1.1

The Deterrability of Common Crimes

Crime or Offender Attributes	Interpersonal Violence	Robbery	Personal Theft	Burglary	Larceny	Auto Theft
Identification						
percent able to cite offender's						
race	96.0	93.9	52.5	4.8	4.2	7.0
age	90.5	92.1	51.0	4.8	4.1	7.1
Visibility						
percent of offenses occurring						
at home	11.7	10.9	2.1	96.3	4.8	0.9
in building	22.5	18.8	47.7	3.7	27.0	1.5
on street or "near home"	53.8	64.8	39.3	.0	60.0	94.8
other	11.6	5.5	10.8	.0	8.2	2.8
Motive						
percent of offenses in which offender was a						
stranger	59.6	85.3	95.0	89.9	78.4	71.3
(don't know)	(0.0)	(0.1)	(0.1)	(90.5)	(92.9)	(91.8)
Reporting						
percent of offenses reported to the police	40.0	49.6	31.6	45.8	22.5	67.2
Total	3777	1023	512	5789	19601	1198

Note: The "in building" category combines events occurring in schools, hotels, office buildings, and commercial establishments. In the "motive" category, the "stranger" percent figure is based only upon those cases in which the victim knew enough about who did it to render a judgment. The "don't know" figure indicates how often they were unable to do so. The number of cases involved in the calculation of individual percentages may vary slightly from the total number of offenses recorded in that category.

Source: Compiled by the author from 1973 national crime panel personal and household incident data.

place. In those categories of criminal activity for which the justice system depends upon citizens to initiate the investigation process this greatly reduces the impact of official responses to crime.

The furtive character of many crimes means that there often is only a small residual of clues available to the police. If a victim is unable to supply much information about an offender, it is unlikely that an arrest will ever be made, for physical evidence plays a small role in ordinary police work. Typically the victims of property crime are unable to supply such rudimentary data as the exact time of the offense, and the lack of personal contact between victim and offender that characterizes such crimes usually means that no descriptions can be rendered either. The result is that clearance rates for property crimes are much lower than those for personal offenses.

The amount of information that is potentially available to the police for particular kinds of crimes can be analyzed by examining the "don't know" responses to items in a victimization survey. Table 1.1 presents the responses of a national sample of victims to questions about the apparent age and race of those who carried off the caper. It indicates the importance of substantial victim-offender interaction in establishing a base of information for later police investigation. Both assaultive violence and robbery offenses typically leave a strong impression of the perpetrator in the minds of victims. Property offenses almost never lead to a personal identification, on the other hand. In the middle lies personal larceny (purse snatching and pickpocketing), crimes in which victim-offender relationships often are fleeting. In those offenses only about one-half of all victims were willing to hazard a guess about the characteristics of their attackers.

The location of crimes also affects the ability of the criminal-justice system to prevent the occurrence or to respond rapidly following the event. Incidents that occur in public places are more visible to passing patrols and are more likely to involve witnesses and bystanders who may be willing to intervene or call the police. Those in private places, on the other hand, are shielded from view, and it is often difficult for the police to intervene legally unless their services are requested.[5] The Census Bureau's national victimization survey suggests that a substantial proportion of offenses occur in closed-off or semipublic places where private efforts are more likely to affect victimization rates. As Table 1.1 indicates, burglary, personal theft, and interpersonal violence often occur in less-visible locations. Many purse snatchings occur in office buildings, commercial establishments, schools, or hotels, however. There the vigilance of private security agents, changes in building design (alarm systems, the availability of exits), and routine self-protective practices by employees are likely to affect victimization patterns. In the robbery and larceny categories, most incidents occur in relatively public places. Programs designed to increase the amount of "street watching" in a community, either by patrol officers or community groups, may pay dividends in those cases.

The relationship between victims and offenders is related by inference to the motive behind many crimes, especially those of violence. Incidents that spring from relationships gone awry are probably less sensitive to variations in the certainty and severity of justice-system responses than are crimes of calculation.[6] While there is some evidence that the Census Bureau's victim surveys greatly undercount incidents within the family and among friends and neighbors, the data may still be useful in comparing the relative concentration of stranger crimes in various categories. The data in Table 1.1 suggest that the only substantial reservoir of nonstranger crime is the interpersonal violence category; there, 40 percent of all offenses registered in the victimization survey for 1973 involved victims and offenders who were at least acquainted. Most of the robberies involving nonstrangers could be described as "school-yard extortion," a serious problem among the young.

The difficulty is that almost none of that extortion nor many robberies are reported to the police. Only in the auto-theft category were a substantial proportion of offenses uncovered in the victim survey reported to the authorities. Petty property thefts were least frequently reported (22 percent), while burglary and robbery hovered around the 50 percent mark.[7] In all of these crimes the police rely primarily upon citizens to initiate the investigation process. Thus, programs aimed at improving response time, the quality of police service, or the effectiveness of other elements of the criminal-justice system are not likely to have much impact on the overall victimization rate. The data on suspect identification suggest that even full reporting probably would not help much in the case of property crime. The high visibility of most vehicle thefts does lend hope that official or civilian patrol programs might make a dent in that rate. On the basis of this data, robbery also looks like a good bet for effective crime-prevention activity: it involves rational calculation on the part of offenders, it takes place in public or semipublic places, and frequently it could lead to the identification of specific suspects. The weak link in the deterrence chain in the case of robbery appears to be citizen reporting.

SOURCES OF THE FEAR OF CRIME

Different types of crime have different effects on the fear of crime, and that effect varies from group to group. Not all victimizations have the same attitudinal effect, and the impact of that experience varies from person to person. Thus, reducing the frequency of certain crimes will have a higher payoff than others, and programs aimed at selected subgroups in the population will have a greater effect than scattershot crime-reduction policies.

In the 1967 analysis of citizen attitudes, the National Crime Commission noted that only crimes against persons appeared to have any direct impact upon the fear of crime. While property crimes reported in their surveys outnumbered

TABLE 1.2

Victimization and the Fear of Crime

Victimization Type	Correlation (Gamma) with:	
	Feelings of Safety	No Change in Activity
Rape	−.25	−.51
Robbery	−.22	−.32
Personal Theft	−.34	−.40
Assault	−.01	−.09
Burglary	−.13	−.14
Larceny	.04	.01
Auto Theft	.02	−.06
	(n = 23,022)	(n = 23,033)

Source: Compiled by the author from the attitude subsample of the 1973 survey of New York, Chicago, Philadelphia, Detroit, and Los Angeles. This analysis is based upon a 50 percent sample of that data.

those involving personal victim-offender contact by a wide margin, their attitudinal impact seemed to be slight.[8] Virtually the same is true among those who were interviewed by the Census Bureau during their survey of victimization and attitudes in the nation's five largest cities, which was conducted early in 1973. The only exception is burglary, which appears to have psychological consequences parallel to—but weaker than—those of personal crime. The incidence of property crime affected the respondent's perceptions of the amount of crime in their neighborhood, but not their personal reactions to it.

Table 1.2 presents bivariate correlations between victimization measures and two indicators of the fear of crime: a composite index that measures the respondents' fear of walking the streets of their neighborhoods during the day and at night (a high score on which indicates feelings of relative safety), and an item probing whether they had changed or limited their activities in the past few years because of crime (a "no" response on which was scored high).[9] The analysis is based upon a 50 percent sample of the 47,000 respondents who were administered an attitudinal inventory during interviewing in New York City, Detroit, Chicago, Los Angeles, and Philadelphia.[10] The independent variables are counts of the number of times each respondent was victimized by each type of offense during the preceding year. These variables ranged in value from zero to four for personal crimes, and up to seven for some property offenses. As Table 1.2 indicates, victimization by rape, robbery, personal theft (pickpocketing and purse snatching), and burglary was related systematically to the fear of crime. As the signs there indicate, victims were less likely than nonvictims to perceive their neighborhood as a place of safety, and they were more likely to report changes in their behavior. Auto theft, simple larceny, and assault were not so related. The limited effect in the latter cases may be due to inadequacies in the measurement of assault in the victimization surveys, or to the large component of interfamily, nonstranger crime in this category. The importance of burglary victimization in structuring attitudes should not be surprising, for it is a crime that violates one of the most important sources of personal security—home walls. The home-as-haven plays an important psychological role in maintaining one's sense of security and order, especially for low-income people who cannot purchase residential distance from high-crime neighborhoods.[11]

As this suggests, the impact of victimization upon the fear of crime varies from group to group in the population. In general, those who are more physically vulnerable to victimization and those who are more likely to have difficulty bearing the consequences of crime are more terrified when their fears are realized. The effect can be illustrated using mean scores on the five-point "safety" index to compare the attitudes of victims and nonvictims of various types. Women who were victimized by personal crimes had an average score of 4.98 on this measure, the nonvictims 5.5. Among men, the comparable scores were 6.12 and 6.3. Male victims felt less insecure than female nonvictims, and the effect of victimization (the difference between the two scores within each group) was twice as great for females. Similarly, the effect of victimization was 2.5 times as great among those making under $10,000 per year as among those with family incomes above that mark, and the security score for those over 30 years of age dropped 3 times as far in response to personal crime as that for those under 30.

Based on the five-city data, it thus is apparent that certain groups in the population are much more fearful than others, and the effect of victimization among those groups is more intense. Programs aimed at alleviating the burdens born by persons in those categories should reap large benefits. One approach to the problem would be to reduce victimization rates, especially among the poor, women, and older people. Given that this strategy may not have many significant payoffs, an alternative response to the fear-of-crime problem may be to provide the victims of crime better services. There is important evidence that quality of police service received by crime victims plays an important role in mediating the relationship between victimization and fear. In an analysis of victimization data collected in a St. Louis area study, Roger Parks reports that victims who received thorough and more satisfactory service from police officers who responded to their call were less frightened by the experience as a result. Faster perceived response time was helpful in mediating the impact of victimization as well.[12] Being more vulnerable, the spirits of women, the poor, and the elderly may be especially buoyed by a sign of support and by the promise of competent protection that good service may hold out.

The fear of crime usually is generated vicariously, and not by direct victimization. Measures of direct victimization cannot explain much of the

TABLE 1.3

Personal Victimization and Perceptions of Safety

Perceptions of Safety		Percentage Distribution of Personal Victimization		N
		No	Yes	
Low	1	21	2	5,338
	2	18	1	4,304
	3	19	1	4,698
	4	23	1	5,524
High	5	13	1	3,159
Total		100%		100%

Source: Compiled by the author from the attitude subsamples of the 1973 survey of New York, Chicago, Detroit, Philadelphia, and Los Angeles. This analysis is based upon a 50 percent sample of that data.

variation in measures of the fear of crime, for many more people express great fear than actually are victimized. Although it has not been investigated systematically, it seems that the roots of most people's perceptions of crime and knowledge about victimization lie in vicarious sources: television programs, newspapers, and the secondhand reports of friends and neighbors.

Attitude studies indicate that experience with personal crime (and burglary) is the only consistent predictor to the fear of crime among victimization measures. However, crimes against the person are relatively rare events, even in these five high-crime cities. Within the one-year reference period used in these (and most other) surveys, most people are not involved in a rape, robbery, assault, or personal theft. In the 5-city survey, only 0.2 percent of all respondents (and less than 0.4 percent of all females) reported that they were raped within the past year; for robbery the overall figure was 2.4 percent, for assault 2.8 percent, and for personal theft 1.2 percent. A few of these victimizations overlapped, leaving about 94 percent of all the respondents in these surveys untouched by personal crime during the 1972 reference year.

The difficulty is that a variable with a highly skewed distribution cannot be related in simple fashion to a variable with a normal distribution. This is illustrated in Table 1.3, which relates victimization experience to perceptions of safety, when the former is collapsed into a simple victim-nonvictim dichotomy for all personal crimes. While the data in Table 1.3 indicate a correlation between victimization and perceptions of safety (a gamma of -.15, which is brought down by the inclusion of assault cases), it is clear that most people falling in the low-safety categories were not victimized during 1972. The roots of fear must be found elsewhere.

One source may be the experiences of those we know and love. An indicator of this which may be generated from the Census Bureau's data is the victimization experiences of others in the household of each respondent. When we measure this using a count of the number of robberies and personal thefts suffered by other household members during 1972 (which ranged in value from 0 to 5), we find that perceptions of safety declined steadily with indirect victimization: mean safety scores dropped from 2.9 among nonvictims to 2.0 among those who lived in households where others suffered 3 or more victimizations.

Beyond this there is no direct data on the importance of vicarious experiences in shaping people's opinions about crime. Robert LeJeune and Nicholas Alex indicate that the victims of robbery spend a great deal of time communicating their experience to others, but there is no evidence of the impact of such "war stories."[13] It seems likely that popular stereotypes about the motives and behavior of criminals, the characteristic features of crimes, and the relative frequency of personal and property offenses are largely passed on through the media, and systematic observations of television programs indicate that information from that source is quite inaccurate.[14] Perhaps information campaigns that "tell the truth" about the crime problem and contribute to a more realistic public assessment of the nature of the crime problem in the United States might contribute to an overall reduction in the aggregate level of fear in urban communities.

Safety and activity are affected by many social factors that have little to do with victimization, directly or indirectly. The fear of crime is mixed up with a number of other fears and aggravations that plague the lives of big-city residents. People do not get along with nor understand their neighbors, they fear what goes on in schools, and they do not like to rub elbows with the people they do in places where they shop or seek recreation. Part of this has to do with the fear of strangers. Strangers are unpredictable: we do not understand their motives and we do not know what they may do. In this sense, people of a different race or class are stranger than those who are not. As a result, the fear of crime is intermingled with racial fears and class-linked differences in behavior.

It is apparent from the Census Bureau's surveys that a number of factors other than crime (as a specific response category) affect people's behavior. For example, the survey asked whether respondents in the five largest cities went out at night for entertainment more or less than they did "a few years ago." Among the 33 percent who indicated that they went out less, 16 percent (5 percent of the total) attributed their decreased mobility to crime. The comparable figure was 11 percent for those who indicated that they do not go downtown to make major purchases. When asked about events close to home people volunteered a number of complaints that were related to perceptions of safety and mobility, but were not specifically "criminal." In response to a question of what they disliked about their present neighborhood, 28 percent indicated that "crime" was the most important response category. An additional 19 percent said that they were unhappy because a "bad element" was moving into the neighborhood, 9 percent cited their dislike of the character of their neighbors, and 5 percent mentioned problems with the schools. This adds up to 62 percent of all those responding to the question. Persons who chose those responses were more likely than those who did not to fall into low-safety and reduced activity categories, suggesting that the "fear of crime" is a diffuse psychological construct affected by a number of aspects of urban life.

The relationship between expressed fear and actual behavior is problematic. It is not always possible to predict behavior on the basis of attitudes. Our behavior is shaped by a variety of opportunities and constraints that may cause us, perhaps even unwillingly, to act in ways that are discrepant with our expressed fears, beliefs, or preferences. People may fear street crime and still have to take the bus home from work after dark; youths may be victimized frequently, yet they may be drawn by sociability and peer pressure to spend a great deal of time in parks and alleys; the elderly may be relatively safe from actual victimization, but they still may take great precautions to avoid injuries that may be slow to heal or losses they cannot recoup. The more indirect the connection between attitudes and behavior, the less programs aimed at one will affect the other. This may have consequences for policies encouraging the adoption of individual self-protective measures against crime.

The Census Bureau's victimization surveys reveal a substantial correspondence between perceptions of safety and self-reports of behavior. The correlation (gamma) between the composite index measuring perceived neighborhood safety and responses to the question, "Have you limited or changed your activities in the past few years because of crime" (with a "no" response scored high), was +.55 among residents of the five largest cities. Twelve percent of all respondents fell in the two "least safe" categories and yet indicated that they had not. Almost 70 percent of these "discrepants" were female, young, working, unmarried women were most likely to report that their neighborhood was unsafe and yet failed to take "appropriate" countermeasures. This perhaps was a consequence of role pressures that led them to behave this way, while their physical vulnerability to personal crime made them more fearful of the consequences.

One explanation for the general discrepancy between belief and behavior may be that for many persons the fear of crime is a relatively abstract concern. Few are victimized, and not many live with others who have fallen victim to a serious personal crime. In general, consistency in attitude (perceptions of safety) and behavior (limits on activity) increases with exposure to crime. For example, the gamma between the two measures was +.54 among nonvictims, while among those who were victimized by rape, robbery, or personal larceny during the preceding year the correlation increased to +.61. The correlation between safety and activity also was higher among those who lived in the same household with the victims of personal crimes. Similarly, the suspicion that one's neighbors are likely to be counted among the criminal class was related to greater consistency between perceptions of neighborhood safety and personal behavior. Respondents were asked: "How about any crimes that may be happening in your neighborhood—would you say they are committed mostly by people who live here in this neighborhood or mostly by outsiders?" Among those who insisted that there was "no crime" in their area, the correlation between the two measures was +.49; among those choosing "outsiders" it was +.52; among those indicating that both outsiders and those in the neighborhood were responsible it was +.58; among those who feared only their neighbors it was +.59. The more immediate the source of the threat, the more consistent were attitudes and behaviors.

IMPLICATIONS FOR CRIME-CONTROL POLICY

The implications of this data for crime-control policy are inferential, but speak to a central issue—citizen participation in crime-prevention activities. By popular image, the urban dweller lives in a state of seige, armed to the teeth and locked behind bolted doors. This contrasts with the picture of the average apathetic citizen lamented by criminal-justice professionals—he does not cooperate with officials in crime-prevention efforts, he leaves his keys in his car door or his back door unlocked with alarming frequency, and he does not even report many crimes to the police. Part of the difference between these stereotypes may be the distinction between attitudes or verbalized opinions and behavior. Most people are not victimized and most people do not suspect their neighbors, even in these five high-crime cities. As a result, it may be difficult to convince nonvictims (or, more appropriately, the not-yet-victimized) to invest time or money in defensive tactics or to change their life-styles. Even among victims, defensive tactics are less than universally pursued. In the five cities, 59 percent of the victims of personal crime reported that they had changed or limited their activities due to crime, as contrasted with 48 percent of nonvictims. This effect is somewhat stronger than that uncovered by the Crime Commission in their surveys in the mid-1960s, but neither the strength of the relationship nor the level of defensive activity is high enough to lend credence to extreme views of the paralysis of big-city life.[15] People are concerned about crime, and there is reason to believe that this concern is on the upswing, but life goes on.

The causal system underlying the fear of crime is characterized by positive feedback and accelerating rates of change. The framework for this discussion, sketched in Figure 1.1, is a dynamic model. Crime, racial and class tensions, and communication of those fears not only contribute to the spread of fear and the reduction of personal mobility, but they in turn lead to increasing rates of crime and demographic and economic changes that further fuel the spiral of fear. The result is that over time we should find exponentially increasing levels of fear in communities that have gotten caught up in that spiral. Although time-series attitudinal data for central cities is lacking, other indicators of social change in large American cities do not portend well for the future.

First, rates of reported crime have increased dramatically in certain cities. In Chicago the number of reported homicides rose from 231 in 1946 to over 1,000 in 1973, while the city's population remained virtually unchanged.[16] Crime rates have risen the most in larger communities, and by 1970 the 32 largest cities in the country—which housed 16 percent of the nation's population—experienced 67 percent of all the robbery known to the police.[17] Whether the linkage between crime rates and the fear of crime is through direct victimization or the contagion of vicarious experiences, we should expect fear to increase in some regular fashion with skyrocketing reported crime rates.

Analysis of the attitudinal data collected by the Bureau of the Census in 26 major cities indicates that rates of officially reported crime are strongly correlated with the level of fear in those communities. Figure 1.2 presents a plot of the relationship between officially reported robbery rates in those communities and a measure of citizen safety, the (projected) proportion of the population who indicated that they were afraid or very afraid to walk the streets of their neighborhood alone at night.[18] The official robbery rate in this case probably reflects both true patterns of victimization and the image of the dimensions of the local crime problem that radiates from the police and the media in these communities. As Figure 1.2 indicates, citizens in cities where reported robbery rates were high (including Newark, Detroit, and Baltimore) felt very insecure, while those in low-crime cities (notably in San Diego) felt safe indeed. The slope of the regression line illustrated in Figure 1.2 suggests that a shift of 10 robberies per 10,000 inhabitants is associated with a 1.8 percent change in aggregate levels of safety in these communities.[19] While it is inappropriate to make firm claims about temporal trends from such cross-sectional parameters, it is likely that the positive relationship displayed in Figure 1.2 has remained constant across time within cities as well.

This is troublesome, for projections of existing trends suggest that large central cities will continue to experience rapidly increasing rates of reported crime. One reason for this is that crime and associated problems appear to be linked in reciprocal fashion with patterns of metropolitan suburbanization.[20] The impact of this process upon the social ecology of central cities has been mammoth. Suburbanization sorts the population along race and class lines, concentrating the poor and the marginally employable in deteriorating physical plants that are cheaper to abandon than repair. The hearts of large cities are peopled by working-class whites and blacks and Latins of various classes who are unable to escape, while job opportunities expand on the fringes of metropolitan areas where land is cheap and expressway connections are handy. Skilled

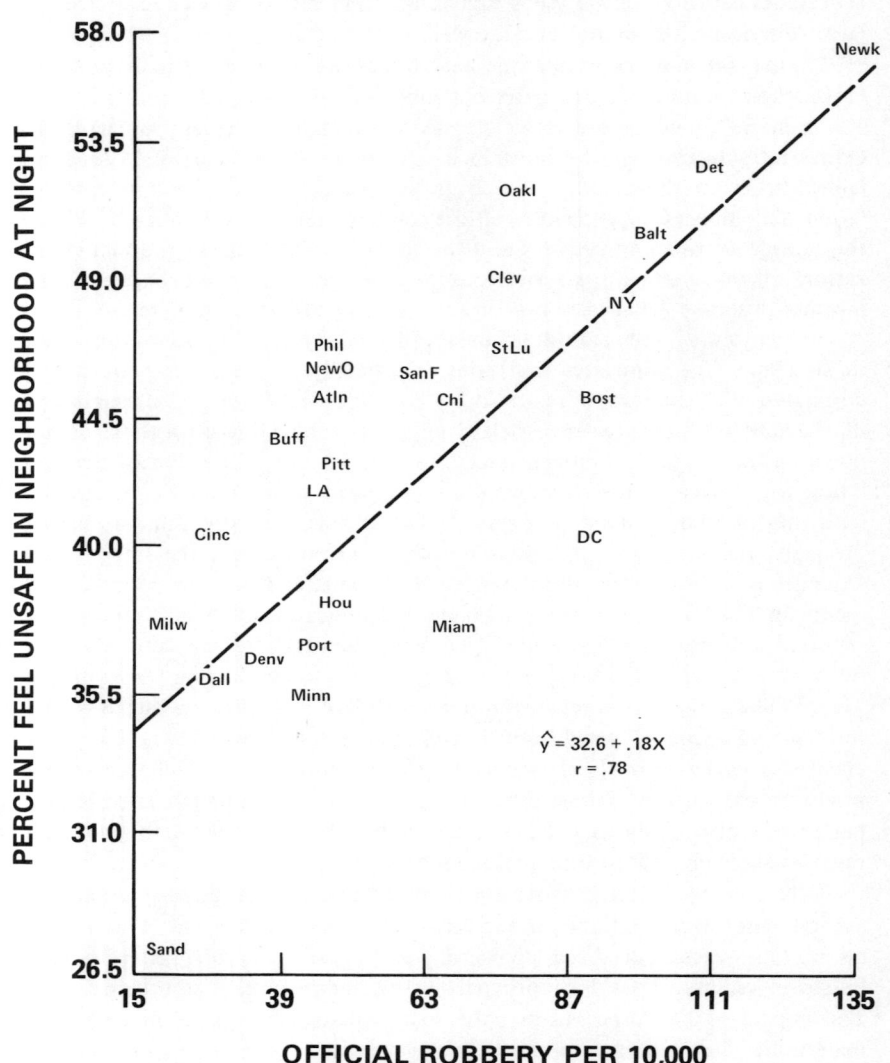

FIGURE 1.2

Robbery Rates and the Fear of Crime

$\hat{y} = 32.6 + .18X$
$r = .78$

Source: Compiled by the author.

labor and the tax base are rapidly following the middle class to suburban areas, pulled by opportunity and pushed by the fear of crime and the financial burden of supporting the services apparently necessary to maintain order in the old neighborhoods. Thus suburbanization is most extensive around central cities with the highest rates of reported crime. Across the nation's 32 largest cities in 1970, the correlation between the crime rate and an index of suburbanization based upon jobs and population was +.62.[21] The correlation between changes in each between 1946 and 1970 was +.57, suggesting that the relationship between suburban growth and central-city crime patterns has been quite powerful.

The difficulty is that those policies that exist about suburban growth have been drafted to encourage it, and it is unlikely that U.S. governments in their present form can do much to reverse demographic trends. The movement of people and jobs is largely a function of market forces and racial discrimination, which usually work in tandem.[22] What limited impact the government has in such affairs has been in the areas of highway construction, mortgage financing, mass-transit policy, and gasoline prices. In the past, these have worked to speed the growth of suburbs, but it is unlikely that incremental changes in any or all of these activities would much affect the course of urban development. Thus the prognosis for large, dense, racially heterogeneous central cities is not good, and it is a sure bet that crime and (perhaps) the fear of crime there will register steady increases for the foreseeable future.

SOME RECOMMENDATIONS

This review has argued that many of the policies we traditionally pursue to affect the fear of crime have little chance of success, and that much of that fear is probably beyond the control of the criminal-justice system in the first place. It has suggested three viable paths that still appear to be open to policymakers, however. These include programs that inform the concern rather than the fears of the public; that mobilize them in support of narrow, crime-specific prevention activities; and that provide services to victims, calling for new skills on the part of criminal-justice practitioners.

It is important to distinguish between the fear of crime (as manifested by reduced activity or an unwillingness to venture onto the street) and concern over crime as a public issue. The latter involves how high we place the issue on the public agenda, relative to other ways of spending our money. Too often the latter issue is approached by playing to the former, drumming up levels of public hysteria that for most people (the data indicate) is quite inappropriate. The result: many people are afraid, many more than are victimized by "crime in the streets," and that fear has negative systemic consequences which probably far overshadow its strategic payoffs. A more responsible (and profitable) strategy

would focus upon those high-volume crimes that strike more uniformly thrrough-
out the population, and that might be reduced in number through simple self-
defensive tactics on the part of potential victims. These include burglary and
property thefts, crimes that cost us a lot (which can easily be measured), rely
largely upon carelessness on the part of victims, and do not evoke high levels of
debilitating fear. This strategy for mobilizing public support of the criminal-
justice system recognizes the "positive functions" of concern and attempts to
focus upon activities where it may do the most good for the greatest number.

The data presented in Table 1.1 also suggest some ways of setting viable
crime-prevention priorities with payoffs in the fear department. Analysis of the
victimization survey data indicates that certain classes of crimes may be amenable to government intervention. Almost 27 percent of all property larceny and
6 percent of all personal violence, for example, were reported to have taken
place in schools in 1973.[23] Schools are places with controlled access, lockers,
and security administrators, all things that governments can improve upon. The
data also indicate that robbery is a good bet for deterrent impact—there is a high
potential for suspect identification, it often occurs in public places, and it
involves rational calculation on the part of offenders. Citizen reporting programs
would help close the biggest gap in the apprehension process, for less than one-
half of all personal robberies are now coming to the attention of the police.

Finally, Roger Parks' analysis of the impact of the quality and quantity of
police service upon the extent to which victimization experiences were translated into generalized fear should suggest training and organization policies to
police administrators.[24] Perhaps the best model for the kind of police intervention style that is called for is Morton Bard's family crisis-intervention
team.[25] They are trained to cope with conflicts that arise out of domestic
problems, which often calls for negotiating between the disputing parties and
arranging for the assistance of other social agencies in the solution of family
difficulties. For police officers, victimization is a routine event, and often they
simply do not understand the crisis that it evokes in the lives of victims. What
the victim needs is information (what to do about insurance, where to locate a
good doctor), advice (is his assailant likely to do it again; what should he do to
protect himself in the future?), and a prognosis (will he get any property back;
will they catch the one who did it; how much of his time will it take if they do?).
The evidence suggests that such assistance—which is not the same thing as
unwarranted reassurance that all is well—helps a lot in assisting victims in
adjusting to their new status.

The fear of crime greatly affects the quality of urban life. It affects it
directly through its impact upon our use of the streets and parks, the bustle of
social activity, shopping, and recreation, and the diversity and anonymity that
have long characterized city dwelling. It affects it indirectly through the debilitating impact of crime upon social intercourse, community morale, and even
the economic base of the city. When shops and restaurants close, when downtown

streets become lonely canyons in the evening, and when families rearing children flee the central city, we all suffer the consequences. The fear of crime has a social, political, and economic reality of its own, quite independent of the true dimensions of the crime problem and the efficacy of crime-reduction policies. The development of social indicators of this aspect of the quality of life and the cultivation of programs that succeed in coping with it should be high on the agenda of innovators in criminal-justice administration.

NOTES

1. "Crime Seen Top Problem for Cities," Washington *Post*, July 27, 1975, p. 1.
2. Ibid.; New York *Times*, January 15, 1974.
3. Washington *Post*, op. cit.
4. For a collection of two dozen of the best studies by economists, see Lee R. McPheters and William B. Stronge, *The Economics of Crime and Law Enforcement* (Springfield, Ill.: Charles C. Thomas, 1976). Some of the manpower studies are reviewed in James Q. Wilson, *Thinking About Crime* (New York: Basic Books, 1975).
5. Arthur Stinchcombe, "Institutions of Privacy in the Determination of Police Practice," *American Journal of Sociology* 69 (1963): 150-60.
6. Lynn A. Curtis, *Criminal Violence: National Patterns and Behavior* (Lexington, Mass.: D. C. Heath, 1975).
7. For a more detailed analysis of the data on reporting, see Wesley G. Skogan, "Citizen Reporting of Crime: Some National Panel Data," *Criminology* 13 (February 1976): 535-49.
8. President's Commission on Law Enforcement and Administration of Justice, *Task Force Report: Crime and Its Impact—An Assessment* (Washington, D.C.: Government Printing Office, 1967), p. 87.
9. For a description of the victimization surveys conducted by the Bureau of the Census, see Wesley G. Skogan, "Sample Surveys of the Victims of Crime," *Review of Public Data Use* 4 (January 1976): 23-28.
10. The composite index added responses to two questions, "How safe do you feel or would you feel being out alone in your neighborhood at night?" and "How about during the day—how safe do you feel or would you feel being out alone in your neighborhood?" Each item featured a four-point response scale ranging from "very safe" to "very unsafe." The two items were correlated (gamma) +.78.
11. Lee Rainwater, "Fear and the House-as-Haven in the Lower Class," *Journal of the American Institute of Planners* 32 (January 1966): 23-31.
12. Roger Parks, "Victims and the Police," in *Sample Surveys of the Victims of Crime*, ed. Wesley G. Skogan (Cambridge, Mass.: Ballinger, 1976).
13. Robert LeJeune and Nicholas Alex, "On Being Mugged," *Urban Life and Culture* 3 (October 1973): 259-387.
14. Joseph Dolminick, "Crime and Law Enforcement on Prime-Time Television," *Public Opinion Quarterly* 37 (Summer 1973): 141-50.
15. President's Commission, op. cit., p. 86.
16. Chicago Police Department, *Annual Report* (Chicago: Chicago Police Department, 1947 and 1974).
17. These figures were calculated from the *Uniform Crime Report 1970* (Washington, D.C.: Federal Bureau of Investigation), and Bureau of the Census, *General Population*

Characteristics: United States Summary (Washington, D.C.: Government Printing Office, 1972).

18. The attitude measures were computed from unpublished item marginals supplied by the Census Bureau.

19. This inference is based upon the observed regression equation, $y = 32.6 + .18X$.

20. For an elaboration of this argument, see Wesley G. Skogan, "The Changing Distribution of Big-City Crime: A Multi-City Time-Series Analysis," unpublished ms., Northwestern University, 1976.

21. The index of suburbanization is a composite score combining standardized values of the proportion of each Standard Metropolitan Statistical Area's (SMSA) population and jobs that were located outside the central city.

22. For an insightful study of these market forces in the housing sector see Harvey Molotoch, *Managed Integration* (Berkeley: University of California Press, 1972).

23. Richard W. Dodge, Harold Lentzner, and Frederick Shenk, "Crime in the United States: A Report on the National Crime Survey," in *Sample Surveys of the Victims of Crime*, ed. Wesley G. Skogan (Cambridge, Mass.: Ballinger, 1976).

24. Parks, op. cit.

25. Morton Bard, "Training Police as Specialists in Family Crisis Intervention: A Community Psychology Action Program," *Community Mental Health Journal* 3 (1967); Raymond Parnas, "Police Discretion and Diversion of Incidents of Intra-Family Violence," in *Police Practices*, ed. John C. Weistart (Dobbs Ferry, N.Y.: Oceana Publications, 1974), pp. 95-121.

CHAPTER 2

THE IMPACT OF DEFENDANT RACE IN TRIAL-COURT SANCTIONING DECISIONS
Thomas M. Uhlman

Since the late 1920s, controversy has existed over the degree and importance of race-related disparities in the criminal-sanctioning process. Social scientists have explored a wide variety of local legal systems to determine whether black and other minority-group defendants receive harsher treatment than their white counterparts and, if so, whether this differential treatment can be considered discriminatory.[1] Notwithstanding the difficulties inherent in this field of study,[2] work continues for one simple but compelling reason. To the extent that it exists, discriminatory sanctioning represents a fundamental distortion of the ideal of equal justice for all before the law.

This chapter extends this research by investigating the sanctioning decisions meted out to 34,258 black and 9,344 white defendants appearing before a major metropolitan trial court between 1968 and 1974. Initially, defendants are compared along three sanctioning dimensions: conviction rates, jail rates, and sentence severity. Next, we undertake the challenging task of trying to interpret and explain both the interracial differences and similarities that emerge. The challenge results in part from the overall complexity of the criminal-justice mechanism and in part from competing theories that are advanced to account for race-related disparities uncovered elsewhere.

In an attempt to incorporate both the complexities and the divergent theories in a realistic assessment of the defendant race question, a causal model

---

I would like to thank Stuart Rabinowitz, George Rabinowitz, Jack Hoadley, and Scott Keeter for their assistance in negotiating several tricky analytic corners. Lance T. LeLoup and Roy B. Flemming also helped by offering valuable comments on earlier versions of this chapter.

of the sanctioning process is then developed. Including additional case characteristics, this model is operationalized using path analytic techniques to determine the relative impact of various legal and extralegal components of the race-sanctioning relationship. From this analysis we are in a position to conclude both the extent to which these relationships exist and the degree to which they may be linked to discriminatory behavior or result from legally justifiable distinctions among defendants.

The issue of primary concern here may have been voiced most eloquently by Frederick Douglass. Speaking in 1883, he stated,

> Justice is often painted with bandaged eyes, she is described in forensic eloquence as utterly blind to wealth or poverty, high or low, white or black, but a mask of iron however thick could never blind American justice when a black man happens to be on trial.[3]

Here it is a system of justice that is on trial as we investigate the truth of Douglass' assertion as it applies to a major metropolitan court system.

THE METRO CITY CRIMINAL COURT

The study focuses on sanctioning activity within the courts of a major metropolitan center, called Metro City for sake of anonymity. Statistical evidence amply supports impressionistic notions of Metro City as one of the nation's principal urban areas.[4] Between July 1, 1968, and June 30, 1974, 62,436 cases were docketed and disposed of in the city's trial court. Of this total, 43,602 computerized case histories comprise the sample analyzed; the unit of analysis is the individual defendant.

In selecting the sample, case deletion criteria are adopted based on the presence or absence of information central to the primary focus of the project. Cases are omitted if they fail to record one or more of the following: valid charge, disposition and sanction codes;[5] race of the defendant;[6] the maximum possible sentence for the charge in the case;[7] and certain variables relating to the trial judge.[8]

This deletion strategy, facilitated by the size of the original data set, results in a solid research base. Each case contains a complete sanctioning record along with defendant race information. In addition, the computerized data-processing techniques adopted by the court increase the reliability of the case histories. A uniform coding scheme was in use during the entire six-year period under investigation. Case records were checked, updated, and rechecked while a file was active, increasing the likelihood that mistakes were caught and corrected.

TABLE 2.1

Independent Variables Included in the Metro City Data

Variable Name	Description
Crime Category	16 individual crimes: murder, manslaughter, aggravated assault, minor assault, burglary, larceny, auto larceny, stolen property, forgery, counterfeiting, rape, driving under the influence (DUI), gambling, contributing to the delinquency of a minor, drug offenses, weapons offenses.
Charge Severity	Maximum possible sentence (in years) for each charge (311) in sample.
Number of Charges	Total number of charges originally lodged against defendant.
Bail Amount	A dollar amount indicating bail requirement.
Bail Status	Defendant's pretrial status, either pretrial release or detention.
Defense Counsel	Legal representation by either court-appointed counsel (public defender or court-appointed private counsel) or private, retained counsel.
Method of Disposition	Case disposed of by either guilty plea or trial (judge or jury).
Evidence of Charge Reduction	Sentencing on either the most serious charge originally lodged or a charge less than the most serious.

Source: Compiled by the author.

    In addition to defendant race and measures of sanctioning, other case characteristics are utilized in the subsequent analysis. They include: selected crime categories; severity of the criminal charges; total number of charges; bail amount; pretrial bail status; type of defense counsel; method of case disposition; and evidence of charge reduction. These variables are summarized in Table 2.1.[9]

    Three frequently explored sanctioning decisions serve as dependent variables in this analysis—conviction rates, jail rates, and sentence severity.[10] The decision to convict or acquit marks a critical turning point for the defendant. Without belaboring the obvious, the added burden a person assumes with a felony conviction will probably have a bearing on the rest of his life. A dichotomous measure of defendant guilt or innocence is utilized. Not-guilty determinations encompass both judge and jury verdicts, and represent 24.9 percent

(10,871) of the total sample. Guilty verdicts (32,731) are achieved by both judge and jury deliberations or result from negotiated pleas.

In a sentencing analysis two measures seem desirable. Qualitatively there is almost an incalculable jump between nonprison sanctions (suspended sentence, probation, fine) and a jail term. This critical decision is measured by a dichotomous variable of jail/no jail. Guilty verdicts were returned in 32,731 cases in Metro City. For 11,769 individuals (36 percent) the eventual result of a guilty verdict was jail. The remaining 20,962 were more fortunate in receiving lesser forms of punishment.

A second measure of sanctioning severity also deals with this subsample of 32,000+ cases. This measure deemphasizes the breaking point between prison and nonimprisonment, and instead taps subtler differences along a broader sanctioning continuum. Joining past theory and practice to the data at hand results in a detailed 93-point sentence severity scale that makes meaningful distinctions between and among degrees of deprivation of individual freedom and the varying severity of nonprison sanctions.[11] The scale breaks down into the following general categories (in increasing order of severity): (1) suspended sentences only (scale value 1); (2) fines only (scale values 2-6); (3) suspended sentences and fines (scale values 7-11); (4) probated sentences and probated sentences and fines (scale values 12-31); and (5) active jail sentences (scale values 32-93). Since all but two of the 93 categories are used, it is evident that judges both perceive and respond to the wide variety of sentencing possibilities available to them.

The Metro City data represent a large and reliable collection of sanctioning information. We can exploit the strength of these data to investigate the impact of racial differences among criminal defendants. The first step is to determine the magnitude of interracial sanctioning disparities.

In studies measuring race-related sanctioning, absolute disparities nearly always favor whites.[12] Frequently restated in other ways, Henry Allen Bullock's comment describes the issue in its broadest terms: "It is generally concluded that Negroes receive differential treatment in arrest, sentencing, and imprisonment . . . ."[13] The research focus is narrower here, but the testable hypotheses remain. We may expect Metro City blacks to be found guilty and sent to jail more often, and also be the recipients of harsher sentences than white offenders.

The first sanctioning choice examined is the decision to convict or acquit. Sanctioning may relate to the type of crime that has been committed. To explore this possibility, 16 divergent crime categories are examined individually. In 4 of the 16, white defendants are found guilty more often than blacks (Table 2.2). The largest absolute disparity remains under 2.5 percent. This difference is not statistically significant. Neither are the three remaining disparities, which are even smaller. In 12 other crime categories black defendants are convicted more frequently than whites. Many of these disparities are also slight. Seven crimes have interracial differences of less than five percent while four others manifest

TABLE 2.2

Percent by Race of Defendants Convicted in Selected Crime Categories

Crime Category	Black Defendants	White Defendants	Percent Difference	r
Murder	80.0 (1,015)	77.9 (86)	+2.1	.01
Manslaughter	87.5 (361)	80.6 (72)	+6.9	.07
Robbery	73.8 (4,855)	75.7 (395)	-1.9	-.01
Aggravated assault	71.1 (2,464)	66.2 (497)	+4.9	.04
Minor assault	76.0 (1,917)	75.6 (761)	+0.4	.00
Burglary	76.9 (5,789)	75.6 (1,727)	+1.3	.01
Larceny	80.1 (3,138)	81.9 (753)	-1.8	-.02
Auto larceny	82.1 (378)	84.4 (77)	-2.3	-.04
Stolen property	86.8 (2,028)	83.9 (601)	+2.9	.03
Forgery-counterfeiting	84.9 (755)	81.2 (309)	+3.7	.04
Rape-serious sex	64.4 (742)	66.0 (144)	-1.6	.01
Drug offenses	71.0 (4,553)	66.2 (1,634)	+4.8	.05*
Weapons offenses	76.6 (2,685)	67.1 (377)	+9.5	.07*
Driving under the influence	73.4 (1,088)	57.2 (327)	+16.2	.16*
Gambling	56.6 (258)	48.7 (156)	+7.9	.07
Contributing to delinquency	78.7 (207)	73.6 (174)	+5.1	.05

*Statistically significant at .01 level.
Note: r = Pearson's Product-Moment Correlation Coefficient.
Source: Compiled by the author.

moderate disparities of between five and ten percent. In only three instances are the interracial differences statistically significant.

Examining conviction rates over all 43,602 cases supports a tentative conclusion that we have tapped at most a small interracial disparity. White defendants (9,344) are found guilty 72 percent of the time while blacks receive guilty dispositions in 75.9 percent of the 34,258 cases heard in Metro City. With a sample this large the difference is, of course, statistically significant and in the hypothesized direction. Yet it remains an open question how important a 4 percent disparity is. For the present it is classified as being meaningful but marginal with a final evaluation deferred until possible explanatory factors are considered.

There is far less maneuverability in evaluating interracial differences in jail rates; convicted black defendants are sentenced to prison substantially more often than whites. Table 2.3 reveals the breadth and consistency of the pattern. In 15 crimes, blacks are recipients of jail terms more frequently, and in the remaining crime, gambling, blacks are only slightly favored. Over all cases, jail sentences are meted out to only 19.6 percent of the convicted white offenders, compared to 40.2 percent of the convicted blacks. In the Metro City criminal court, blacks are twice as likely to go to prison as are whites.

Considering the positioning of the jail/no jail dichotomy in the overall sentence severity scale, it is not surprising that black defendants also receive harsher sentences of all types. Blacks average more severe punishments in 15 of the 16 individual crime categories (Table 2.4). With two exceptions, crimes that manifest large interracial jail disparities also tend to be associated with sizable overall sentencing differentials.[14] The same relationship holds in categories where the disparities are smaller. Averaging over all cases, white defendants receive mean sentences of 19.9 scale units while blacks average sentences of 26.4 units. This 6.5 unit difference translates into a correlation coefficient equaling .16, which is comparable to the interracial disparity in jail rates ($r = .17$).

In Metro City we find similar absolute disparities in prison rates and sentence severity. Along both measures blacks are sanctioned more severely than whites with most of the differences appearing substantial. The evidence is less clear as far as determinations of guilt or innocence are concerned. Marginal differences mark most of the defendant race-conviction relationships. These disparities may be interpreted as being significant, but the argument is more difficult to make. In light of these findings it seems necessary to group race-related jail and sentencing disparities together and to distinguish them from conviction rates.

We have carefully avoided labeling any relationship discriminatory. Absolute race-related disparities exist, but at present one cannot conclude more. Caution is necessary because other explanations have been advanced to account for similar differences found elsewhere. After charting these initial disparities, the difficult and challenging task of interpretation lies ahead.

TABLE 2.3

Percent by Race of Defendants Jailed in Selected Crime Categories

Crime Category	Black Defendants	White Defendants	Percent Difference	r
Murder	85.8 (812)	82.1 (67)	+3.7	.02
Manslaughter	52.8 (316)	50.0 (58)	+2.8	.01
Robbery	71.1 (3,582)	46.8 (299)	+24.3	.14*
Aggravated assault	40.2 (1,751)	25.2 (329)	+15.0	.11*
Minor assault	30.6 (1,456)	13.7 (575)	+16.9	.17*
Burglary	46.7 (4,451)	25.3 (1,305)	+21.4	.18*
Larceny	36.3 (2,515)	18.2 (617)	+18.1	.15*
Auto larceny	29.8 (299)	23.1 (65)	+6.7	.05
Stolen property	31.0 (1,761)	18.7 (504)	+12.3	.11*
Forgery-counterfeiting	19.0 (641)	16.3 (251)	+2.7	.03
Rape-serious sex	57.9 (478)	41.1 (95)	+16.8	.12*
Drug offenses	23.0 (3,232)	11.1 (1,082)	+11.9	.13*
Weapons offenses	28.7 (2,056)	17.8 (253)	+10.9	.08*
Driving under the influence	7.6 (799)	2.4 (327)	+5.2	.09*
Gambling	4.8 (146)	5.3 (76)	−0.5	−.01
Contributing to delinquency	30.1 (163)	15.6 (128)	+14.5	.16*

*Statistically significant at the .01 level.
Note: r = Pearson's Product-Moment Correlation Coefficient.
Source: Compiled by the author.

TABLE 2.4

Mean-Sentence Severity by Race in Selected Crime Categories

Crime Category	Black Defendants	White Defendants	Unit Difference	r
Murder	66.5	61.9	+4.6	.05
	(812)	(67)		
Manslaughter	36.5	31.4	+5.1	.10
	(316)	(58)		
Robbery	40.6	33.1	+7.5	.11*
	(3,582)	(299)		
Aggravated assault	26.4	23.0	+3.4	.09*
	(1,751)	(329)		
Minor assault	19.0	15.0	+4.0	.17*
	(1,456)	(575)		
Burglary	26.9	23.5	+3.4	.12*
	(4,451)	(1,305)		
Larceny	22.6	19.7	+2.9	.12*
	(2,515)	(617)		
Auto larceny	20.4	18.1	+2.3	.08
	(299)	(65)		
Stolen property	22.0	19.5	+2.5	.10*
	(1,761)	(504)		
Forgery-counterfeiting	20.8	20.3	+0.5	.02
	(641)	(251)		
Rape-serious sex	37.9	29.1	+8.8	.15*
	(478)	(95)		
Drug offenses	20.2	17.0	+3.2	.14*
	(3,232)	(1,082)		
Weapons offenses	19.0	17.0	+2.0	.07*
	(2,056)	(253)		
Driving under the influence	11.9	8.8	+3.1	.16*
	(799)	(327)		
Gambling	8.8	9.6	−0.8	−.05
	(146)	(76)		
Contributing to delinquency	20.7	19.2	+1.5	.07
	(163)	(128)		

*Statistically significant at .01 level.

Note: Mean sentence based on 93-point sentence severity scale. r = Pearson's Product-Moment Correlation Coefficient.

Source: Compiled by the author.

ALTERNATIVE EXPLANATIONS FOR INTERRACIAL SENTENCING DISPARITIES

Alternative explanations for interracial disparities are directly attributable to the inherent complexity of the santioning process. Believing the direct link between race and sanctioning is an inaccurate oversimplification of a multifaceted relationship, researchers have incorporated intervening variables into broader analyses of the question. In general, these are attempts to view sanctioning in more comprehensive terms by including several variables of which race is only one.

These efforts represent notable advancements in exploring the impact of race in adjudicatory proceedings. Complex interrelationships among a series of variables describe the reality of the process. While giving full credit to these studies, frequently they also are limited. Restricted either by missing variables or a narrrow theoretical focus, many fail to examine the full spectrum of explanatory alternatives. To mitigate this problem it is useful to develop a more general race-sanctioning model unencumbered by either limitations on the available data or a favored explanatory theory.

An approach to constructing this model is to introduce and define a network of direct and indirect causal relationships between defendant race and sanctioning outcomes. The principles of path analysis are applicable to such a complex causal structure.[15] Specifically, a multistage, multivariate, recursive path model enables us to explicitly state theoretical propositions and describe potential pathways of influence linking race and sanctioning decisions.

This formulation is more than an intellectual exercise. We need to interpret the disparities found in Metro City. Within the framework of a general model, we can make explicit omissions that are due to data limitations. Not every explanatory option can be explored but at least we can specify where gaps remain. Finally, the general model is useful for theory-building by functioning as a convenient reference in developing alternative theoretical structures and/or analytic approaches.

A recent critic of sanctioning studies concludes that nearly every project is incomplete, fragmentary, and "... necessarily inadequate to the question at issue."[16] Beginning with a general model and then operationalizing it within the limitations imposed by the data represents a comprehensive approach to analyzing an emotionally charged issue, set in a complex environment, and already subject to a variety of interpretations.

Criminality Component

Edward Green is one of the strongest and most persuasive advocates of what will be referred to as the criminality component of the race-sanctioning

FIGURE 2.1

Criminality Component

Source: Compiled by the author.

model.[17] Green contends that while absolute race-related disparities exist, they most likely are the indirect result of differing patterns of criminal behavior. Subsequent research has supported his contention.[18] According to Green, "When the effect of these variant patterns of criminal behavior is controlled ... the differences in the severity of the sentences [by defendant race] become negligible."[19] Here the defendant race-sanctioning relationship is indirectly operative through various determinants of criminality. (See Figure 2.1.)

The factors most frequently used to gauge criminality are a defendant's prior record and the severity of the criminal act that has been committed. In Green's studies, black defendants not only had more extensive prior criminal records but also committed more serious offenses.[20] Similar patterns are evident elsewhere as absolute race-sanctioning relationships vanish when criminality variables are controlled.[21]

When race acts through differences in criminality, it is argued that resulting disparities are legitimate and even necessary responses to legally relevant and justifiable distinctions among cases. This indirect linkage is not considered discriminatory. Blacks are sanctioned more harshly because of the greater extent of their criminal activity.[22] Bluntly stated, proponents of the criminality component of a general race-sanctioning model contend that if blacks receive harsher punishment as a result of committing more serious crimes or committing crimes more frequently, they are receiving their due.

Class/Status Component

An interpretation of race-related sanctioning disparities giving primary emphasis to legally relevant criteria presents the criminal-justice mechanism in a favorable light. Alternative explanations are far less complimentary. Links between race and wealth or class differentials among defendants may affect sanctioning outcomes. Labeled the class/status component of the general model, this explanatory alternative posits that inequities arise as middle- and upper-class defendants receive more favorable treatment in the criminal-justice process than do their lower-class counterparts. Differential impacts can be hypothesized as being both direct and indirect. Class and status differences affect sanctioning outcomes as well as a series of important presanctioning decisions, such as bail-bond proceedings and plea negotiations. Racial disparities emerge to the extent that black and other minority-group members are poor and lower class or are so perceived by criminal-justice decision makers. The class/status component is depicted in Figure 2.2.

FIGURE 2.2

Class/Status Component

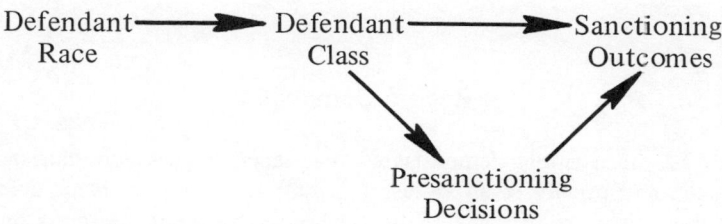

Source: Compiled by the author.

Specifically, defendant race and class status can be related with whites generally perceived as predominantly middle and upper class and blacks predominantly lower class. Blacks again are expected to fare worse than whites in the criminal-justice process. The disparity is attributed, in part, to income differentials between poorer blacks and more affluent whites.[23] But it is more than poverty that is operative. Stuart Nagel sees the indigent facing "... the handicap that he is and looks lower class while those who determine his destiny ... are middle class."[24] So in addition to the tangible burdens of poverty, the poor black confronts a criminal-justice mechanism that may more readily or perhaps only identify with and respond equitably to economically privileged defendants.

One effect of this race-class relationship may be a direct impact on sanctioning outcomes. Representative is William Chambliss' finding that, "The lower class person was more likely to be found guilty and if found guilty, more likely to receive harsh punishment than his middle and upper class counterpart."[25]

As Figure 2.2 indicates, the effect may also be indirect and operate through one or more presanctioning decisions that ultimately affect case disposition. For example, class differences among defendants have been found related to representation by private counsel, favorable bail determinations, and successful plea negotiations—decisions subsequently linked to differential sanctioning.[26]

Like the criminality component, the class/status interpretation proposes no direct race-sanctioning linkage. This is their only point in common as the general thrust and implications stemming from each differ markedly. It may be argued that race-related disparities are acceptable when tied to variations in legal criteria. One would be hard-pressed, however, to justify disparities that are related to class and income differentials among defendants. Thus, to the extent it can be supported by actual data, the class/status dimension represents injustice that is operative in the criminal process. The inequities described, though related to racial differences, are filtered through class disparities; as such this component of the general race-sanctioning model can be distinguished from both the criminality linkage already described and the explanatory path we have yet to discuss—"pure" racism.

Racism Component

It has been amply demonstrated that race-related sanctioning disparities both exist and usually result in less favorable treatment for black defendants. Often these data are offered by those whose subsequent interpretations place them in either the criminality or class/status components of the general model. For some, however, these findings are clear and convincing proof that racism directed against black Americans is commonplace in the sanctioning process.[27] Representative is Marvin Wolfgang's and Marc Reidel's conclusion that, "Far from being 'freakish' or capricious . . . the significant racial differentials found in the imposition of the death penalty are indeed produced by racial discrimination."[28]

Thus, a third and perhaps the most ominous interpretation of absolute race-sanctioning disparities is posited. To the extent that race-related differences

FIGURE 2.3

Racism Component

Defendant Race ⟶ Sanctioning Outcomes

Source: Compiled by the author.

FIGURE 2.4

General Race-Sanctioning Model

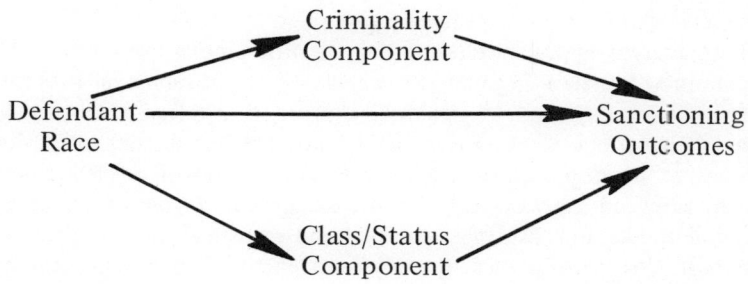

Source: Compiled by the author.

in sanctioning appear, they are hypothesized to result from racist or discriminatory behavior on the part of the key decision makers. Depicted in Figure 2.3, this component of the general path model is viewed as a clear and direct relationship linking racial differences to sanctioning outcomes; the minority group defendant is victimized by unfavorable sanctioning decisions based solely upon his or her racial identification.

Proponents of the racism explanation usually do not attack alternative interpretations, but they often ignore or fail to test them. It is now evident how misleading these omissions might be. Figure 2.4 depicts the three major components of the race-sanctioning model. When one also includes possible linkages between the criminality and class/status components,[29] we see that labeling absolute sanctioning differences as racist is only one of three or more viable explanations for the disparities uncovered. One can interpret as racist or discriminatory that portion of the association that remains after the criminality and class/status components have had chances to operate. The same approach is required in interpreting the other two explanatory paths. Each one could be the major determinant of the race-related disparities. But their impacts can only be gauged accurately after taking into account the influence of other factors.

A PATH ANALYSIS OF METRO CITY DATA

Having described the model in general form, we are in a position to examine it within the context of the Metro City criminal-justice system. Without the restrictions imposed by the reality of available data, a more complete version has been outlined. An attempt to operationalize it will entail simplifying assumptions and limitations. But this effort is worthwhile. Disparate—and in some ways contradictory—explanations have been offered by others to account for race-related sanctioning disparities such as those found in Metro City. Individually these explanations have been tested haphazardly; they have yet to be explored jointly. Therefore, even a limited test of the model will provide useful insights into the relative influences of its three principal components.

Path analysis appears well-suited to the interpretive task outlined.[30] We have determined that a fragmentary analysis of the absolute race-sanctioning relationship using any single explanatory component can lead to erroneous conclusions. This serious shortcoming can be avoided by utilizing path analytic techniques to develop simple and compound pathways of influence between defendant race and sanctioning.[31] To the extent we are able to operationalize the general model and also meet the required statistical assumptions,[32] path analysis will allow us to observe the relative strengths of the racism, criminality, and class/status components evident in Metro City.

Of immediate concern is the assumption in path analysis that residuals of error terms not be correlated among themselves or with more than one variable in the causal system. To approximate this, all relevant variables should be specified in the model. In the operational version, a defendant's prior record and class/status do not appear, raising the prospect to correlated residuals. These unmeasured variables create a regrettable but unavoidable loss of information. Their absence, however, does not undermine the rest of the analysis.

The effects of the defendant's socioeconomic status (SES) and prior record are merged with the impact of racial differences. Figures 2.5 and 2.6

FIGURE 2.5

Race-Sanctioning Model, Including SES and Prior Record

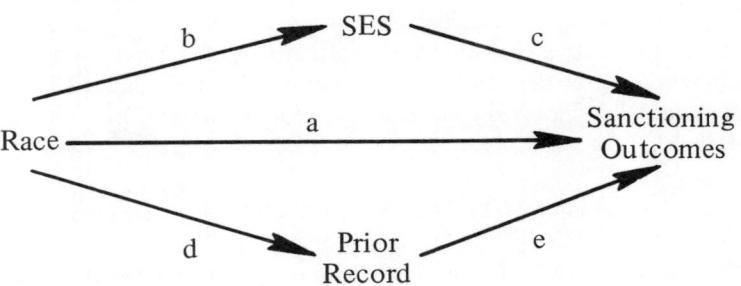

Source: Compiled by the author.

FIGURE 2.6

Race-Sanctioning Model Where SES and Prior Record Remain Unmeasured

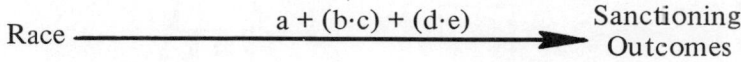

Source: Compiled by the author.

describe the situation in simplified form. In Figure 2.5 we specify the direct effect of race on sanctioning as path a and indirect effects via defendant SES (path b × c) and defendant prior record (d × e). This figure approximates the original path model. Figure 2.6 represents the operational version where SES and prior record remain unmeasured. The race-sanctioning relationship now includes both the direct and indirect effects of race. Therefore, what we will measure as a race impact is really an upper bound for racial influences that also includes class and prior record. These variables are not eliminated from the causal system and do not become correlated residuals. Instead, they may be conceived of as "phantom" variables whose influence is joined to that of race.

Of the numerous models that could be developed from these data, only a general defendant race-sentencing path model is actually operationalized.[33] First, we briefly survey a fully defined or "just-identified" model and from it construct a more easily interpreted and parsimoniously reduced version based on the strongest simple and compound paths linking race and sentencing outcomes. Path coefficients in the reduced model are then reestimated to gauge the relative impact of the remaining pathways. At this point we are able to compare the contributions made by the three major components of the general model to the absolute disparities noted previously.

Figure 2.7 depicts the fully defined race-sentencing path model for the Metro City court. For ease of reference, individual variables are numbered in causal sequence, and the figure is presented along with a summary table (Table 2.5) describing the operationalization in detail. (The simple correlations among the variables in the model appear in Table 2.7.)

In Figure 2.7, the total defendant race-sentence correlation is $r = .16$. We hypothesize defendant race (1) as having a direct effect on sentence severity (9), p_{91}, in addition to indirect effects through the criminality and class/status components. Portions of both of these components are examined. The number of charges (2) and charge severity (3) represent the extensiveness and seriousness of the criminal behavior alleged (criminality component). Bail amount (4), type of counsel (5), bail status (6), disposition (7), and charge reduction (8) describe

FIGURE 2.7

A Fully Defined Race-Sentencing Path Model

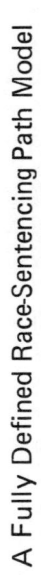

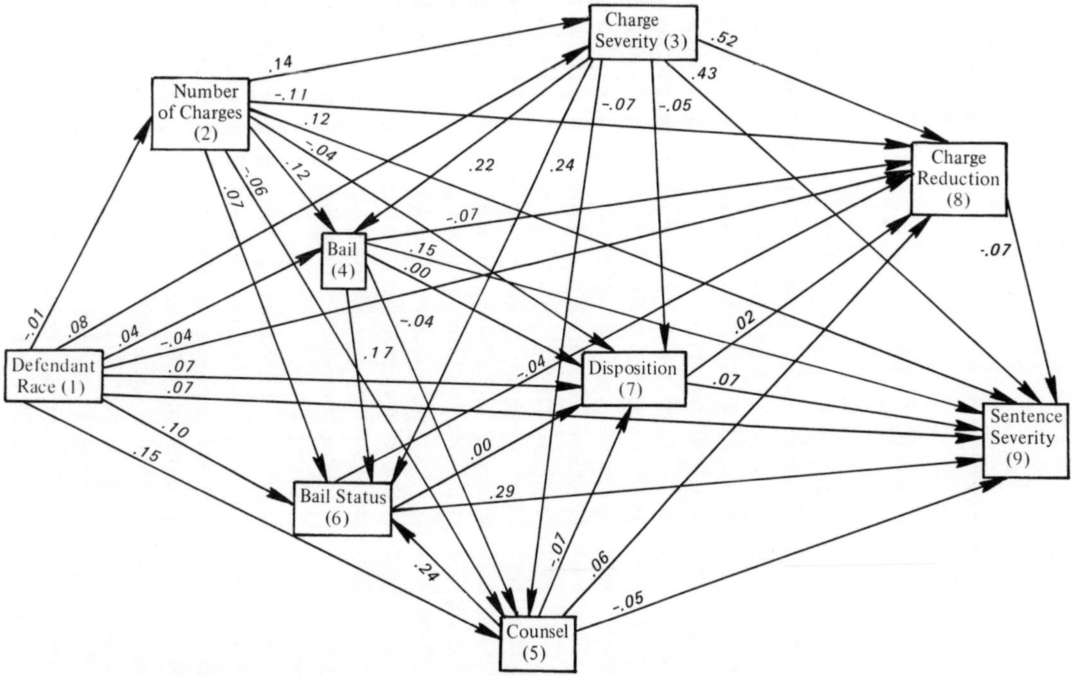

*All path coefficients larger than .00 are statistically significant at the .01 level.
Source: Compiled by the author.

TABLE 2.5

Variables Included in Race-Sentencing Path Model

Variable	Code Description
Race of defendant (1)	1 = black defendant
	0 = white defendant
Number of charges lodged against defendant (2)	—
Maximum potential sentence for charge/crime (3)[a]	—
Amount of bail (4)[b]	—
Type of defense counsel (5)	1 = court-appointed public or private defender
	0 = retained counsel
Defendant pretrial bail status (6)	1 = pretrial detention
	0 = pretrial release
Disposition (7)	1 = judge or jury guilty verdict
	0 = guilty plea
Charge reduction—evidence of plea negotiation (8)	1 = sentenced on most serious charge or charge tied as most serious
	0 = sentenced on less than most serious charge
Sentence severity (9)	93-point sentence severity scale[c]

[a]Measured in years.
[b]Measured in dollars.
[c]See note 11 at end of chapter.
Source: Compiled by the author.

presanctioning decisions or institutional responses that may differentially affect various defendant groups (class/status component). Relationships are hypothesized between defendant race and the criminality and the class/status components, between elements of the criminality and the class/status components themselves, among individual factors within each component, and between each variable and sentence outcome.

The model as described is quite complex and space limitations prohibit analyzing each path. Some general observations are, however, in order. Lending credibility to the entire model is evidence that the direction and magnitude of the most frequently described paths are in accord with prior research.

Within the criminality component, positive relationships exist between the number of charges and eventual sentence ($p_{92} = .12$) and charge severity and sentence severity ($p_{93} = .43$). The extent of alleged criminal activity can also be expected to influence presanctioning decisions (class/status). The number of charges is positively related to both bail amounts ($p_{42} = .12$) and bail status ($p_{62} = .07$). The charge severity-bond paths are substantially stronger ($p_{43} = .22$; $p_{63} = .24$). The more serious the alleged offense the higher the bail requirement and the less likely the defendant is to obtain pretrial release.

Logical relationships also link the number of charges to both charge severity and charge reduction. Charging a defendant with more offenses increases both the prospect that at least one of the charged offenses will be serious ($p_{32} = .14$) and the likelihood of eventual sentencing on a reduced charge ($p_{82} = -.11$). Finally, the strong, positive path between charge severity and charge reduction ($p_{83} = .52$) indicates that reduced charges are much less likely to be given in more serious and perhaps more visible cases.

Bail amount and bail status are both interpreted as intermediate stages in the sanctioning process that may affect final case dispositions directly or indirectly through the plea-bargaining process. Only direct effects materialize. Higher bail amounts are related to more severe sentences. The marked drop-off ($p_{94} = .15$) from the simple correlation ($p_{49} = .35$) indicates that part of the impact of bail amount on sentence severity operates through bail status. This interpretation is supported as we observe a strong relationship between bail amount and bail status ($p_{64} = .17$) and also find an important path linking bail status and sentencing ($p_{96} = .29$). The latter relationship concurs with previous studies, indicating that harsher sanctions are more likely to be accorded defendants unable to win pretrial release.

The remaining class/status variables yield a mixed set of relationships with sentencing outcomes. The generally accepted notion that the criminal-justice system rewards those who cooperate and punishes those who do not receives some support. A defendant whose case proceeds to trial does indeed wind up with a higher average sentence ($p_{97} = .07$). The path between charge reduction and sentence ($p_{98} = -.07$) indicates that in cases where charges are reduced, relatively more severe sentences are meted out. With crime severity held constant, defendants convicted on a reduced charge are more likely to be sentenced closer to the maximum on the reduced charge while those convicted on more serious charges tend to be given less than maximum sentences. Plea "bargains" in Metro City may be more apparent than real.

One of the few relationships running counter to general expectations links type of defense counsel to sentence severity. In Metro City, defendants represented by court-appointed counsel receive less severe sentences than do defendants with privately retained counsel ($p_{95} = -.05$). While a similar finding has been reported elsewhere,[34] the pattern contradicts the notion that private counsel are more successful advocates.

This path marks one of the few exceptions to a broad range of relationships that are close to previously observed patterns. Therefore, the operational path model appears to be a realistic portrayal of a complex network of interrelationships among critical variables in the sanctioning process. The paths from defendant race to other variables in the causal system provide further evidence in this regard. They also demonstrate support for the three major components of the general model.

Despite a marginal path to the number-of-charges variable ($p_{21} = -.01$), the criminality explanation is evident as black defendants are convicted of more serious offenses than are whites ($p_{31} = .08$). The class/status component is also supported with blacks more frequently recipients of unfavorable presanctioning decisions. They are given higher bail ($p_{41} = .04$), are less likely to obtain pretrial release ($p_{61} = .10$), are more likely to go to trial ($p_{71} = .07$), and are more likely to be represented by court-appointed counsel ($p_{51} = .15$). Even their apparent advantage in charge reduction ($p_{81} = -.04$) is largely eliminated by harsher sentences on reduced charges.

Finally, the racism component is left. After removing the effects of portions of the criminality and class/status interpretations, a significant, direct race-related disparity remains. The path coefficient ($p_{91} = .07$) may confirm charges that behavior most accurately termed racist exists in the sanctioning process. This conclusion must still be guarded because the direct race-sentencing path may include the unmeasured effects of defendant class/status and prior record.

A REDUCED MODEL

Interpreting the impact of defendant race within the context of the fully defined model is a difficult task at best. It is hard to gauge the relative impacts of the criminality and class/status components or identify the specific indirect paths that are most important to each. Well over 50 individual pathways can be followed linking defendant race to sentence outcome. Since most of these compound paths contribute extremely little to the total race-sentencing association, it becomes useful to construct a more parsimonious model.

The goal in developing this reduced model is the retention of the strongest, simple and compound paths of influence between defendant race and sentencing outcomes. The standard to be used is not simply the size of the paths emanating from race or flowing into sentencing but rather the total impact of a particular pathway, derived by multiplying together the individual coefficients that comprise the path. This was done for every compound path. No standard measure of significance is available in determining which pathways to keep and which to discard,[35] but a reasonable cutoff did emerge. Remembering that the sum of all possible paths is .16 (equaling the simple correlation between race and sentence severity), it was decided that compound paths of less than .01 would be too weak to be considered theoretically meaningful. After eliminating them, three

FIGURE 2.8

A Reduced Race-Sentencing Path Model

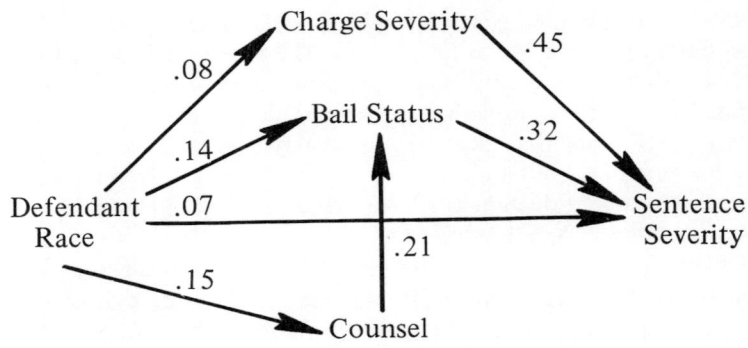

Source: Compiled by the author.

compound paths and three intervening variables remained in addition to the direct race-sentencing relationship. Figure 2.8 depicts the reduced race-sentencing model including reestimated path coefficients.

This model describes in much clearer fashion the key linkages between defendant race and sentencing outcomes. The three intervening variables represent two of the primary components of the general race model with the direct path representing the third. Table 2.6 presents the individual pathways and their relative strengths in the model.

The criminality component is represented by charge severity and shows blacks receiving more severe punishment, in part at least, because they are charged with more serious offenses. The path from charge into sentence is clearly the strongest in the model, but the path from race is the weakest. The product of both (.036) describes about 22 percent of the total race-sentencing relationship. This is less than either of the two remaining general interpretations.

The class/status component is described by two paths. Both include a defendant's bail status as an intervening variable with one also incorporating type of defense counsel. The race → counsel → bail status → sentence linkage is the weakest in the reduced model, accounting for about 6 percent of the observed disparity. It indicates that black defendants are more likely to be represented by court-appointed counsel. These attorneys appear less effective than privately retained counsel at getting defendants released pending trial. The bail status disparity is also linked directly to racial differences. Black defendants are less likely to make bail and be released, with the compound path of .045

TABLE 2.6

A Reduced Race-Sentencing Model: Significant Pathways of Influence

Pathway and Component	Path Coefficients and Products		Percent of Total Relationship
Criminality			
Race → Charge → Sentence	(.08)(.45) = .036		22.4
Class/Status			
Race → Bail Status → Sentence	(.14)(.32) = .045	28.0	
Race → Counsel → Bail Status → Sentence	(.15)(.21)(.32) = .010	6.2	
			34.2
Racism			
Race → Sentence	.07		43.5
	Total Correlation = .161		100.0

Source: Compiled by the author.

representing nearly 28 percent of the total race-related difference. Both paths describe inequities because the direct consequence of pretrial detention status is harsher sentencing.

Bail status unquestionably emerges as the key class/status variable in the model. Besides being unjust punishment if later found innocent, prisoner status may create unfavorable stereotypes among court officials as well as result in decreased opportunities to prepare a defense. Thus, blacks are indeed disadvantaged to the extent that they are less likely to make bail. What we are probably witnessing are race-related inequities caused primarily by the limited financial resources of Metro City blacks. Being poorer than their white counterparts, they are less able to retain private counsel and, more importantly, less able to raise bail that has been set. While this pattern is more class-related than racist, it clearly describes a disturbing inequity in the criminal-justice mechanism.

The last path connecting defendant race and sentence outcome is the direct one between the two variables. With a coefficient equalling .07, it accounts for over 40 percent of the total association. This component has been labeled racist and except for the unmeasured, intervening influence of defendant prior record and SES, no other interpretation is tenable. After taking out the influence of both the criminality and class/status variables, race-related differences in sentencing severity remain.

CONCLUSIONS

The reduced model allows us to reach some tentative conclusions in interpreting the absolute race-sentencing relationship noted previously. The actual pathways of influence between race and sentence outcome do approximate the major components of the general path model. This means that while proponents of a criminality interpretation are correct in advocating the inclusion of legally relevant variables, greater criminality by blacks does not emerge as the sole explanation for the disparities reported. Also, the criminal-justice mechanism responds, either by conscious design or circumstance, to defendants favored by private counsel and pretrial release status. On the average, white defendants are the primary recipients of these favorable institutional responses that later affect sentencing. Finally, all the observed race-related disparities cannot be "explained away" using either the criminality or class/status explanations. The largest proportion of the total race-sentencing relationship may describe unjustified, discriminatory treatment.

In light of the available evidence, defendant race makes meaningful differences in the Metro City criminal-justice sanctioning process. These differences are significant and unjust to the extent they operate through a class-oriented institutional structure or spring directly from discriminatory decisions on the part of key actors. However, considerable caution must still be exercised in reaching this conclusion. Care is needed because of major differences in the impact of defendant race on conviction rates and sentence severity. A priori, there is no reason why one would hypothesize behavior labeled as discriminatory occurring at one point in the highly interrelated sanctioning process and not the next; one would expect that discrimination is either present or it is not. Therefore, the finding that racism may exist in sentencing while race-related disparities are minimal in determinations of guilt leads us to at least suggest an alternative explanation.

The answer may be found in the varying impact of a defendant's prior criminal record on these two sanctioning decisions. As previously noted, prior record and sentence severity have been strongly and positively related.[36] On the other hand, the relationship between record and case verdict should be minimal, given that information on prior record is not usually in evidence at trial.[37] Juxtaposing our findings and the conventional wisdom regarding prior record encourages speculation that record and not defendant race may be responsible for a major portion of the absolute disparity left unexplained by the other independent variables. Likewise, the small race-related disparities in conviction rates may simply reflect the minimal influence of record on this sanctioning decision.

This interpretation is offered as a logical but untested alternative. It must remain so until prior record can be investigated in conjunction with the variables examined here.

TABLE 2.7

An Operational Race-Sentencing Path Model: Simple Correlations

	Sentence	Race	Bail Amount	Bail Status	Number of Charges	Charge Severity	Charge Reduction	Plea	Counsel
Sentence	—								
Race	.16	—							
Bail Amount	.35	.05	—						
Bail Status	.46	.17	.23	—					
Number of Charges	.24	-.01	.15	.11	—				
Charge Severity	.54	.08	.25	.29	.14	—			
Charge Reduction	.15	.00	.03	.09	-.06	.47	—		
Plea	.05	.05	-.01	-.02	-.04	-.04	.00	—	
Counsel	-.02	.15	-.06	.23	-.08	-.06	.02	-.05	—

Note: All correlation coefficients larger than .00 are statistically significant at .01 level. N = 32,731.
Source: Compiled by the author.

Operationalizing prior record is just one of several possible extensions of the conceptual framework and method of analysis utilized in this chapter.[38] We have attempted to broaden the interpretation and refine the analysis of the complex race-sanctioning relationship. While these objectives may have been achieved in part, there remains a need for further development on both the theoretical and operational levels. From this initial effort, path-analytic techniques appear well-suited to both tasks. The approach has the flexibility to incorporate sanctioning complexities in a systematic analysis of what remains an important criminal-justice issue.

NOTES

1. Many of the major race-sanctioning studies are cited in John Hagan, "Extra-Legal Attributes and Criminal Sentencing: An Assessment of a Sociological Viewpoint," *Law and Society Review* 8 (1974): 357-83. See also George William Baab and William Royal Furgeson, "Texas Sentencing Practices: A Statistical Study," *Texas Law Review* 45 (1967): 471-503; Donald Bartlett and James Steele, "Crime and Injustice," Philadelphia *Inquirer*, February 18-24, 1973; Jules B. Gerard and T. Rankin Terry, "Discrimination Against Negroes in the Administration of Criminal Law in Missouri," *Washington University Law Quarterly* (1970): 415-37; James L. Gibson, "Racial Discrimination in Criminal Courts: Some Theoretical and Methodological Considerations" (mimeographed paper available upon request from the author at the University of Wisconsin-Milwaukee); Herbert Jacob and James Eisenstein, "Sentences and Other Sanctions Imposed on Felony Defendants in Baltimore, Chicago, and Detroit" (Paper read at the annual meeting of the American Political Science Association, Chicago, August 29-September 2, 1974); Terence P. Thornberry, "Race, Socioeconomic Status and Sentencing in the Juvenile Justice System," *The Journal of Criminal Law and Criminology* 64 (1973): 90-98.

2. Stuart S. Nagel and Marian Neef touch on many of the difficulties and potential problems in a recent manuscript entitled "The Racial Disparity that Supposedly Wasn't There: Some Pitfalls to Watch for in Analyzing Court Statistics" (mimeographed paper available upon request from the authors at the University of Illinois at Champaign-Urbana).

3. Frederick Douglass, as quoted in A. Leon Higgenbotham, "The Black Lawyer in America Today," *Harvard Law School Bulletin* 22 (1971): 57.

4. The similarities between Metro City and other large urban centers, such as black in-migration, "white flight," low measures of personal income and wealth, and high crime rates, might increase representativeness and, hence, our ability to generalize from these data. No matter how representative it is, however, the city and the court constitute a single sample point containing unmeasured and uncontrolled dimensions of uniqueness.

5. Invalid charge codes include 40 cases falling outside the general classification of crime categories established by the court administrator's office. Of more importance are the 19.7 percent of these data deleted because of problematic disposition codes. The criterion determining validity is whether a clear determination of guilt or innocence is rendered. Omitted are cases: nolle prosequi (5,995); transferred (291); dropped on a technicality (2,661); dismissed by grand jury (2,081); routed through preindictment probation (964); containing apparent coding errors (313). Finally, 162 cases contain invalid sentence codes—sentences to mental institutions or cases where not-guilty dispositions indicated punishment and vice versa.

Within the remaining sample, a single charge, disposition, and sentence frequently have to be selected among several in multiple-charge cases. Prior research serves as a general guide with three criteria selected to break successive ties. The initial basis for charge selection is actual sentence severity (Engle). That is, in multiple-charge cases, if one charge carries a sentence more severe than any other, it represents the "crime" for that particular case. This charge is judged to be most representative of the actual punishment accorded a defendant.

In many cases, however, a single sentence does not emerge from this procedure as most severe. Ties remain because not-guilty verdicts are rendered or several charges receive equally severe sentences. In these instances, among those charges with maximum tied sentences, the charge carrying the most severe potential maximum penalty is selected (Green). Maximum sentences are calculated from a list of standard offenses in Metro City and state.

At this point, fewer than 5 percent of the cases remain tied on maximum-sentence severity and maximum-charge severity. Charges still tied are grouped into general-crime categories and the crime categories ranked as to severity (Baab and Furgeson). Ties are broken with the charge falling in the most serious category chosen.

Finally, random selection is used to choose among a few charges that are now virtually indistinguishable—falling in the same general-crime category, carrying the same maximum potential punishment, and accorded the same actual sentence. See Charles Engle, "Criminal Justice in the City: A Study of Sentence Severity and Variation in the Philadelphia Criminal Court System" (Ph.D. dissertation, Temple University, 1971), pp. 79-80; Edward Green, *Judicial Attitudes in Sentencing* (New York: St. Martin's Press, 1961), p. 26; Baab and Furgeson, op. cit., pp. 490-91.

6. For several reasons 5,135 cases are dropped because of invalid defendant race data. Initially, the 3,430 cases failing to contain a race code are eliminated. Most of these data appear in 1968, the year the computerized record-keeping system was initiated, and can be attributed to early mechanical and procedural flaws. Since our primary interest is in the treatment accorded black and white defendants, the inclusion of additional racial or ethnic factors adds unnecessary and undesired complexity to the analysis. Because of this problem and evidence that sanctioning patterns may vary between other ethnic groups and both black and white defendants, 1,705 defendants coded as being of "other" races (Mexican-American, Puerto Rican, American Indian) are also eliminated. See Peter Greenwood et al., *Prosecution of Adult Felony Defendants in Los Angeles County: A Policy Perspective* (Santa Monica: The Rand Corporation, 1973); Markham, op. cit.

7. This information, important in controlling for the varying severity of different criminal charges, is not located in 160 cases.

8. Cases with invalid judge codes (1,643), missing background data (986), or those cases decided by visiting and/or semiretired judges (3,210) are excluded. These deletions result from other analyses of these data but should not affect a randomness assumption here.

9. Missing data are deleted pairwise or variable by variable. Because of the case-deletion criteria adopted there are no missing data for the crime category, charge severity, number of charges, or method of disposition variables. Missing data on bail amounts include 18.1 percent of the cases where defendants remain in pretrial custody with no dollar bail established. Instead of setting arbitrary dollar figures in these cases, they are omitted in bail calculations. In determining bail status, the 2.3 percent of the defendants classified as "fugitives" are also treated as missing. Valid defense-counsel codes appear in 98.9 percent of the cases. Cases containing only a single charge are classified as missing on the evidence charge-reduction variable.

10. Clearly these are critical decisions in the sanctioning process. They are not, however, the only important ones. Pretrial actions, such as a decision to dismiss or route a case through preindictment probation, may have already determined the fate of a criminal defendant.

11. Since the use and abuse of sentence severity scales have engendered controversy, further explanation is in order. Suspended sentences are considered the least serious form of punishment handed down by a court. Usually involving little or no supervision and rarely revoked, suspended sentences are termed "judicial warnings" by Green. Next in increasing order of severity stand five fine categories. Unlike suspended sentences, they carry with them a penalty resulting in deprivation but the potential for actual punishment is considered less than either probated or active jail sentences. The logical extension of both of these major divisions is a set of scale values for cases disposed of with both suspended sentences and fines.

Probationary sentences are ranked next in severity (scale values 12-31). Occasionally treated as less or equally severe as fines and suspended sentences, they are generally operationalized as more severe than both. This relative positioning is due to the conditional nature of the sentence as well as the greater restrictions placed on the offender. Probationary sentences vary, making it appropriate to differentiate among them on the sentencing scale. Finally, to avoid an unnecessary loss of sanctioning information, probated sentences alone are distinguished from sentences of a similar length that include a fine.

The final 61 scale values represent the active sentencing options available to Metro City judges. Severity rankings in this project, as in nearly every previous work, are keyed to the minimum sentence as the most reliable indicator of the actual period of imprisonment expected. But additional sanctioning information is incorporated by making secondary differentiations based on the maximum sentences included in a decision.

A detailed description of the entire scale is available from the author at the University of Missouri-St. Louis. For the development, discussion, and application of sentencing scales see, Baab and Furgeson, op. cit.; Engle, op. cit.; Green, op. cit.; Jacob and Eisenstein, op. cit.; Markham, op. cit.; Gibson, op. cit.

The potential pitfalls attending the adoption of this scale are similar to those developed previously. There is an inevitable degree of arbitrariness in the ranking scheme. One must assume that this factor and others possibly distorting the scale values are randomly distributed and not systematically related to the independent variables studied. Also, sentence severity as measured here is most precisely an ordinal scale. The index is, however, open to interval interpretations. With the expectation that the results will be roughly linear to the scale, we may take advantage of stronger interval statistical techniques. While some valid ordinal transformation of the scale might be possible, it is unlikely to change the results significantly. See Hubert M. Blalock, Jr., *Causal Inferences in Nonexperimental Research* (Chapel Hill: University of North Carolina Press, 1964), pp. 34-35, W. Phillips Shively, *The Craft of Political Research* (Englewood Cliffs, N.J.: Prentice-Hall, 1974), pp. 71-76.

12. For example, see Marvin E. Wolfgang and Marc Reidel, "Race, Judicial Discretion and the Death Penalty," *Annals of the American Academy of Political and Social Science* 407 (1973): 119-33; Stuart S. Nagel, *The Legal Process From a Behavioral Perspective* (Homewood, Ill.: Dorsey Press, 1969): pp. 81-112; Henry Allen Bullock, "Significance of the Racial Factor in the Length of Prison Sentences," *Journal of Criminal Law, Criminology and Police Science* 52 (1961): 411-17; Morris A. Forslund, "Age, Occupation and Conviction Rates of White and Negro Males: A Case Study," *Rocky Mountain Social Science Journal* 6 (1969): 141-46. Many of these studies do, however, part ways either over the size of the interracial disparity or its interpretation.

A few exceptions to this general pattern exist. See Dean Jaros and Robert I. Mendelsohn, "The Judicial Role and Sentencing Behavior," *Midwest Journal of Political Science*

11 (1967): 471-88; Robert M. Terry, "The Screening of Juvenile Offenders," *Journal of Criminal Law, Criminology and Police Science* 58 (1967): 178.

13. Bullock, op. cit., p. 412.

14. The two exceptions occur in the crimes of manslaughter and contributing to the delinquency of a minor.

15. Donald E. Stokes, "Compound Paths: An Expository Note," *American Journal of Political Science* 18 (1974): 191-214; Kenneth C. Land, "Principles of Path Analysis," in *Sociological Methodology 1969*, ed. Edgar F. Borgatta (San Francisco: Jossey-Bass, 1969), pp. 3-37.

16. Hagan, op. cit., p. 379.

17. Green, op. cit., pp. 56-63.

18. See, for example, Hagan, op. cit., p. 379; Gibson, op. cit., p. 15; Maureen Mileski, "Courtroom Encounters: An Observation Study of a Lower Criminal Court," *Law and Society Review* 5 (1971): 505-10; Thornberry, op. cit., p. 92; Robert M. Terry, "Discrimination in the Handling of Juvenile Offenders by Social-Control Agencies," *Journal of Research in Crime and Delinquency* 4 (1967): 227-28.

19. Green, op. cit., p. 63.

20. Edward Green, "Inter- and Intra-Racial Crime Relative to Sentencing," *Journal of Criminal Law, Criminology and Police Science* 105 (1964): 348-58; Green, *Judicial Attitudes*, op. cit., pp. 56-63.

21. See note 18.

22. One important caveat is in order. The criminality component of the race-sanctioning model is characterized as nondiscriminatory, but inequities exist to the extent that, as alleged, blacks are more frequently arrested and/or victimized by overcharging. See Bullock, op. cit., p. 412; Markham, op. cit., p. 5.

This overlap indicates the difficulty in trying to compartmentalize an entire process where decisions at one stage inevitably influence decisions made subsequently. In order to carry out research in the area, simplifications must be made. With equal certainty, however, problems will inevitably arise. The trade-off is as unfortunate as it is unavoidable.

23. Nagel is a most persuasive proponent of this view, see *Legal Process*, op. cit., pp. 87-95. See also Stephen Bing and S. Stephen Rosenfeld, "The Quality of Justice: In the Lower Courts of Metropolitan Boston," *Criminal Law Bulletin* 7 (1971): 398.

24. Stuart S. Nagel, "The Tipped Scales of American Justice," in *The Politics of Local Justice*, eds. James R. Klonoski and Robert I. Mendelsohn (Boston Little, Brown, 1970), p. 120.

25. William J. Chambliss, *Crime and the Legal Process* (New York: McGraw-Hill, 1969), p. 294. See also, Patricia M. Wald, "Poverty and Criminal Justice," in *The Criminal in the Arms of the Law*, eds. Leon Radzinowicz and Marvin E. Wolfgang (New York: Basic Books, 1971), pp. 582-614; William J. Chambliss and Robert B. Seidman, *Law, Order, and Power* (Reading, Mass.: Addison-Wesley, 1971), p. 475.

26. Research on these questions is steadily increasing. See for example, Anne Rankin, "The Effect of Pre-Trial Detention," *New York University Law Review* 39 (1964): 631-41; David N. Atkinson and Dale A. Neuman, "Judicial Attitudes and Defendant Attributes: Some Consequences for Municipal Court Decision-Making," *Journal of Public Law* 19 (1970): 69-88; Nagel, *Legal Process*, op. cit., pp. 87-92.

27. The sophistication of these projects varies widely. Some control for nonracial factors and others do not. See Bullock, op. cit., p. 412; Gerard and Terry, op. cit., pp. 432-37; Southern Regional Council, *Race Makes the Difference: An Analysis of Sentence Disparity Among Black and White Offenders in Southern Prisons* (Atlanta: Southern Regional Council, 1969); Marvin E. Wolfgang, Arlene Kelly, and Hans C. Nolde, "Comparison of the Executed and the Commuted Among Admissions to Death Row," *Journal of Criminal Law, Criminology and Police Science* 53 (1962): 301-11; Richard Quinney, *The Social Reality of Crime* (Boston: Little, Brown, 1970), p. 220.

28. Wolfgang and Reidel, op. cit., p. 133.

29. A natural time sequence indicates how the expected pathways of influence between the criminality and class/status components are structured. Defendant class/status precedes a defendant's prior record and both are established before the particular crime and the presanctioning, class-related decisions. Figure 2.9 displays the hypothesized interconnections between the two criminality (prior record, crime severity) and two class/status (defendant class/status, presanctioning decisions) factors.

Figure 2.9

Criminality and Class/Status Linkages

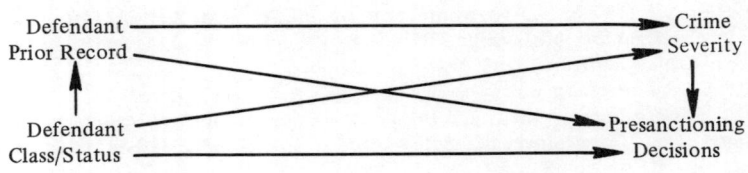

Source: Compiled by the author.

30. More detailed statistical treatments of the subject should be consulted, see Stokes, op. cit.; Land, op. cit.; Fred Kerlinger and Elazar Pedhazur, *Multiple Regression in Behavioral Research* (New York: Holt, Rinehart and Winston, 1973); Samuel A. Kirkpatrick, *Quantitative Analysis of Political Data* (Columbus, Ohio: Charles E. Merrill, 1974); Blalock, op. cit.; Hubert M. Blalock, Jr., *Causal Models in the Social Sciences* (Chicago: Aldine, 1971).

31. Using the technique, we are able to partition a correlation between variables in the path model into alternative pathways of influence. With variables expressed in standard scores (z) a path coefficient (p_{ij}) can be derived that is the standardized-regression coefficient (beta weight) obtained from ordinary least-squares analysis and measures the faction of the standard deviation of an endogenous (dependent) variable for which a particular independent variable is directly responsible. Correlation coefficients can, therefore, be broken down into simple and compound paths with each segment in a diagram or term in a structural equation representing the product of the elementary path coefficients linking the individual steps in a unique pathway.

For example, in the three-variable case (Figure 2.10) $r_{13} = p_{31} + p_{32}p_{21}$; where $p_{31} = B_{31.2}$; $p_{32} = B_{32.1}$; $p_{21} = B_{21} = r_{12}$. The first term (p_{31}) is the simple path

Figure 2.10

Three-Variable Path Model

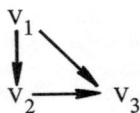

Source: Compiled by the author.

coefficient (standardized beta) between V_3 and V_1, indicating the direct effect of 1 on 3. The second term, the compound path $p_{32}p_{21}$, measures the indirect impact of V_1 and V_3, acting through the intervening variable, V_2.

The sum of the simple and compound pathways describes the total association (correlation) between V_1 and V_3 but in a form that makes meaningful distinctions among patterns of influence.

32. The appropriateness and validity of the technique rely upon meeting or approximating a rather strict set of assumptions. Two meriting special attention are the assumed existence of causal relationships and the assumed absence of reciprocal causation. The absence of reciprocal causation, also called the recursiveness assumption, means that the causal flow is unidirectional, thus eliminating feedback loops.

Though feedback can never be ruled out entirely or causality proven conclusively, an important contributing factor in meeting these assumptions is the presence of natural time intervals between events. Time sequences imply causal ordering, thereby lessening the chances for feedback. Natural time intervals are present in both the general path model outlined and the Metro City data on which the operational version is based.

The time sequences for the general model are illustrated in Figure 2.11. The main components of the race-sanctioning model are divided into four time periods that correspond to the occurrence of events in the life of a defendant and the history of his eventual criminal case. Clearly a defendant's racial identity, the variable whose impact we want to chart, is established first in the causal sequence. Nothing in our system determines race, thus making it an exogenous variable.

FIGURE 2.11

Time Sequences in the General Race-Sanctioning Model

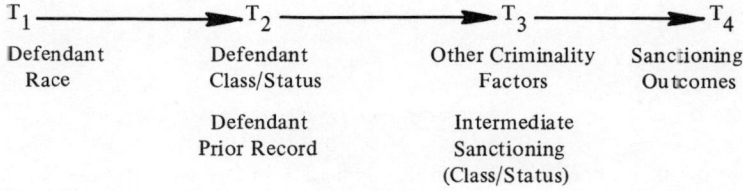

Source: Compiled by the author.

The second time period (T_2) begins after birth and ends just prior to the commission of the criminal act under consideration. Variables of importance included within it are the criminality component factor, prior record, and the class/status component, defendant class/status. While an argument may be made that race and SES are so interrelated as to render them virtually indistinguishable, class cannot cause race. Prior record falls in the latter stages of time period 2 and is subject to the influences of both defendant race and class/status. All three factors clearly precede the events in period 3.

The variables falling in the third time frame (T_3) encompass the elements of the criminal case under consideration prior to final sanctioning decisions on guilt and sentencing. A logical time sequence can be established within this period as cases flow from arrest to arraignment to adjudication. The extent and seriousness of the criminal act(s) are determined at arrest or early in case proceedings. Following closely are presanctioning decisions on counsel type and bail amounts. Then just prior to final case disposition, plea bargaining and charge reduction may occur. Finally, sanctioning outcomes in T_4 are viewed as causally dependent directly and indirectly upon one, several, or all of the variables that have preceded them in T_1, T_2, and T_3.

Other assumptions are those required in regression analysis. Interval levels of measurement are assumed using interval variables, dummy variables, and an approximated interval sentence-severity scale. Because of the large sample size, normal distributions can be assumed. Minimal measurement error is assumed to result from accurate coding and a rigorous case deletion policy. In instances where a complex causal model has been developed, certain simplifying assumptions have usually been necessary. Two are made here. They are the appropriateness of a linear and additive path model. For a more elaborate discussion of these assumptions see the citations in note 30.

33. This initial effort will focus on a full sample of cases with attempts to operationalize crime specific models deferred at present. Large samples are advantageous in path analysis and working with a wide variety of criminal charges increases the potential utility of the findings. Conviction rates are not analyzed because the interracial disparity is small in relation to sentence and jail disparities. Sentence outcomes are selected over jail rates because path analysis has usually been employed in research where interval dependent variables are available. Omission of the jail/no jail dichotomy is acceptable; at nearly every point of comparison, interracial sentence-severity and jail-rate disparities approximate each other.

34. Greenwood et al., op. cit., p. vii.

35. Land, op. cit., pp. 34-35.

36. Refer to the discussion of the criminality component supra.

37. While information on prior record does not come out directly at trial, the indirect effect may be substantial. Prior record may affect presanctioning decisions (such as the amount of bail), which in turn can influence ultimate sanctioning decisions.

38. Other important extensions would be incorporating the trial judge and the race of the victim within the general model and then testing their impacts on various defendant race-sanctioning relationships.

REFERENCES

Atkinson, David, N., and Dale A. Neuman. "Judicial Attitudes and Defendant Attributes: Some Consequences for Municipal Court Decision-Making." *Journal of Public Law* 19 (1970): 69-87.

Baab, George William, and William Royal Furgeson. "Texas Sentencing Practices: A Statistical Study." *Texas Law Review* 45 (February 1967): 471-503.

Bartlett, Donald, and James Steele. "Crime and Injustice." Philadelphia *Inquirer*, February 18-24, 1973.

Bing, Stephen, and S. Stephen Rosenfeld. "The Quality of Justice: In the Lower Courts of Metropolitan Boston." *Criminal Law Bulletin* 7 (June 1971): 393-443.

Blalock, Hubert M., Jr. *Causal Inferences in Nonexperimental Research.* Chapel Hill: University of North Carolina Press, 1964.

———. *Causal Models in the Social Sciences.* Chicago: Aldine, 1971.

Bullock, Henry Allen. "Significance of the Racial Factor in the Length of Prison Sentences." *Journal of Criminal Law, Criminology and Police Science* 52 (November/December 1961): 411-17.

Chambliss, William J. *Crime and the Legal Process.* New York: McGraw-Hill, 1969.

Chambliss, William J., and Robert B. Seidman. *Law, Order, and Power.* Reading, Mass.: Addison-Wesley, 1971.

Engle, Charles. "Criminal Justice in the City: A Study of Sentence Severity and Variation in the Philadelphia Criminal Court System." Ph.D. dissertation, Temple University, 1971.

Forslund, Morris A. "Age, Occupation and Conviction Rates of White and Negro Males: A Case Study." *Rocky Mountain Social Science Journal* 6 (1969): 141-46.

Gerard, Jules B., and T. Rankin Terry. "Discrimination Against Negroes in the Administration of Criminal Law in Missouri." *Washington University Law Quarterly* (Fall 1970): 415-37.

Gibson, James L. "Racial Discrimination in Criminal Courts: Some Theoretical and Methodological Considerations." Mimeographed. Milwaukee: University of Wisconsin-Milwaukee, 1975.

Green, Edward. *Judicial Attitudes in Sentencing.* New York: St. Martin's Press, 1961.

———. "Inter- and Intra-Racial Crime Relative to Sentencing." *Journal of Criminal Law, Criminology, and Police Science* 105 (September 1964): 348-58.

Greenwood, Peter et al. *Prosecution of Adult Felony Defendants in Los Angeles County: A Policy Perspective.* Santa Monica: Rand Corporation, 1973.

Hagan, John. "Extra-Legal Attributes and Criminal Sentencing: An Assessment of a Sociological Viewpoint." *Law and Society Review* 8 (Spring 1974): 257-83.

Higgenbotham, A. Leon. "The Black Lawyer in America Today." *Harvard Law School Bulletin* 22 (February 1971): 55-59.

Jacob, Herbert, and James Eisenstein. "Sentences and Other Sanctions Imposed on Felony Defendants in Baltimore, Chicago, and Detroit." Paper read at the annual meeting of the American Political Science Association, August 29-September 2, 1974, Chicago.

Jaros, Dean, and Robert I. Mendelsohn. "The Judicial Role and Sentencing Behavior." *Midwest Journal of Political Science* 11 (1967): 471-88.

Jones, Nolan E. "Differential Legal Treatment between Blacks and Whites as a Function of Social Contact." Paper read at the annual meeting of the American Political Science Association, September 4-8, 1973, New Orleans.

Kerlinger, Fred, and Elazar Pedhazur. *Multiple Regression in Behavioral Research.* New York: Holt, Rinehart, and Winston, 1973.

Kirkpatrick, Samuel A. *Quantitative Analysis of Political Data.* Columbus, Ohio: Charles E. Merrill, 1974.

Land, Kenneth C. "Principles of Path Analysis." In *Sociological Methodology,* edited by Edgar F. Borgatta, pp. 3-37. San Francisco: Jossey-Bass, 1969.

Markham, Walter Gray. "Chromatic Justice: Color as an Element of the Offense." Paper read at the annual meeting of the American Political Science Association, August 29-September 2, 1974, Chicago.

Mileski, Maureen. "Courtroom Encounters: An Observation Study of a Lower Criminal Court." *Law and Society Review* 5 (May 1971): 473-538.

Nagel, Stuart S. *The Legal Process From a Behavioral Perspective.* Homewood, Ill.: Dorsey Press, 1969.

――――. "The Tipped Scales of American Justice." In *The Politics of Local Justice,* edited by James Klonoski and Robert Mendelsohn, pp. 114-27. Boston: Little, Brown, 1970.

Nagel, Stuart S., and Marian Neef. "The Racial Disparity that Supposedly Wasn't There: Some Pitfalls to Watch for in Analyzing Court Statistics." Mimeographed. Champaign-Urbana: University of Illinois, 1975.

Quinney, Richard. *The Social Reality of Crime.* Boston: Little, Brown, 1970.

Rankin, Anne. "The Effect of Pre-Trial Detention." *New York University Law Review* 39 (June 1964): 631-41.

Shively, W. Phillips. *The Craft of Political Research: A Primer.* Englewood Cliffs, N.J.: Prentice-Hall, 1974.

Southern Regional Council. *Race Makes the Difference: An Analysis of Sentence Disparity Among Black and White Offenders in Southern Prisons.* Atlanta: Southern Regional Council, 1969.

Stokes, Donald E. "Compound Paths: An Expository Note." *The American Journal of Political Science* 18 (February 1974): 191-214.

Terry, Robert M. "The Screening of Juvenile Offenders." *The Journal of Criminal Law, Criminology, and Police Science* 58 (1967): 173-81.

――――. "Discrimination in the Handling of Juvenile Offenders by Social-Control Agencies." *Journal of Research in Crime and Delinquency* 4 (July 1967): 218-30.

Thornberry, Terence P. "Race, Socioeconomic Status and Sentencing in the Juvenile Justice System." *The Journal of Criminal Law and Criminology* 64 (1973): 90-98.

Wald, Patricia M. "Poverty and Criminal Justice." In *The Criminal in the Arms of the Law,* edited by Leon Radzinowicz and Marvin E. Wolfgang, pp. 582-614. New York: Basic Books, 1971.

Wolfgang, Marvin E.; Arlene Kelly; and Hans C. Nolde. "Comparison of the Executed and the Commuted Among Admissions to Death Row." *The Journal of Criminal Law, Criminology, and Police Science* 53 (1962): 301-11.

Wolfgang, Marvin E., and Marc Reidel. "Race, Judicial Discretion and the Death Penalty." *Annals of the American Academy of Political and Social Science* 407 (May 1973): 119-33.

CHAPTER
3

ETHNOGRAPHY AND THE
STUDY OF TRIAL COURTS
Lynn M. Mather

What we have here, Your Honor, is a garden variety 288a. No priors on either one. We'd like to make it 647(b), a misdemeanor.

The above comment occurred in Los Angeles Superior Court after a defense attorney and prosecutor had agreed upon a charge reduction from Penal Code Sec. 288a (sex perversion, a felony) to Penal Code Sec. 647(b) (disorderly conduct, a misdemeanor). The attorneys were in the judge's chambers to tell him of their guilty plea agreement and the only description given of the case was this statement.[1] What is the meaning of the words, "a garden variety 288a. No priors on either one"? California Penal Code Section 288a prohibits "sex perversions," specifically oral copulation. Most 288a cases in Los Angeles involved acts of male homosexuality between consenting adults with little or no criminal record The defense attorney, in describing his clients' case as a "garden variety 288a," was presuming a specific kind of knowledge on the part of the judge and prosecutor: a knowledge of the typical characteristics of the defendants and the offense situation involved in the charge of Penal Code Sec. 288a. By adding "no priors on either one," the attorney was emphasizing the defendants' lack of prior criminal record so that the case fit clearly into the normal or "garden variety" category. Having so categorized the case, the attorney could then refer to the typical 288a disposition—a plea to a reduced charge.

Lawyers, judges, and others in a local criminal-law community share a common knowledge of the typical or normal features of cases and they use this

---

I am indebted to David Neubauer, Richard Winters, and Mike Mather for their helpful comments and suggestions on an earlier draft of this paper.

knowledge in planning pretrial strategies, in plea bargaining, and in decisions about sentencing (Mather 1974a, n.d.; Sudnow 1965). If we are interested in explaining the exercise of discretion by the key actors in criminal courts, then we must be able to describe the perceptions and shared knowledge of these actors. The methodology most appropriate to that task is ethnography. The ethnographic approach is that of anthropology and, to a limited extent, sociology. But the approach has been used less frequently in political science.

This chapter will describe the methodology of ethnography as it has been used in the study of law, focusing on ethnographic studies of trial courts in the United States. Nader (1965), Moore (1969), and Nader and Yngvesson (1973) have discussed the literature in the field of anthropology of law, summarizing and critically evaluating works in the area. Unfortunately most research on law by anthropologists has been conducted outside of the United States. But there are some interesting works on American courts that exemplify an ethnographic perspective.

THE ETHNOGRAPHY OF LAW

The concept of ethnography is basic to cultural anthropology. Essentially, an ethnography is a description of a culture. Conklin (1968, p. 172) defines an ethnographer as "an anthropologist who attempts . . . to record and describe the culturally significant behaviors of a particular society." Ethnography examines how people think about what they do and how they organize and interpret the actions of others. This is what is meant by the task of describing a culture; the task is not simply to describe the customary behaviors, but is also to describe the cultural meaning of those behaviors. As Goodenough (1964, p. 36) noted:

> Culture is not a material phenomenon; it does not consist of things, people, behavior, or emotions. It is rather an organization of these things. It is the forms of things that people have in mind, their models for perceiving, relating, and otherwise interpreting them.

An ethnographic approach to the study of law can be contrasted with a legalistic approach. Where a legalistic perspective views legal processes and decisions in the context of formal legal rules and procedures, an ethnographic perspective sees these processes in the context of informal rules and social interactions of the participants. An ethnographic approach focuses on the network and interactions of persons dealing with "things legal" so that legal ideas, rules, and behaviors are but another aspect of ongoing social life (Nader and Yngvesson 1973).

Frake (1969a, p. 124) describes two important attributes of ethnography:[2]

> First, it is not, I think, the ethnographer's task to predict behavior per se, but rather to state rules of culturally appropriate behavior. ... The model of an ethnographic statement is not: "if a person is confronted with stimulus X, he will do Y," but: "if a person is in situation X, performance Y will be judged appropriate by native actors."

Frake explains this point further in another paper (1969b, p. 471) when he notes that,

> a failure of an ethnographic statement to predict correctly does not necessarily imply descriptive inadequacy as long as the members of the described society are as surprised by the failure as is the ethnographer.

A second attribute of ethnography is that "the ethnographer seeks to discover, not prescribe, the significant stimuli in the subject's world" (Frake 1969a, p. 124). This point is of particular importance in ethnographic work. The ethnographer must learn in the field the objects and behaviors that are culturally significant for the particular society. In contrast, the survey researcher, for example, must define the data he considers to be significant before he begins his study.

In order to describe a culture, the researcher must spend considerable time in direct contact with the people he is studying; indeed, the fieldwork experience is essential for an ethnographic work. Conklin (1968, p. 172) describes the components of anthropological fieldwork:

> a long period of intimate study and residence in a small, well-defined community, knowledge of the spoken language, and the employment of a wide range of observational techniques including prolonged face-to-face contacts with members of the local group, direct participation in some of that group's activities, and a greater emphasis on intensive work with informants than on the use of documentary or survey data.

Most sociologists use the term "participant observation" rather than "fieldwork" to encompass this range of observational techniques. McCall and Simmons (1969, p. 1), for example, suggest that participant observation refers to a

> characteristic blend of techniques, as exemplified by the work of the lone anthropologist living amongst an isolated people, [which] involves some amount of genuinely social interaction in the field with the subjects of the study, some direct observation of relevant events, some systematic counting, some collection of documents and artifacts, and open-endedness in the directions the study takes.

McCall and Simmons note, however, that some sociologists prefer to reserve the term "participant observation" for situations in which the researcher is a genuine participant or member of the group being observed.

Most fieldwork is conducted in small, well-defined communities. The "community study," which developed from the idea of intensive long-term fieldwork, has been a central concern of anthropologists and sociologists since the 1920s (Pelto and Pelto 1973).[3] But, more recently, ethnographic techniques have been used to study cultural aspects of complex societies. Thus there is a growing literature on urban subcultures, deviant subcultures, informal groups, occupations, and complex social organizations.[4] One of the problems of ethnography in complex society is to distinguish one cultural scene from all the others, since superficially everyone seems to share the same language and culture. Spradley and McCurdy (1972, p. 24) define a cultural scene as "the information shared by two or more people that defines some aspect of their experience" and they comment:

> Cultural scenes are closely linked to recurrent social situations . . . . However, it is important not to confuse a cultural scene with a social situation. The former is the knowledge which actors employ in a social situation; the latter is the observable place, events, objects and persons seen by an investigator. There are many ways in which a particular social situation can be defined by those who perceive it. [1972, pp. 24, 27]

A number of field-workers have discussed methodological issues and techniques involved in acquiring an understanding of a culture. Important issues here include how to gain acceptance by the people being studied, how to establish good field relations, how to know if your informant is telling the truth, how to organize and interpret field data, and how to generate and test hypotheses using field data. Wax's (1971) *Doing Fieldwork* and Pelto and Pelto's (1973) "Ethnography: The Fieldwork Enterprise" provide excellent introductions to fieldwork in anthropology. Spradley and McCurdy (1972) also outline research techniques for doing ethnography in complex society. Important sociological works on fieldwork research include McCall and Simmons (1969), Habenstein (1970), Cicourel (1964, chapters 2 and 8), and Polsky (1967, pp. 117-49).

As applied to the study of law, ethnography includes a focus on shared perceptions and knowledge of the law. Particularly in a complex, stratified society, these perceptions will vary among different social groups. It seems obvious, for example, that attitudes on the use of courts and civil litigation in this country would vary according to the availability of legal services. To explain how law actually operates in a society, it is necessary to examine the cultural variations in the law, for example, the variation in shared legal perceptions across racial, ethnic, class, and geographic (urban versus rural) lines. Friedman (1969) writes that a working legal system can be analyzed by its structural, substantive, and cultural components, with legal culture as perhaps the key concept. Legal culture refers to "the network of values and attitudes relating to law" (Friedman 1969, p. 34) and Friedman stresses the fact that

> legal culture is not "public opinion," in the crude sense of a public opinion poll. There is no such thing as *the* public; to understand legal culture, one must carefully define *a* relevant public; for various issues, this will be a different group of people. [1969, p. 40]

Studying the cultural component of law also entails research on the shared perceptions of legal actors—lawyers, judges, and other "officials" in the legal system. This includes both the formal socialization of lawyers in their law-school training and their informal socialization in learning the local norms of their courts and communities. Simonett (1963), for example, suggests the importance of "The Common Law of Morrison County," an area of local legal folk knowledge that exists beside the statutory law and the common law.

The networks of values and knowledge about the law are part of the living law; that is, the culture provides the context for the operation of legal processes and the use of the law by different individuals and groups. An ethnographic study of law investigates patterns in the legal process as they are related to the legal culture. Or, more precisely, the law is studied within its sociocultural context:

> ... an ethnography of law is not simply a description of "the law," a framework for social life, but rather a description of social processes deeply embedded in social contexts. [Nader and Yngvesson 1973, p. 887]

Viewing law in this way leads to an interest in dispute resolution and the process and strategies involved in the choice of one method of dispute resolution over another. The case method has been an especially significant tool for gathering systematic data on disputes and the alternative processes for resolution within a given society (See, for example, Malinowski 1926; Llewellyn and Hoebel 1941; Gulliver 1963). But the limitations of the case method for developing a complete ethnography of law have also been noted (Nader and Yngvesson 1973; Gluckman 1973).

Given a focus on legal process in ethnography, there are two kinds of process that can be distinguished:

> (1) Process to be described in the connections between the court system and other dispute-settling mechanisms in any society, and also (2) process within the court system as well. [Nader and Yngvesson 1973, p. 895]

The review section below is organized according to this distinction. Thus, in the next section, studies are discussed that place American trial courts in the context of other dispute-settling mechanisms; following that are studies describing process within the courts themselves. This discussion is not intended as a comprehensive review of the literature on trial courts. Instead, the aim is to present some key works that exemplify an ethnographic approach to the study of trial courts.

COURTS IN THE WIDER CONTEXT OF DISPUTE RESOLUTION

Cases in court obviously represent only a small segment of all disputes being resolved in this country. What is the range of other dispute-settling processes and what is the role of the courts in this wider context? Sarat and Grossman (1975) propose a typology of adjudicative dispute-settling alternatives based upon the public or private nature of the institutions and on the formality or informality of the processes. For example, they contrast private-informal dispute settlement (such as marriage counseling, settlement of accident claims) with private-formal dispute settlement (such as religious courts, labor arbitration, professional grievance committees); and public-informal processes (such as police action in family quarrels, plea bargaining, civil rights commission hearings) with public-formal processes (such as court trials). Although these processes are described as "adjudicative" mechanisms by Sarat and Grossman (1975, p. 1202), it appears that negotiation and mediation may also be included in their typology. Felstiner (1974; 1975) and Danzig and Lowy (1975) have examined dispute processing in the United States according to the modes of adjudication, mediation, and avoidance ("withdrawal from or contraction of the dispute-producing relationship," Felstiner 1974, p. 70) and they debate the relative costs in the choice of one mode over another. These writers and others (for example, Galanter 1974; Black 1973) are especially concerned with the development of general models to organize information on dispute resolution—information on the processes of mobilization, the structural influences on disputing, the relation of social development to dispute resolution, and the consequences of using different processes. But these writers generally agree that,

> the void in the data is considerable and distressing. To my knowledge, no anthropologist has studied the dispute processing behavior of any non-ethnic American community with the thoroughness and comprehensive perspective that characterize many studies of Mexican towns, African tribes and Indian villages. [Felstiner 1975, pp. 704-05]

Perhaps the best ethnographic data on the wider context of dispute resolution lies in the studies of police. Police are critical actors in settling disputes because of their role as "peace officers" (Banton 1964; compare the order-maintenance function described by Wilson 1968) and their role as "law officers" or law enforcers. In their latter role, police perform a gatekeeping function for the criminal courts in deciding which cases should be advanced for prosecution. There are a number of excellent fieldwork studies of police,[5] such as Skolnick's (1966) study of police in "Westville." Over a period of 15 months, Skolnick investigated police behavior (particularly the vice squad) using the methodology of participant observation. He rode with police at night, joined them on daytime investigations, observed their actions, and interviewed them about their work. Skolnick found that,

> the most informative method was not to ask predetermined questions, but rather to question actions the policeman had just taken or failed to take, about events or objects just encountered, such as certain categories of people or places in the city. [1966, p. 33]

In this way, Skolnick attempted to see the world as the police themselves saw it, showing the operational meaning of legal rules and regulations within the context of the policeman's working environment. Similarly, Black's (1971) observational study of the social organization of arrest explored the situational demands shaping police actions. Black commented that,

> a study of arrest can inform and benefit from the sociology of face-to-face interaction. The police encounter is a small group with its own morphology, its own dynamics. What happens in an encounter may have less to do with crime and law than with the demands of situational order, with social etiquette or the pressures of group size or spatial configuration. [1971, p. 110]

The methodology employed by Black (1971) is noteworthy for the development of comparative data using fieldwork techniques; he employed 36 trained researchers to systematically observe (and later make notes on) police-citizen transactions in Boston, Chicago, and Washington, D.C.

The participant-observation studies by Van Maanen (1973, 1974) and Rubenstein (1973) add another dimension to an understanding of the police culture. Each researcher went through the entire police academy program (Van Maanen in "Union City" and Rubenstein in Philadelphia) before his fieldwork on police patrol. Van Maanen's analysis focused on the occupational socialization of the policeman, describing the critical phases in the development of the patrolman's point of view. Rubenstein's (1973) *City Police* is an exhaustive, detailed study of routine police work from the policeman's perspective, undoubtedly the most complete ethnography of police so far.

While the police initiate criminal actions in certain cases (for example, traffic, vice, narcotics, drunkenness), most of the cases they send to court are in response to a citizen complainant (Black 1973). Thus it is important to investigate the perspectives of injured individuals in the decision on whether to seek punitive action. This area has received little attention, with the exception of Robin's (1967) study of department stores' handling of cases involving employee theft and Cameron's (1964) investigation of department stores' prosecution of shoplifting cases. See also Ennis (1967) for survey data on criminal victimization and the reporting of crime.

In most civil disputes, there are other forums besides the courts that a citizen will choose instead of, or before, formal litigation. Ross (1975) provides an interesting account of one such process—the appellate division of a large insurance company. By close examination of case files within the company, Ross analyzed the type of case disposition by the nature of the complaint. He then speculated on the differences between the outcomes obtained by this private complaints process and those that might have resulted had the cases been decided in court, commenting that a significant group of complainants were probably more successful in this procedure than they would have been in court. Ross' conclusion argues forcefully for more research in this area:

> It is by informal negotiations, complaints to the heads of bureaucratic organizations, letters to Better Business Bureaus and calls to newspaper Action Lines, that most legal claims of the ordinary citizen are ultimately determined. Certainly, the rules of formal law cast long shadows on the informal process. But, if our understanding and our practice of law are to be satisfactory, we should distinguish shadow from substance and broaden our concern and research beyond the courts. [1975, p. 292]

In order to see civil courts in their wider context of dispute resolution, one must also consider the availability of legal services. Jacob (1973, p. 34) notes that "[j]ust as the police are the principal gatekeepers regulating the flow of criminal cases to the courts, so the legal profession is the chief regulator of the flow of civil cases." Mayhew (1975, p. 405) suggests that it is simplistic to view the problem of the distribution of legal services as "a problem of facilitating the access of persons experiencing legal difficulties to qualified professionals." Instead, Mayhew develops the argument that,

> the particular distribution of cases coming to the legal profession reflects the institutional organization of the legal system, not merely the inability of those who think they want lawyers to pay for them. [1975, p. 426]

Data to support this position are also found in Fitzgerald's (1975) study of the Contract Buyers League and its litigation.

THE COURT PROCESS

Process within the criminal court may be defined and perceived very differently according to whether one is a regular participant in the court's activities (for example, judge, prosecuting attorney, most defense attorneys) or an occasional participant (defendants). It is difficult as well to integrate the perspectives of both the "rule enforcers" and the "rule breakers," as pointed out by Becker (1963, p. 173) in discussions of the sociology of deviance. Spradley (1970) and Casper (1972) each describe criminal court processes from the defendant's perspective, but the methodological approach and the results of the two works are quite different. Spradley's (1970) study of urban nomads (or drunks) and their interaction with the criminal process was explicitly ethnographic in method. He began his work "by months of listening to men talk about their experiences with law enforcement agencies in order to discover which questions could appropriately be asked of informants and, further, to ascertain the wording of these questions" (1970, p. 7). These months of participant observation were spent on skid row, as well as in criminal courts and alcoholism treatment centers. Spradley then administered lengthy questionnaires and conducted formal ethnographic interviewing[6] with his informants. In contrast, Casper's (1972) study of criminal defendants was based on a more structured method. Casper interviewed a sample of defendants about their experience with the police and courts; two-thirds of the defendants were in prison during their interviews.[7] The interviews averaged an hour and a half in length and they were tape-recorded.

Emerson (1969) examined the perspective and behavior of the regular participants in a juvenile court to see how the court defines and reacts to the cases brought before it. His work was based upon participant observation, focusing on the interaction between court officials and delinquents in their informal and formal encounters. Observations were supplemented by study of case reports and interviews with the court staff. Juvenile court processes are described and analyzed according to the shared legal perceptions of the court staff. For example, some cases are seen to present "real" trouble to the court and these are handled differently than those which are "mild" or "normal," and thus require little attention (p. 84).

In my research on criminal case disposition in Los Angeles, I found that attorneys and court staff categorize cases according to the seriousness and the strength of the case (Mather n.d., 1974a, 1974b). The "serious" case in the adult felony court is one with a probability of severe punishment (similar to Emerson's "trouble case")—this case requires special attention in developing pretrial strategies and in plea bargaining. The cultural perspective of the adult court (unlike the juvenile court) also emphasizes the strength or weakness of the case in deciding upon appropriate disposition. My research methods were similar to Emerson's (1969) above, using observation of attorneys' informal discussions and of formal court proceedings, open-ended interviews with participants, examination of case files, and statistical analysis of case dispositions. I found that attorneys learned to identify typical or normal types of crime (compare Sudnow 1965); they learned to recognize a "dead-bang" case and to evaluate "what a case is worth" for bargaining over charge and sentencing. Other fieldwork studies of plea bargaining include Newman (1966), Blumberg (1967), Sudnow (1965), Skolnick (1967), and Neubauer (1974).

The important perspective of the criminal prosecutor has been described in a number of field studies, such as Carter (1974), Cole (1970), Castberg (1968), McCall (1975), and Eisenstein (1973). Carter's (1974) research focused on the prosecutor's working environment and the difficulties that superiors had in directing or programming the behavior of their assistants. Carter's data came from extensive observations and informal questioning of prosecutors, review of office files, questionnaires, and semistructured, tape-recorded interviews. As a political scientist, Carter notes that his research objectives were "quasi-anthropological" in that he attempted:

> to describe and to understand criminal prosecution in terms of the means/ends calculations of the prosecutors themselves and in terms of their personal values and the perceptions they had of each other and of others with whom they worked. [1974, p. 6]

Mileski (1971) studied courtroom encounters in a lower court that had little plea bargaining. Her observations focus on the situational factors associated with encounters in different kinds of cases and the patterns of disposition according to characteristics of defendants and their attorneys. Mileski systematically recorded her case observations to obtain quantitative data on certain aspects of the courtroom experience, such as the length of time of the encounter between the judge and defendant, any lecturing to the defendant by the judge, the judge's demeanor and whether or not the defendant attempted to excuse himself before the judge. Clearly none of this material would have been available without the direct observation in court, and it does provide a much more complete description of the court process.

With the exception of the literature on the small-claims courts, there is little fieldwork data on processes within civil courts (see, however, Jacob 1969 and Dolbeare 1967). Yngvesson and Hennessey (1975) provide a comprehensive survey of the literature on small-claims courts, comparing the data in various empirical studies on who is using the courts, how the cases are handled, and on the patterns of case disposition. They also discuss the problems and assumptions of the small-claims model, and they suggest reforms in the procedures and structure of dispute settlement in this area.

Rosenthal's (1974) *Lawyer and Client: Who's in Charge?*, although not a fieldwork study, is noteworthy for its concern with the litigants' perspective on settlement of personal-injury claims. The focus of the study was on the attorney-client relationship in the settlement process. Rosenthal related differences in client participation to case outcomes and found that active clients obtained better results than did passive ones. See also Ross (1970) for discussion of the process of negotiation in adjustment of insurance claims.

CONCLUSION

While political scientists formerly gave exclusive attention to appellate courts, more recently those interested in legal processes have turned to look at the operation of trial courts. Trial courts are important in their role of implementing the rules of the higher courts (compare Wasby 1970). And, more importantly, trial courts are political institutions in their own right, enforcing legal norms and resolving conflicts. Political scientists have done excellent work analyzing the political context of trial courts (Jacob 1965, 1973; Eisenstein 1973; Cole 1973), but more needs to be done to place courts within a broader social and cultural context.

The purpose of this chapter is to suggest the value of ethnography for research on trial courts. First, ethnography is useful for the substantive issues it raises for research on law. For example, an ethnographic approach leads us to ask questions about the perceptions and knowledge of law held by different groups within society, about informal social norms that guide the actions of those within the legal process, and about the relationship between courts and other processes for dispute resolution.

Second, ethnography provides a methodology for answering these and other questions about law. A guiding principle of anthropology is to "discover the native point of view" (Spradley 1970, p. 6). Through extensive fieldwork, or participant observation, the ethnographer learns to perceive and interpret actions and events from the point of view of the people he is studying. This is especially important for doing research within our own society, where we may mistakenly assume a common language and common set of values. Unless one learns the native language (that is, the language with all its nuances and meanings for a particular social group), a researcher may not really understand what is said to him; and even worse, he may not understand that he does not understand and is thus likely to make errors in interpretation (Becker and Geer 1969). To the extent that we want to reform legal processes, we must first understand the perspective or point of view of the legal actors we wish to "reform." Otherwise, these changes in the legal process may have little chance for success.

NOTES

1. This example comes from the author's research on plea bargaining in Los Angeles. See Mather (D. C. Heath, n.d.).

2. Frake notes that these two attributes of ethnography distinguish it from stimulus-response psychology. Ethnography emphasizes mental processes, or "what is going on in people's heads," to account for social behavior. In contrast, s-r psychology accounts for behavior by examination of observable physical actions or stimuli and responses. Discussion of cognitive versus behaviorist approaches appears in psychology (Skinner 1957; compare Chomsky 1959), in sociology (Cicourel 1964, 1974) and in anthropology (Tyler 1969). Behavioralism in political science shares an empirical orientation with psychological behaviorism, but the behavioralist uses data on attitudes, personality, and other mental concepts, in addition to data on observable behavior (Isaak 1975). Ethnography then can be included within behavioralism, although there are differences between ethnography and other behavioral approaches (compare Nagel 1969), as discussed in the text.

3. See Pelto and Pelto (1973) and Wax (1971, chapter 3) for the historical development of fieldwork techniques and concerns within anthropology and sociology.

4. Ethnographies of urban subcultures include works such as Whyte (1943), Gans (1962), Liebow (1968), and Hannerz (1969). See Gulick (1973) for review of studies in urban anthropology. Works on deviant subcultures include Becker (1963), Polsky (1967), and Humphreys (1970). Other ethnographic studies in complex societies include such diverse works as Goffman (1961), Emerson (1969), Becker et al. (1961), and Rubenstein (1973).

5. See McCall (1975) for a recent review of the literature.

6. This interview procedure uses eliciting techniques to arrive at taxonomic definitions and componential definitions of terms used within a culture. See Spradley (1970, chapter 2), Spradley and McCurdy (1972), and Black and Metzger (1965).

7. Polsky (1967, p. 116) warns of the possible bias in gathering data from "caught criminals": it is too heavily retrospective and often involves "the kind of 'cooperativeness' in which you get told what the criminal thinks you want to hear so you will get off his back or maybe do him some good with the judge or parole board."

REFERENCES

Banton, Michael. 1964. *The Policeman in the Community.* New York: Basic Books.

Becker, Howard S. 1963. *Outsiders: Studies in the Sociology of Deviance.* New York: Free Press.

Becker, Howard S., and Blanche Geer. 1969. "Participant Observation and Interviewing: A Comparison." In *Issues in Participant Observation,* eds. George McCall and J. L. Simmons. Reading, Mass.: Addison-Wesley, 1969.

Becker, Howard; Blanche Geer; Everett C. Hughes; and Anselm L. Strauss. 1961. *Boys in White.* Chicago: Aldine.

Black, Donald J. 1973. "The Mobilization of Law." *Journal of Legal Studies* 23 (6): 1087-1111.

Black, Mary, and Duane Metzger. 1965. "Ethnographic Description and the Study of Law." *American Anthropologist* 67 (6, part 2): 141-65.

Blumberg, Abraham. 1967. *Criminal Justice.* Chicago: Quadrangle Books.

Cameron, Mary Owen. 1964. *The Booster and the Snitch.* New York: The Free Press of Glencoe.

Carter, Leif H. 1974. *The Limits of Order.* Lexington, Mass.: D. C. Heath.

Casper, Jonathan D. 1972. *American Criminal Justice: The Defendant's Perspective.* Englewood Cliffs, N.J.: Prentice-Hall.

Castberg, A. Didrick. 1968. "Prosecutorial Discretion." Ph.D. dissertation, Northwestern University.

Chomsky, Noam. 1959. "Verbal Behavior (A Review)." *Language* 35: 26-58.

Cicourel, Aaron. 1974. *Cognitive Sociology: Language and Meaning in Social Interaction.* New York: Free Press.

———. 1964. *Method and Measurement in Sociology.* New York: Free Press of Glencoe.

Cole, George F. 1973. *Politics and the Administration of Justice.* Beverly Hills: Sage Publications.

———. 1970. "The Decision to Prosecute." *Law and Society Review* 4: 331-43.

Conklin, Harold. 1968. "Ethnography." In *International Encyclopedia of the Social Sciences,* Vol. 5, ed. David L. Sills. New York: Macmillan, Free Press, 1968.

Danzig, Richard, and Michael J. Lowy. 1975. "Everyday Disputes and Mediation in the United States: A Reply to Professor Felstiner." *Law and Society Review* 9: 675-94.

Dolbeare, Kenneth. 1967. *Trial Courts in Urban Politics.* New York: John Wiley.

Eisenstein, James. 1973. *Politics and the Legal Process.* New York: Harper and Row.

Emerson, Robert M. 1969. *Judging Delinquents: Context and Process in Juvenile Court.* Chicago: Aldine.

Ennis, Philip H. 1967. "Criminal Victimization in the United States." In *Field Surveys II,* The President's Commission on Law Enforcement and the Administration of Justice. Washington, D.C.: Government Printing Office.

Felstiner, William. 1975. "Avoidance as Dispute Processing: An Elaboration." *Law and Society Review* 9 (4): 695-706.

———. 1974. "Influences of Social Organization on Dispute Processing." *Law and Society Review* 9 (1): 63-94.

Fitzgerald, Jeffrey M. 1975. "The Contract Buyers League and the Courts: A Case Study of Poverty Litigation." *Law and Society Review* 9 (2): 165-95.

Frake, Charles O. 1969a. "Notes on Queries in Ethnography." In *Cognitive Anthropology,* ed. Stephen A. Tyler, pp. 123-37. New York: Holt, Rinehart and Winston, 1969.

———. 1969b. "A Structural Description of Subanun 'Religious Behavior'." In *Cognitive Anthropology*, ed. Stephen A. Tyler, pp. 470-87. New York: Holt, Rinehart and Winston, 1969.

Friedman, Lawrence M. 1969. "Legal Culture and Social Development." *Law and Society Review* 4 (1): 29-44.

Galanter, Marc. 1974. "Why the 'Haves' Come Out Ahead: Speculations on the Limits of Legal Change." *Law and Society Review* 9 (1): 95-160.

Gans, Herbert J. 1962. *The Urban Villagers: Group and Class in the Life of Italian-Americans*. New York: Free Press of Glencoe.

Gluckman, Max. 1973. "Limitations of the Case-Method in the Study of Tribal Law." *Law and Society Review* 7 (4): 611-41.

Goffman, Erving. 1961. *Asylums: Essays on the Social Situation of Mental Patients and Other Inmates*. Garden City, N.Y.: Anchor Books.

Goodenough, Ward. 1964. "Cultural Anthropology and Linguistics." In *Language in Culture and Society*, ed. Dell Hymes, pp. 36-39. New York: Harper and Row, 1964.

Gulick, John. 1973. *Social Control in an African Society: A Study of the Arusha, Agricultural Masai of Northern Tanganyika*. Boston: Boston University Press.

Habenstein, Robert W., ed. 1970. *Pathways to Data: Field Methods for Studying Ongoing Social Organizations*. Chicago: Aldine.

Hannerz, Ulf. 1969. *Soulside: Inquiries into Ghetto Culture and Community*. New York: Columbia University Press.

Humphreys, L. 1970. *Tearoom Trade: Impersonal Sex in Public Places*. Chicago: Aldine.

Isaak, Alan C. 1975. *Scope and Methods of Political Science*. Homewood, Ill.: Dorsey Press.

Jacob, Herbert. 1973. *Urban Justice*. Englewood Cliffs, N.J.: Prentice-Hall.

———. 1969. *Debtors in Court*. Chicago: Rand McNally.

———. 1965. *Justice in America*. Boston: Little, Brown.

Liebow, Elliott. 1967. *Tally's Corner: A Study of Negro Streetcorner Men*. Boston: Little, Brown.

Llewelyn, K. N., and E. A. Hoebel. 1941. *The Cheyenne Way: Conflict and Case Law in Primitive Jurisprudence*. Norman: University of Oklahoma Press.

Malinowski, B. 1926. *Crime and Custom in Savage Society*. London: Kegan Paul, Trench, Trubner.

Mather, Lynn. (n.d.) *Plea Bargaining or Trial? The Dynamics of Criminal Case Disposition* (forthcoming). Lexington, Mass.: D. C. Heath.

———. 1974a. "Some Determinants of the Method of Case Disposition: Decision-Making by Public Defenders in Los Angeles." *Law and Society Review* 8 (2): 187-216.

———. 1974b. "The Outsider in the Courtroom." In *The Potential for Reform of Criminal Justice,* ed. Herbert Jacob, pp. 263-89. Beverly Hills: Sage Publications, 1974.

Mayhew, Leon. 1975. "Institutions of Representation: Civil Justice and the Public." *Law and Society Review* 9 (3): 401-29.

McCall, George J. 1975. *Observing the Law: Applications of Field Methods to the Study of the Criminal Justice System.* Washington, D.C.: Government Printing Office.

McCall, George J., and J. L. Simmons, eds. 1969. *Issues in Participant Observation: A Text and Reader.* Reading, Mass.: Addison-Wesley.

Mileski, Maureen. 1971. "Courtroom Encounters: An Observation Study of a Lower Criminal Court." *Law and Society Review* 5 (4): 473-538.

Moore, S. F. 1969. "Law and Anthropology." In *Biennial Review of Anthropology,* ed. B. J. Siegel, pp. 252-95. Palo Alto: Stanford University Press, 1969.

Nader, Laura. 1965. "The Anthropological Study of Law." *American Anthropologist* 67 (6, part 2): 3-32.

Nader, Laura, and Barbara Yngvesson. 1973. "On Studying the Ethnography of Law and Its Consequences." In *Handbook of Social and Cultural Anthropology,* ed. John J. Honigmann, pp. 883-921. Chicago: Rand McNally, 1973.

Nagel, Stuart S. 1969. *The Legal Process from a Behavioral Perspective.* Homewood, Ill.: Dorsey Press.

Neubauer, David W. 1974. *Criminal Justice in Middle America.* Morristown, N.J.: General Learning Corporation.

Newman, Donald J. 1966. *Conviction: The Determination of Guilt or Innocence.* Boston: Little, Brown.

Pelto, Pertti, and Gretel H. Pelto. 1973. "Ethnography: The Fieldwork Enterprise." In *Handbook of Social and Cultural Anthropology,* ed. John J. Honigmann, pp. 241-88. Chicago: Rand McNally, 1973.

Polsky, Ned. 1967. *Hustlers, Beats, and Others.* Chicago: Aldine.

Robin, Gerald D. 1967. "The Corporate and Judicial Disposition of Employee Thieves." *Wisconsin Law Review* 1967: 685-702.

Rosenthal, Douglas E. 1974. *Lawyer and Client: Who's in Charge?* New York: Russell Sage Foundation.

Ross, H. Lawrence. 1975. "Insurance Claims Complaints: A Private Appeals Procedure." *Law and Society Review* 9 (2): 275-92.

———. 1970. *Settled Out of Court*. Chicago: Aldine.

Rubinstein, Jonathan. 1974. *City Police*. New York: Ballantine Books.

Sarat, Austin, and Joel B. Grossman. 1975. "Courts and Conflict Resolution." *American Political Science Review* 69 (4): 1200-1217.

Simonett, John E. 1957. *Verbal Behavior*. New York: Appleton-Century-Crofts.

Skolnick, Jerome. 1967. "Social Control in the Adversary System." *Journal of Conflict Resolution* 11: 52-70.

———. 1966. *Justice Without Trial*. New York: John Wiley.

Spradley, James. 1970. *You Owe Yourself a Drunk*. Boston: Little, Brown.

Sudnow, David. 1965. "Normal Crimes: Sociological Features of the Penal Code in a Public Defender Office." *Social Problems* 12: 255-76.

Tyler, Stephen A., ed. 1969. *Cognitive Anthropology*. New York: Holt, Rinehart and Winston.

Van Maanen, John. 1974. "Working the Street: A Developmental View of Police Behavior." In *The Potential for Reform of Criminal Justice*, ed. Herbert Jacob, pp. 83-130. Beverly Hills: Sage Publications, 1974.

———. 1973. "Observations on the Making of Policemen." *Human Organizations* 32: 407-18.

Wasby, Stephen. 1970. *The Impact of the United States Supreme Court*. Homewood, Ill.: Dorsey Press.

Wax, Rosalie H. 1971. *Doing Fieldwork: Warnings and Advice*. Chicago: University of Chicago Press.

Whyte, William F. 1943. *Street Corner Society: The Social Structure of an Italian Slum*. Chicago: University of Chicago Press.

Wilson, James Q. 1968. *Varieties of Police Behavior: The Management of Law and Order in Eight Communities*. Cambridge, Mass.: Harvard University Press.

Yngvesson, Barbara, and Patricia Hennessey. 1975. "Small Claims, Complex Disputes: A Review of the Small Claims Literature." *Law and Society Review* 9 (2): 219-74.

CHAPTER 4

ECONOMIC ANALYSIS OF
CRIME AND THE
CRIMINAL-JUSTICE SYSTEM
Nicholas Elliott

By almost any standard the incidence of crime in this country must be considered a major problem. In 1965, when crime rates were considerably lower than they presently are, the estimated annual cost of crime was $21 billion.[1] Among segments of the population such as older citizens in urban areas, the fear of crime supersedes all other issues of importance.[2] Crime occurs in communities of all sizes, and in recent years many types of crimes have been increasing faster in smaller communities than in the large cities. Between 1973 and 1974 reported crime grew fastest in cities under 10,000 in population. Violent crime increased most in cities between 25,000 and 50,000.[3] Crime appears to have proven resistant to the onslaught of efforts to reduce its occurrence. Traditional mechanisms for control as well as more innovative approaches have generally been found wanting. There appears to be a general pessimism prevailing among those charged with law enforcement. This is indicated by the following statement made by Don Byrd, the Chief of Police in Dallas, Texas:

> In the community what turns a youngster into a criminal? What makes him graduate from one crime to another? I tell you we have no control over that. The churches, the schools, the families, the communities have that control. We do not.[4]

Although scholars have long recognized crime as a legitimate area of study, there has been a failure to develop adequate theory or to provide much useful information to policymakers. This failure has not been due to lack of effort. Criminology is a well-established and active subdiscipline of sociology. Scholars in other fields as well have directed their attention to crime. However, virtually without exception, these efforts have produced results that are inadequate either in their usefulness as scientific explanations or in their usefulness as paradigms suitable for policy development. Many efforts have failed on both counts.

THEORIES OF THE ETIOLOGY OF CRIME

The earliest attempts at scientifically explaining crime were based on biological concepts. In the latter third of the nineteenth century Cesare Lombroso developed the atavistic theory of crime. According to this theory, many criminals—and especially those responsible for a disproportionate share of serious crimes—demonstrated morphological characteristics of more primitive humans.[5] While Lombroso's theory was refuted by Goring in 1936,[6] the search for a biological explanation of crime continued.[7] The best known of the contemporary manifestations of the biological theories is based on the supposed relationship between criminal behavior and the occurrence of the XYY genotype.[8]

Other disciplines have joined in the study of the etiology of crime. A substantial body of literature exists in the related fields of psychiatry and psychology.[9] However, it has been argued that psychology has failed to offer a paradigm applicable to the study of crime.[10] Urban design[11] and geography[12] are two disciplines that have recently provided research attempting to explain the incidence of crime.

It is within the discipline of sociology that the etiology of crime has received the greatest attention. A number of influential paradigms have emerged from sociology, including Sutherland's theory of differential association. This theory was first presented in 1939[13] and refined to its contemporary version in 1947.[14]

Differential association is essentially a learning theory. It posits that the learning relevant to engaging in criminal behavior takes place in intimate social groups. What one learns in these groups are definitions of behavior that are either favorable or unfavorable to violations of the law. When an individual is associated with a group from which he receives an "excessive number of behavioral definitions favorable to violating the law," the individual is likely to engage in criminal activities. In addition to learning the specific direction of motives, drives, rationalizations, and attitudes associated with criminal behavior, the individual must also learn the techniques of committing crimes. The theory also attributes this learning to intimate social groups.[15]

While the differential association thesis has demonstrated considerable longevity, its standing as a scientific theory must be considered suspect. Gibbons has pointed out that the key concepts of the theory, such as "an excess of definitions favorable to violations of the law," are unclear and ambiguous.[16] This in turn leads to difficulties in operationalizing the theory. Indeed empirical tests of the theory are comparatively rare.[17] Recently attempts have been made to solve the problems discussed above by incorporating differential associations into learning theory.[18] It would be premature to comment on the success of these efforts at this time.

The second major sociological theory is labeling theory. This theory was originally developed by Tannenbaum at approximately the same time Sutherland was developing differential association.[19] Labeling theory asserts that criminality is not a function of individual action but rather a function of the reaction of authority to individual behavior.[20] Once identified as a criminal, the offender rejects those who have rejected him. As a result, the offender is likely to reject the values of those he rejects and see himself in opposition to society with right on his side.[21] Thus the offender who might have initially committed a rather innocuous crime is driven into a life of crime.

While labeling theory appears to have some validity, there are several difficulties inherent in the theory. Wellford has analyzed the assumptions of labeling theory and reports that in general the validity of the assumptions is not supported by relevant empirical research.[22] The theory tends to put the blame for crime on the labelers, that is, those who are charged with law enforcement. The theory asserts that continued criminal activity is a result of the labeling process. However, this does not account for continuing criminal behavior on the part of individuals who are never labeled as criminals. It is also obvious that many individuals who are at one time labeled as criminals do not develop criminal careers. Thus it seems clear that labeling is neither a necessary nor a sufficient condition to induce criminality.[23]

The preceding discussion has pointed out weaknesses of the most influential etiological theories as scientific paradigms. Of equal importance is the failure of these theories to offer useful policy guides. Wilson argues that criminological theory looks for the sources of crime in factors which themselves are not caused.[24] While this is probably an overstatement of the objectives of criminologists, it does point out that criminological theory deals with conditions that are rather basic and often extremely difficult to change. When the condition described by Wilson is combined with the causal fallacy, the assumption is that no problem is adequately addressed unless its causes are eliminated,[25] it is clear that those who look at criminological theory for policy guides are faced with heroic tasks. The same situation exists with regard to the biological theories. However, as they currently exist, the biological theories do not appear to warrant serious consideration as policy guides.

The criminological theories appear to offer the potential for dealing with crime only if the resources are available for major alterations to the society. While this is not necessarily something to be avoided, political realities would appear to make this a long term endeavor. The magnitude of crime in this country is such that a more immediate remedy would be far more useful. The primary purpose of the remainder of this chapter is to describe and comment on a paradigm that appears to offer a considerable potential for explaining the incidence of crime while at the same time providing policymakers with a useful

THE ECONOMIC THEORY OF CRIME

The study of crime has not been until very recently a major concern of economists. Viewed historically, this is somewhat surprising. Jeremy Bentham, one of the intellectual precursors of modern economics, was greatly concerned with crime. His concern was more than academic. Bentham invested a considerable share of his own funds in an attempt to establish a model prison to be named the Panopticon.[26] He was also instrumental in developing a police force for London.[27] It is to Bentham's principle of utility and utility theory that contemporary economists have returned to develop the economic theory of crime.

Bentham argued that human behavior is governed by pain and pleasure. The principle of utility follows from this assumption. This principle states that individuals will behave so as to maximize the amount of pleasure possible from a situation or to minimize the amount of pain.[28] It follows from this that public policies which increase the costs of crime or which reduce the returns from crime will reduce the incidence of crime. If this is correct, it is possible to reduce the incidence of crime without dealing with those factors that cause a unique form of behavior termed crime.

The economic theory of crime approaches criminal activity in a manner significantly different from that of other paradigms. As indicated above, this theory makes no attempt to identify the ultimate causes of crime. Rather the theory attempts to identify variables, including public policy outputs, which—by structuring the costs of and the returns from engaging in criminal activity—are related to the incidence of crime. The economic theory has one other very important characteristic. Unlike other theories that view crime as resulting from either a single variable or from multiple variables in an additive relationship, the economic theory conceptualizes crime as resulting from a situation analogous to classical supply-and-demand functions. Like the supply of and the demand for any good or service, the supply of crime and the demand for sanctions are jointly determined.[29] This is made clear in the expositions of the theory presented by Becker,[30] Orsagh,[31] and Ehrlich.[32] In its simplest form the theory can be represented by the following:

$$\text{Crime} = a_1 + B_1 \text{Sanctions} + B_2 X + u_1 \qquad \text{1a}$$
$$\text{Sanctions} = a_2 + B_3 \text{Crime} + B_4 Y + u_2 \qquad \text{1b}$$

where X is a collective variable reflecting all other factors influencing the costs and returns of crime; Y is a collective variable reflecting constraints imposed on devoting resources to sanctioning, and u_1 and u_2 are error terms.

The first equation yields a measure of the number of offenses individuals are willing to commit (supply). The second equation yields a measure of the demand for sanctions. That is, it is a measure of the demand to utilize public resources to increase the costs of engaging in criminal activities. In order to ascertain the incidence of crime it is necessary to resolve the two functions simultaneously.

In a somewhat more developed form, the theory can be represented by the following:

$$C = a_1 + b_1 R_p + b_2 R_x + b_4 S + u_1 \qquad 2a$$
$$S = a_2 + b_5 C + b_6 I + b_7 B + b_8 X + u_2 \qquad 2b$$

where

C = Supply of criminal offenses
R_p = Pecuniary returns
R_x = Psychic returns
O = Opportunity costs incurred by foregoing legal activities
S = Sanctions imposed by the criminal justice system for engaging in illegal activities
I = Income available for all public policy outputs
B = Budgetary constraints imposed by demand for other public services
X = Cultural factors influencing the taste for sanctioning of criminal activities.[33]

It follows from utility theory that a negative sign would be expected for b_3, b_4, and b_7 while the expected sign for the remaining coefficients would be positive. Equations 2a and 2b clearly do not represent an operationalized model but rather demonstrate factors that various economic theorists have viewed as being important.

Paradigms of this variety have guided the overwhelming portion of the empirical research based on the economic theory of crime. The works of Becker, Orsagh and Ehrlich form the core of the economic theory. However, recently Block and Heineke have argued that the assumptions from which Becker and Ehrlich argue are special conditions and that the negative relation between crime and sanctions that Becker and Ehrlich deduce from theory may not necessarily follow under more general conditions. Block and Heineke argue that the sign of the coefficients must be determined empirically.[34] While this critique does not negate the theory, it does point out the need for empirical research to find the conditions under which the theory applies. More will be said later concerning the need for empirical testing.

Methodological Implications

In addition to the conceptual differences between the economic theory of crime and alternative theories, there is one very important related methodological difference. As is made clear by equations 1 and 2, the economic theory views crime and sanctions as endogenous variables in a system of simultaneous equations. Thus they are jointly determined. If the economic theory of crime expresses the true relationship between crime and sanctions, then virtually all of the research predating the economic theory of crime that examines the impact of sanctions is flawed and of limited utility in measuring the impact of the criminal justice system's outputs on criminal activity.

As Blalock points out, the "laws" of social science are expressed as regression equations.[35] Much of the research on the impact of policies of the criminal justice system is weakened by the fact that it does not attempt to estimate the parameters of the relationship between crime and sanctions by using regression analysis. Virtually all of the research that has attempted parameter estimation has employed ordinary least squares regression analysis. However for simultaneous equations, ordinary least squares yield biased and inconsistent estimates of regression coefficients.[36] This bias can be eliminated through the use of an appropriate technique; the technique most often employed by economic theorists is two-stage least squares. The two-stage least squares technique eliminates the problems produced by simultaneity without producing distortions when the model is not as predicted by the economic theory but is rather a single equation model.[37]

The possibility of bias existing in research employing ordinary least squares can explain certain perverse findings concerning the relationship between outputs of the criminal-justice system and the incidence of crime such as has been found by several researchers. Using two samples, one composed of the 49 largest cities in Ohio, Cho found several examples of positive relationships between the incidence of crime and outputs of police departments.[38] It makes little sense to take the position that high levels of police outputs produce more crime. It makes more sense to argue, as indeed Cho does, that the positive relationships are due to policy responses to the rising crime rate.[39] However, while Cho recognizes the existence of this key element of the economic theory of crime, he fails to adjust his model or to alter his statistical techniques.

A researcher who assumed a single equation model, such as:

$$\text{Crime} = a + B_1 \text{Sanctions} + B_2 X \qquad 3$$

where X represents a collection of additional independent variables would probably take the data represented in Figure 4.1 as support for the existence of a positive relationship between crime and sanctions. Figure 4.1 shows the relationship between crime and sanctions on the crime-sanction plane. However

FIGURE 4.1

Hypothetical Crime and Sanction Data

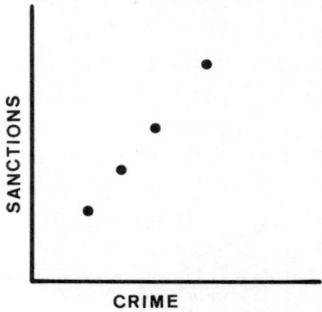

Source: Compiled by the author.

the economic theory offers alternative explanations. For example, the same results could be obtained from the situation represented in Figure 4.2 (top graph). In this situation, the apparent positive relationship results from collecting data from communities with differing crime functions but a single sanction function. The same results could be produced from the situation represented in the bottom graph of Figure 4.2. In this case, the results are produced by each city having a differing crime and sanction function. In either case or in any other representing a supply-and-demand situation, B_1, as estimated by equation 3, is a biased estimate of the true parameter.[40] The bias is such that both the magnitude of the estimate and the sign of the estimate might be in error.[41]

The Economic Theory of Irrational Behavior

It might be argued that the economic theory of crime requires the assumption that criminals are rational. Psychiatrists might very well choose to dispute this assumption. Halleck points out that even criminals who engage in crimes that appear to be motivated primarily by economic considerations fail to exhibit rational restraint and caution.[42] Schmideberg argues that criminals' attitudes toward punishment differ from those of the ordinary citizens in that they are not normally deterred or influenced by the possibility of punishment.[43]

It is probably possible to argue against the conclusion of criminal irrationality that can be drawn from the findings stated above. However, it does not seem necessary for individual behavior to be rational for the economic theory of crime to be valid. Becker points out that the laws of economics assume a rational

FIGURE 4.2

Data as the Result of the Interaction of
Supply-and-Demand Functions

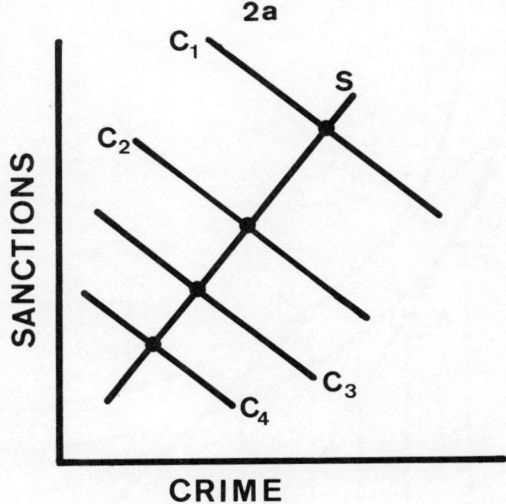

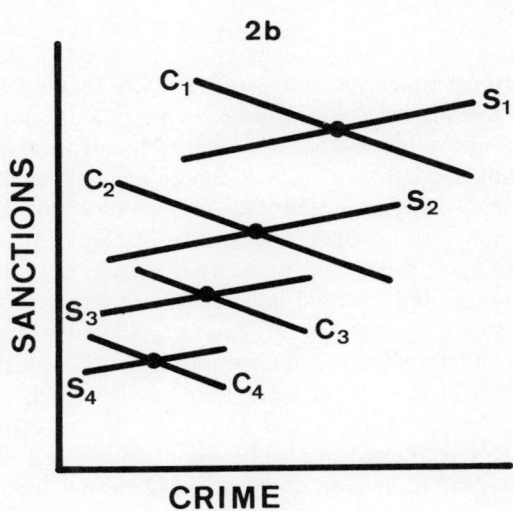

Source: Compiled by the author.

FIGURE 4.3

The Behavioral Impact of Increasing the Costs of Engaging in Illegal Activities under Differing Decision-Making Rules

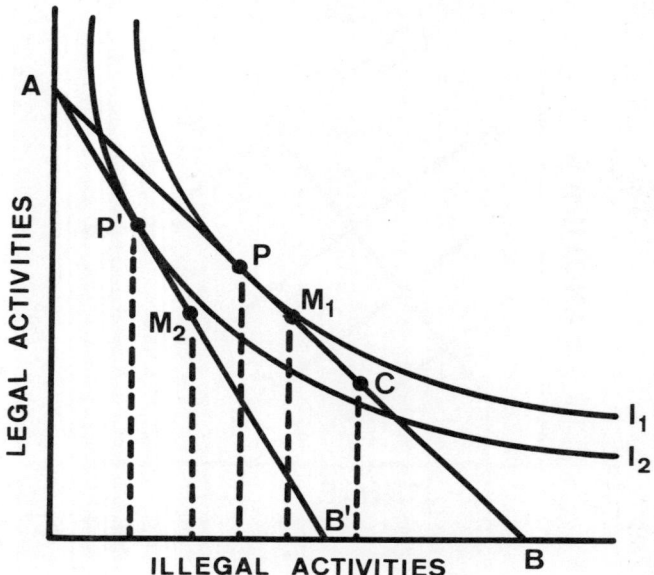

Source: Compiled by the author.

market and not rational individual behavior.[44] To infer that individual rationality exists in a rational market could be an example of Robinson's classical ecological fallacy.[45] However there does not seem to be adequate reason to pursue the issue of individual rationality since it can be demonstrated that a rational market can result from conditions other than rational individual behavior.[46]

The following in a somewhat oversimplified manner demonstrates that the economic theory of crime can be valid under a wide variety of individual decision-making rules.[47] Line AB in Figure 4.3 represents an opportunity boundary. That is, it connects all points representing maximum combinations of legal and illegal activities possible under a given set of constraints. An individual could be constrained by a number of factors, including time, his skill level, and wealth available to devote to legal and illegal activities. With the opportunity boundary defined as line AB, the rational individual would engage in a mix of activities represented by point P. The division of activities represented by point P provides the individual with the greatest possible satisfaction. Since point P is on the opportunity boundary, it represents a condition of maximum possible consumption. At point P the opportunity boundary is intersected by an indifference curve. Points along an indifference curve represent equal satisfaction. At points on the opportunity boundary not intersected by an indifference curve an individual can gain greater satisfaction by sacrificing some of one activity to gain more of the other. Although a division of activities at other points along I_1 would provide equal satisfaction, it is not possible. Point P is the only place where that indifference curve intersects the opportunity boundary. It would be possible for an individual to have consumption points along an alternative indifference curve such as I_2. However I_2 does not provide as much utility as is provided by I_1. Indifference curves representing greater utility than I_1 do not intersect the opportunity boundary and do not represent possible consumption points. Therefore a division of activities represented by point P provides the greatest possible utility and is the point indicating how the rational individual will divide his time between legal and illegal activities.

If public policies were instituted that reduced the opportunities to engage in illegal activities then the opportunity boundary could shift to AB'. This could be accomplished through policies that would make it more time consuming to engage in criminal activities, or force a larger interval of time to elapse between the commission of each illegal activity. It could even result from policies that create the psychological impression that the costs of engaging in crime have increased. In such a situation the rational individual would alter his mix of activities to correspond to the point P'. Thus the level of criminal activity would be reduced.

It is also possible for nonrational individuals to experience reductions in criminal activity by reducing the possibility for engaging in illegal activities. Some individuals might wish to retain a given quantity of illegal activities and sacrifice any amount of legal activities that would be necessary, but this might not always be possible. An individual whose initial mix of activities was represented by point C would find it impossible to maintain his level of activities if the opportunity boundary were shifted to AB'. Even with zero legal activities it is impossible to maintain that quantity of illegal activites. He would have no alternative but to reduce his level of criminal activity. The effectiveness of policies designed to reduce the amount of crime committed by such inflexible criminals would depend on the extent to which these individuals would be found in the area of impossible illegal activities. This is essentially an empirical issue and points up the need for greatly expanded research efforts based upon economic theory.

Even if individuals randomly decided on the mix of legal and illegal activities, the economic theory indicates that lowering the opportunity boundary for illegal activities will reduce the crime rate. Assume that line AB represents the opportunity boundary for a number of individuals rather than for just one. If these individuals randomly selected their behavior mix, it is reasonable to assume that M_1, the midpoint of line AB, would represent the average amount of illegal activity. With a shift in the opportunity boundary to AB', the midpoint becomes M_2. Clearly M_2 represents a lower level of illegal activity.

The Impact of the Criminal-Justice System

As demonstrated above, it can be argued that the economic theory of crime is valid under a number of decision-making rules and that individual rationality is not necessary for the crime rate to be reduced by increasing the sanctioning outputs of the criminal-justice system. However it is necessary to assume that individual behavior is somehow constrained by the outputs of the criminal-justice system. There appears to be a tendency on the part of the public and among scholars to dismiss the criminal-justice system as a deterrent to crime,[48] yet there is ample evidence to indicate that the outputs of at least some of the components of the criminal-justice system can deter crime.

Sanctioning can be thought of as involving two components. The first is the probability of sanctions being imposed. The second is the severity of the sanctions imposed. It follows from the economic theory of crime that when sanctions are more likely to be imposed or when sanctions become more severe that crime is less likely. It also follows from the economic theory that the same is true when the potential offender perceives that sanctions are more likely to be imposed or that sanctions are likely to be more severe. The evidence is strongest for certainty of punishment deterring crime. In a study of homicide rates, Gibbs found that certainty of punishment was a deterrent.[49] Tittle expanded the analysis to all seven of the Part I crimes reported by the FBI. He also introduced controls for environmental factors. Tittle found negative relationships between certainty of punishment and crime rates, although for several crimes, the magnitude of the coefficients was small.[50] Chiricos and Waldo found inconsistent relationships between certainty of punishment and crime rates using longitudinal data. However, certainty of punishment appeared to deter robbery, assault, and burglary.[51] Logan found negative correlations between certainty of imprisonment and crime rates for all felonies studied.[52] Antunes and Hunt also reported moderate but consistently negative relationships between certainty of punishment and crime rates.[53] Baily, Martin, and Gray reported similar results.[54] Thus there does appear to be ample evidence to support the notion that one output of the criminal-justice system, certainty of punishment, deters crime. Since none of the studies took into account the possibility of a mutually determinant relationship between crime and sanctions, the deterrent impact of certainty of punishment was probably underestimated.

The role of severity of punishment is much less clear. Much of the early research on this topic focused on the death penalty. Generally this research failed to show a significant relationship between murder rates and capital punishment.[55] However a number of studies have reported that the severity of punishment is negatively related to homicide rates.[56]

While the focus of research has been on the deterring impact of criminal-justice system outputs, there is also evidence that the outputs of the criminal justice system can reduce crime due to incapacitation. Andenaes states that deterrence refers to the motivating impact of conscious fear.[57] Incapacitation results from the removal of the offender from society. Shinnar and Shinnar found that changes in public policies that result in lessened incapacitation resulted in higher crime rates.[58] It follows from this that policies that increase incapacitation, such as increasing length of sentences and increasing the certainty that an offender spends some time in prison, would serve to reduce the crime rate even if there were no deterrent effect.

Thus while the contours remain unclear, there is sufficient justification to take the position that the outputs of the criminal-justice system can deter or otherwise reduce crime. It would seem useful to turn the focus of the research to the questions of what components and what policies of the criminal justice system deter crime and to what extent they do deter it. The economic theory of crime is a powerful research tool for this task.

Empirical Tests of the Theory

Empirical research conducted within the conceptual and methodological framework of the economic theory of crime has supported the theory. In addition, the research has indicated that coefficients estimated by employing a single-equation model and ordinary least squares are frequently biased. The use of two-stage least squares often produces a change of sign from positive to negative for the relationship between crime and sanctions. Ehrlich found that when using two-stage least squares both the number of offenders imprisoned per known offense and the average time served by offenders in state prisons were negatively related to crime rates for all FBI Part I crimes. While ordinary least squares estimates were also frequently negative, they inevitably underestimated the magnitude of the coefficients.[59] Orsagh reports similar results.[60]

While the above studies used only cross-sectional data, Pogue employed both longitudinal and cross-sectional data. For the cross-sectional data, total crimes, rape, burglary, and larceny clearance rates were found to be negatively related to their respective crime rates.[61] Swimmer reported that total per capita police expenditures were negatively related to murder and rape.[62] Swimmer also provided estimates of the degree to which ordinary least squares underestimated the regression coefficients. Assault was underestimated by 439 percent. All coefficients were underestimated except auto theft, which was overestimated by 49 percent.[63] Furthermore, Swimmer found that spending additional funds for police would be cost efficient.[64] Finally Swimmer found that the effectiveness of police in deterring crime results from manpower rather than other outputs of police departments.[65] Of all the research utilizing the economic theory of crime, Swimmer's probably most clearly demonstrates the potential usefulness of the economic theory of crime to the policymaker.

McPheters and Stronge recognize the problem of crime and sanctions being jointly determined. However, unlike most other researchers, they approach the problem through the use of a Koyck transformation, a lagging technique. They found that police expenditures are negatively associated with the total crime rate.[66]

PROBLEMS WITH THE ECONOMIC THEORY OF CRIME

The existing research indicates considerable support for the economic theory of crime. Both property crimes and violent crimes appear to be deterred by outputs from the criminal-justice system. There are, however, a number of problems that must be resolved before the full utility of the economic theory can be measured. Included in the list of problems are the assumption of diminishing returns for criminal-justice outputs, the operationalization of the endogenous variables—especially the crime variables—and the limited scope of the research in terms of the extent to which the criminal-justice system has been investigated.

The Assumption of Diminishing Returns

Most of the empirical research based on the economic theory of crime has made the assumption that increased expenditures by criminal-justice agencies would yield diminishing returns. To build this assumption into the empirical examinations most researchers have employed a logarithmic model, despite the fact that diminishing returns were not assumed for the environmental variables. Researchers have been willing to accept errors in the estimates of the environmental parameters in order to obtain better estimates of the sanction parameters.

However, it is not logically necessary for outputs of the criminal-justice system to yield diminishing returns. It is possible that the policies of the criminal-justice system are "critical mass" politics. That is, a certain level of output must be reached in order for the policies to become fully effective.[67] In an examination of 22 police policy variables, Elliott found little evidence to support the notion of diminishing returns for police policy outputs. Correlation coefficients indicated that log transformations of the police variables generally provided no better fit with crime indicators than the untransformed data.[68] This indicates that the diminishing-returns assumption may not be justified and that a linear model would be more appropriate and give better estimates of the environmental parameters.

Measuring Crime

Another weakness of the empirical tests of the economic theory of crime is to be found in the endogenous variables employed. This problem reaches its greatest magnitude with the crime indicators. Generally a heavy reliance has been placed on FBI Uniform Crime Reports (UCR). The weaknesses and limitations of these data have long been topics for academic discussion.[69] What is probably the most common critique of UCR data and the one most relevant to the economic theory of crime is that reported crimes are only a fraction of total crimes. However it does not appear that UCR data are unrelated to actual crime rates. Skogan reported that UCR data is related to estimates of the incidence of crime obtained from the assumedly more accurate victimization surveys. Generally survey data and UCR data show similar patterns of correlations with predictor variables.[70]

Underreporting is in itself not a major problem for the economic theory of crime. Swimmer pointed out that the impact of uniform underreporting is to attentuate the estimates of the regression coefficients.[71] Thus underreporting could result in underestimation of the strength of criminal-justice policies. Bias that would make the economic theory appear more powerful than it actually is could result only if underreporting is not uniform. Unfortunately there is evidence that indicated that underreporting is not uniform and is therefore a potential source of bias. Skogan found that the estimates of the regression coefficients obtained when survey rates were regressed on independent variables differed significantly from the estimates obtained using UCR data.[72] Thus the estimates of parameters obtained using UCR data are possibly biased.

A major source of this bias appears to be region. Ennis reported that the underreporting of violent crime is twice as great in the western states as it is in the northeastern states. Property crime underreporting is approximately 50 percent greater in North Central states than in other regions. The differences observed when looking at UCR Part I crimes individually are frequently even greater.[73] Obviously region can be controlled for in a number of different ways. Data could be selected from the communities in a single state. It would be useful in this situation to select a state where greater care was exercised over the reporting practices of the local police agencies than is exercised by the FBI. In a study where this was done, support was found for the hypothesis that outputs of police departments deterred property crime in Kansas.[74]

Perhaps as significant as underreporting of crime is underrecording of crime by the police. Skogan reports that the percentage of crimes that go unrecorded after being reported by the public is approximately equal to the percentage of crime occurring that go unreported.[75] Furthermore there is wide variation in recording rates among cities.[76] The impact of this is to distort the relationship between outputs of municipal police forces and their effectiveness. Skogan found that reporting is positively related to police professionalism and police resources.[77] Complete recording decreases the clearance rates.[78] This makes the use of clearance rates as measures of police effectiveness very questionable.

While Skogan very effectively illustrates some serious problems with crime data, these problems do not appear to make existing crime data unsuitable for empirical tests of the economic theory of crime. This can be demonstrated by looking at Figure 4.4. Following the economic theory of crime it would be expected that there would be a negative relationship between police outputs and crime. However, assuming that points A and B were observed data points (only two data points are utilized to provide graphic simplicity), the finding would be that there was no relationship between police outputs and crime. It can be assumed that there was unrecorded crime in both cases. It would be expected that the greatest actual amount of unrecorded crime would be in case A because it had a lower level of police outputs. Therefore allowing for an adjustment of both crime rates upward with the greater increase for A due to its lower level of police resources, it can be seen that there is actually a negative relationship. Thus it appears that the actual impact of discrepancies in police recording practices is

FIGURE 4.4

The Impact of the Underrecording of Crime on Measuring the Relationship between Police Outputs and Crime

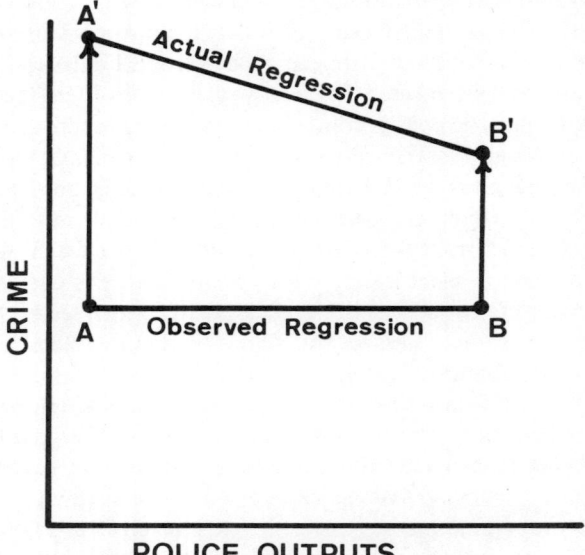

Source: Compiled by the author.

to provide estimates of the impact of police policies that attenuate the negative magnitude of the true relationship.

It appears that the empirical support that has been provided for the economic theory of crime is not an artifact of statistical bias. It is also likely that little confidence can be placed in the precision of figures purporting to indicate the exact amount of deterrence provided by a change in any criminal-justice output. The same reservations must be held concerning reported cost-benefit ratios.

FUTURE APPLICATIONS

To date, the economic theory of crime has been utilized to examine only a very limited range of criminal-justice-system policies. The theory is of such recent origin that it would be unrealistic to expect all aspects of the criminal-justice system to have been investigated at this time. However the scope of existing research seems needlessly narrow. Police outputs have received most of the attention. The economic theory of crime is eminently suited to study virtually any aspect of criminal justice when the goal of the research is to ascertain the impact of that component or policy of the system on the incidence of crime. The theory is uniquely suited for dealing with those situations where there is an a priori reason to suspect that crime has an influence on the demand for sanctions. There are many instances of this to be found in the criminal justice system.

For example, there is, as was indicated earlier, a tendency to dismiss severity of punishment as being rather unimportant in deterring crime. This position is supported by a sizable but somewhat questionable body of research that is now being challenged by research built on the economic theory of crime. Ehrlich argues that each execution saves between seven and eight lives.[79] As was indicated earlier, data limitations probably make it impossible to give much credence to the actual number, but it seems unlikely than an elasticity that high would be reported if the true value were zero. The economic theory offers a mechanism for researching an issue that again appears to be a topic of public concern.

There are a number of aspects of the sentencing procedure that could be investigated. The obvious one is the extent to which variations in sentencing influence crime rates. Another possibility is to investigate the impact of determinant versus indeterminant sentencing. Still another investigation could examine how judges and juries react to variations in the crime rate. Sanctioning as well as crime is an endogenous variable and therefore it would be inappropriate to use a single-equation model in this situation.

Currently the economic theory is most commonly used to investigate the impact of police policies. This research indicates that policing can deter crime[80] and that it is police personnel that is effective.[81] These findings probably are of little use to policymakers. The findings do suggest that police departments would probably be advised to shift resources away from hardware acquisition and into augmenting personnel. Although the dynamics of the relationship between the numerical strength of police and deterrence remain very unclear at this time, there is an indication that it is the visibility of police that is important.[82]

Becker, one of the developers of the economic theory of crime, offers some interesting suggestions for research. He presents a case for the substitution of fines for imprisonment in many criminal cases. He argues that fines could be used to compensate the victim while imprisonment of the offender offers no compensation. In addition, fines do not use up social resources as does institutionalization.[83] The economic theory of crime could be used to ascertain what levels of fines correspond to what durations of imprisonment in terms of having equal deterring capabilities. Decisions could then be made concerning the equity of allowing the substitution.

Stover and Brown suggest that in general it would be useful to study legislatures and their role in deterring criminal activity. They argue that while agencies in the criminal-justice system can influence the severity or likelihood of punishment, legislatures can do this, and in addition they are in a position to alter the benefits of compliance with the law.[84] Furthermore, if it can be assumed that legislative behavior is influenced by criminal behavior, then the economic theory of crime could be used to examine the degree of this influence as well as the nature of the relationship.

This discussion by no means exhausts the possible topics of investigation for which the economic theory of crime offers a reasonable model. For example, the whole question of the division of resources within the criminal-justice system would be a proper subject as would the division of resources between the criminal-justice system and the providers of social services. In situations where there is reason to believe that crime responds to sanctions and that the level of sanctioning responds to the level of crime, the economic theory is currently the only appropriate paradigm.

The economic theory of crime appears to be a paradigm with extremely high potential for scholars, policy analysts and policymakers. While most existing criminological theories have as their goal the identification of the causes of crime, they are deficient on two counts. None of the most commonly known theories have demonstrated that they have identified the causes of crime. Even if it could be demonstrated that a theory had empirically been verified this would still be information of limited utility. The hypothesized causes of crime are of such a nature that they would prove extremely intractable when confronted with public policy. The etiological theories deal with factors that might well be beyond the capabilities of the existing political system to change.

The economic theory of crime is less ambitious. The economic theory asserts that whatever the causes of crime, offenders and potential offenders will curtail their criminal activities as the actual or perceived costs of engaging in crime increase. Although derived from utility theory, the economic theory of crime is not dependent on individual rationality for validity. Rather the theory is valid under a number of individual decision-making rules, including intransigency and random decision making. The theory is not made unverifiable by the well-discussed problems of crime incidence data. The only major problems in this area appear to be biases in the underreporting of crime. This problem can be eliminated by careful selection of research sites. When these biases are eliminated the impact of underreporting is to reduce the estimated impact of sanctioning below the actual impact. Another potential problem, underrecording by police, appears to make estimates of the impact of the criminal-justice component, or at least the law-enforcement component, conservative.

It is hoped that others will be encouraged to apply the economic theory of crime in their research. By doing so, the potential exists to discover more efficient and effective ways of dealing with the problems generated by crime.

NOTES

1. President's Commission on Law Enforcement and Administration of Justice, *Task Force Report: Crime and Its Impact; An Assessment* (Washington, D.C.: Government Printing Office, 1967), p. 44.

2. New York *Times*, January 16, 1974.

3. *Uniform Crime Reports* (Washington, D.C.: U.S. Department of Justice, 1975), pp. 153-54.

4. Dallas *Times-Herald*, December 19, 1973.

5. Cesare Lombroso, *Crime: Its Causes and Remedies*, trans. Henry P. Horton (Montclair, N.J.: Patterson-Smith, 1968), pp. 365-84.

6. Charles Goring, *The English Convict* (London: His Majesty's Stationery Office, 1913).

7. For example, see Earnest A. Hooton, *Crime and the Man* (New York: Greenwood Press, 1968). While not employing an atavistic notion, Hooton places strong emphasis on the relationship between physical characteristics and criminal behavior.

8. For a review of this literature see Ernest B. Hack, "Behavioral Implications of the Human XYY Genotype," *Science* 179 (January 12, 1973): 139-50; and Richard S. Fox, "The XYY Offender: A Myth?," *Journal of Criminal Law, Criminology and Police Science* 62 (March 1971): 59-73.

9. See Walter Bromberg, *Crime and the Mind: A Psychiatric Analysis of Crime and Punishment* (New York: Macmillan, 1965) for a work in this tradition. For a review of psychiatric research related to crime see Seymour L. Halleck, *Psychiatry and the Dilemmas of Crime* (New York: Harper and Row, 1967). For an overview of the role of psychology in the criminal-justice system see Stanley L. Brodsky, et al., *Psychologists in the Criminal Justice System* (Urbana: University of Illinois Press, 1973).

10. Don M. Gottfredson, "Five Challenges," in Brodsky, op. cit., pp. 26-31.

11. Oscar Newman, *Defensible Space: Crime Prevention Through Urban Design* (New York: Collier, 1973).
12. Keith D. Harries, *The Geography of Crime and Justice* (New York: McGraw-Hill, 1974).
13. Edwin H. Sutherland, *Principles of Criminology*, 3rd ed. (Philadelphia: J.B. Lippincott, 1939).
14. Edwin H. Sutherland, *Principles of Criminology*, 4th ed. (Philadelphia: J.B. Lippincott, 1947), pp. 5-9.
15. Edwin H. Sutherland and Donald R. Cressey, *Principles of Criminology*, 9th ed. (Philadelphia: J.B. Lippincott, 1974), pp. 75-76.
16. Don C. Gibbons, "Observations on the Study of Crime Causation," *American Journal of Sociology* 77 (September 1971): 263.
17. For a discussion of the problems of operationalization and an attempt at empirical testing see James F. Short, Jr., "Differential Association as a Hypothesis: Problems of Empirical Testing," *Social Problems* 8 (Summer 1960): 14-25.
18. Reed Adams, "Differential Association and Learning Principles Revisited," *Social Problems* 20 (Spring 1973): 458-70.
19. See Frank Tannenbaum, *Crime and the Community* (Lexington, Mass.: Ginn and Co., 1938).
20. Clarence Schrag, *Crime and Justice: American Style*, National Institute of Mental Health, Center for Studies of Crime and Delinquency publication NO. HSM-72-9052 (Washington, D.C.: Government Printing Office, 1971), p. 89.
21. Ibid., pp. 89-92.
22. Charles Wellford, "Labeling Theory and Criminology: An Assessment," *Social Problems* 22 (February 1975): 332-45.
23. Nanette J. Davis, "Labeling Theory in Deviance Research: A Critique and Consideration," *Sociological Quarterly* 13 (Fall 1972): 332-45.
24. James Q. Wilson, *Thinking About Crime* (New York: Basic Books, 1975), p. 50.
25. Ibid., p. 51.
26. John Plamenatz, *The English Utilitarians* (Oxford, England: Basil Blackwell, 1958), p. 62.
27. Jonathan Rubinstein, *City Police* (New York: Ballantine, 1973), p. 10.
28. Jeremy Bentham, *An Introduction to the Principles of Morals and Legislation* (New York: Hafner Publishing, 1948), pp. 1-2.
29. For a discussion of dealing with supply-and-demand functions see Hubert M. Blalock, Jr., *Theory Construction* (Englewood Cliffs, N.J.: Prentice-Hall, 1969), pp. 50-54.
30. Gary S. Becker, "Crime and Punishment: An Economic Approach," *The Journal of Political Economy* 76 (March/April 1968): 169-217.
31. Thomas Orsagh, "Crime, Sanctions and Scientific Explanation," *The Journal of Criminal Law and Criminology* 64 (September 1973): 354-61.
32. Isaac Ehrlich, "Participation in Illegitimate Activities: A Theoretical and Empirical Investigation," *Journal of Political Economy* 81 (May/June 1973): 521-67.
33. Taken with slight modification from Nicholas Elliott, "Police Policies and the Deterrence of Crime: An Econometric Approach." Paper presented at the meeting of the Southwestern Political Science Association, Dallas, Texas, April 1976. Similar but slightly different versions of these formulations are presented by Eugene Swimmer, "Measurement of the Effectiveness of Urban Law Enforcement: A Simultaneous Approach,"*Southern Economics Journal* 40 (April 1974): 618-22; David Lawrence Sjoquist, "Property Crime and Economic Behavior: Some Empirical Results," *American Economic Review* 63 (June 1973): 441; Orsagh, op. cit.; Lee R. McPheters and William B. Stronge, "Law Enforcement Expenditures and Urban Crime," *National Tax Journal* 27 (December 1974): 635-36; and

Thomas F. Pogue, "Effect of Police Expenditures on Crime Rates: Some Evidence," *Public Finance Quarterly* 3 (January 1975): 17.

34. M. K. Block and J. M. Heineke, "A Labor Theoretic Analysis of the Criminal Choice," *American Economic Review* 65 (July 1975): 314-25.

35. Hubert M. Blalock, Jr., "Theory Building and Causal Inferences," in *Methodology in Social Research*, eds. Hubert M. Blalock, Jr. and Ann B. Blalock (New York: McGraw-Hill, 1962), p. 187-91.

36. For a discussion of this problem see Harry H. Kelejian and Wallace Oates, *Introduction to Econometrics* (New York: Harper and Row, 1974), pp. 224-39; Ronald J. Wonnacott and Thomas J. Wonnacott, *Econometrics* (New York: John Wiley, 1970), pp. 149-71; and J. Johnston, *Econometric Methods*, 2nd ed. (New York: McGraw-Hill, 1972), pp. 341-51.

37. See Kelejian and Oates, op. cit., pp. 228-32; and Johnston, op. cit., pp. 347-48 for discussions of two-stage least squares.

38. Yong Hyo Cho, *Public Policy and Urban Crime* (Cambridge, Mass.: Ballinger, 1974), pp. 165-78.

39. Ibid., p. 168.

40. Orsagh, op. cit.

41. Ibid., p. 361.

42. Halleck, op. cit., p. 49.

43. Melitta Schmideberg, "The Offender's Attitude Toward Punishment," *The Journal of Criminal Law, Criminology and Police Science* 51 (September/October 1960): 333.

44. Gary S. Becker, "Irrational Behavior and Economic Theory," *The Journal of Political Economy* 70 (February 1962): 1-2.

45. William S. Robinson, "Ecological Correlations and the Behavior of Individuals," *American Sociological Review* 15 (June 1950): 351-57.

46. The following discussion draws from Becker, "Irrational Behavior," op. cit., pp. 2-12. It also utilizes Becker's notion of rationality, that is, rational behavior implies consistent maximization of a well-ordered function. A well-ordered function would display the characteristic of transitivity.

47. The oversimplification results primarily from dealing with crime only as consumption and not as production. If, however, the assumption is made that the producers of crime have constraints that limit the amount of crime they can produce the simplification does not detract from the validity of the argument (see Becker, "Irrational Behavior," op. cit., pp. 9-12). The graphic presentation can be made with greater clarity with this assumption. Becker argues that the constraint assumption can be reasonably made for firms (producers) as well as individuals (consumers). This appears to be valid for the production of crime given the point made by Block and Heineke that the analysis of illegal activity requires an examination of the expenditure of time (Block and Heineke, op. cit., p. 314). Clearly the quantity of time available is constrained.

48. For a discussion of this problem see Johannes Andenaes, "General Prevention Research and Policy Implications," *The Journal of Criminal Law and Criminology* 66 (September 1975): 338-39.

49. Jack P. Gibbs, "Crime, Punishment and Deterrence," *Southwest Social Science Quarterly* 48 (March 1968): 515-30.

50. Charles Tittle, "Crime Rates and Legal Sanctions," *Social Problems* 16 (1969): 409.

51. Theodore G. Chiricos and Gordon P. Waldo, "Punishment and Crime: An Examination of Some Empirical Evidence," *Social Problems* 18 (Fall 1970): 200-17.

52. Charles H. Logan, "General Deterrent Effects of Imprisonment," *Social Forces* 51 (September 1972): 64-73.

53. George Antunes and A. Lee Hunt, "The Impact of Certainty and Severity of Punishment on Levels of Crime in American States: An Extended Analysis," *The Journal of Criminal Law and Criminology* 64 (December 1973): 486-93.

54. William C. Bailey, J. David Martin, and Louis Gray, "Crime and Deterrence: A Correlation Analysis," *Journal of Research in Crime and Delinquency* 11 (July 1974): 124-43.

55. See Karl Schuessler, "The Deterrent Influence of the Death Penalty," *The Annals* 284 (November 1952): 54-62; Royal Commission on Capital Punishment 1949-53, *Report* (London: His Majesty's Stationery Office, 1953); Thorsten Sellin, "Homicides in Retentionist and Abolitionist States," in *Capital Punishment*, ed. Thorsten Sellin (New York: Harper and Row, 1967), pp. 135-38.

56. Tittle, op. cit., p. 417; Chiricos and Waldo, op. cit., p. 207; Bailey, Martin, and Gray, op. cit., pp. 136-37.

57. Andenaes, op. cit., p. 341.

58. Shlomo Shinnar and Reuel Shinnar, "The Effects of the Criminal Justice System on the Control of Crime: A Quantitative Approach," *Law and Society Review* 9 (Summer 1975): 581-611.

59. Isaac Ehrlich, "Participation in Illegal Activities: An Economic Analysis," in *Essays in the Economics of Crime and Punishment*, eds. Gary S. Becker and William M. Landes (New York: National Bureau of Economic Research, 1974), pp. 95-101.

60. Orsagh, op. cit.

61. Pogue, op. cit.

62. Swimmer, op. cit.

63. Ibid., p. 624.

64. Ibid., pp. 626-28.

65. Eugene Swimmer, "Measurement of the Effectiveness of Urban Law Enforcement: A Simultaneous Equations Approach," (Ph.D. dissertation, Cornell University, 1972), pp. 108-17.

66. McPheters and Stronge, op. cit.

67. For a discussion of this concept see Paul R. Schulman, "Nonincremental Policy Making: Notes Toward an Alternative Paradigm," *American Political Science Review* 69 (December 1975): 1354-70.

68. Elliott, op. cit., p. 27.

69. For summaries of these objections see Elinor Ostrom, "Institutional Arrangements and the Measurement of Policy Consequences: Applications to Evaluating Police Performance," *Urban Affairs Quarterly* 6 (June 1971): 458-59; and Eugene Doleschal, *Criminal Statistics*, Dept. of Health, Education and Welfare Publication No. (HSM) 72-9094 (Washington, D.C.: Government Printing Office, 1972).

70. Wesley G. Skogan, "The Validity of Official Crime Statistics: An Empirical Investigation," *Social Science Quarterly* 55 (June 1974): 34.

71. Swimmer, op. cit., pp. 50-53.

72. Skogan, op. cit., p. 37.

73. Phillip Ennis, *Criminal Victimization in the United States*: A Report of a National Survey, Field Survey II conducted for the President's Commission for Law Enforcement and Administration of Justice (Washington, D.C.: Government Printing Office, 1967).

74. Elliott, op. cit.

75. Wesley G. Skogan, "Crime and Crime Rates," in *Sample Surveys of the Victims of Crime*, ed. Wesley G. Skogan (Cambridge, Mass.: Ballinger, 1976).

76. Ibid. For an account of the factors that determine whether or not police act on a citizen complaint, see Rubinstein, op. cit., pp. 129-340.

77. Skogan, "Crime and Crime Rates," op. cit.

78. Ibid.

79. Isaac Ehrlich, "The Deterrent Effect of Capital Punishment: A Question of Life and Death," *American Economic Review* 65 (June 1975): 414.

80. Swimmer, op. cit.; McPheters and Stronge, op. cit.

81. Swimmer, op. cit.

82. Elliott, op. cit., pp. 34-35.

83. Becker, "Participation," op. cit., pp. 193-98.

84. Robert V. Stover and Don W. Brown, "Understanding Compliance and Noncompliance with Law: The Contribution of Utility Theory," *Social Science Quarterly* 56 (December 1975): 371.

CHAPTER 5

DETERMINING THE IMPACT OF LEGAL POLICY CHANGES BEFORE THE CHANGES OCCUR

Stuart Nagel
Marian Neef

In recent years there has been a substantial increase in evaluation studies in political and social science, and of impact studies within the public law field of political science.[1] Virtually all evaluation and impact studies, however, require the policy (that is being evaluated or whose impact is being determined) to be adopted somewhere before the evaluation or the impact analysis can be done. Methodologically speaking, evaluation and impact studies tend to emphasize before and after analyses or comparisons between places having the policy and those not having it.[2] In spite of the insights that can be obtained from such studies, they do have some serious defects that a supplementary approach based on deductive modeling does not have. By deductive modeling in this context, we mean deducing the effects of adopting a policy before it has been adopted from what is known about related policies and related situations. It is the purpose of this chapter to discuss deductive policy evaluation, particularly as applied to legal-policy changes relating to the operation of the judicial process.

POST-IMPACT ANALYSIS VERSUS PRE-IMPACT ANALYSIS

As implied, the most obvious defect of an overtime or overspace policy evaluation is that the adoption of the policy is required and no place or not

---

Thanks are owed to the LEAA National Institute of Law Enforcement and Criminal Justice, the Ford Foundation Public Policy Committee, and the University of Illinois Law and Society Program for financing some aspects of the illustrative examples that are used in this chapter. The ideas advocated herein, however, are original with the authors rather than the funding agencies.

enough places may be willing to adopt the policy to be able to make a meaningful empirical analysis. Another defect is that virtually all places may adopt a policy simultaneously, leaving no places for a control group. Some places may adopt a policy and some not, but unfortunately not in a random way. Therefore other things may be disproportionately present or change among the places that adopt the policy, and those other hard-to-statistically-control things may cause the alleged effects, not the policy. The policy may also be adopted for too short a time to determine its effects, or data may be unavailable for the period before. Even with a highly sound social experiment, there are normative problems if not methodological ones. These include the difficulty of retracting the policy if it is found to be defective, and especially restoring the damage that it may have done to people or places subjected to it.

Closely related to a before-and-after analysis is the extension of a trend line whereby one observes, for example, that policy X increases two units each year and effect Y increases four units each year. From that information, one can deduce that if the future is like the past and if two more units of the policy are adopted next year, then four more units of the effect will occur without having to wait for the policy to be adopted next year. That extrapolation methodology, however, requires that the policy have been adopted to some degree in the past in order to have a trend line to extend. Also closely related to a comparison of places is an analysis that finds that if each place is plotted as a dot on a graph relating effect Y to policy X, then a line fitted to those dots can be represented by the equation $Y = 2X$. From that equation, one can deduce that if those are a representative set of places and if a place not included in the analysis were specified to have adopted the policy to the extent of 10 X units, then that place should have 20 Y units as a result. That methodology of predicting from indicator variables requires, however, that the policy have been adopted in some places to some degree in order to create the predictive equation. Sometimes one can test a policy's effects by adopting it in a pretend or simulated situation, for example, having students engage in plea bargaining or pretend they are jurors. It may, however, be virtually impossible to capture reality sufficiently through that kind of methodology, especially if one has limited financial resources.

Deductive policy evaluation or pre-impact analysis in its simplest form involves saying that X_1 policy or situation (which has been adopted) has been found to cause Y effect; X_2 policy (which has not been adopted) is like X_1 policy, with regard to all that we know to be relevant to the occurrence of Y effect; and therefore we predict X_2 policy will also cause Y effect if it is adopted. That kind of deductive policy evaluation involves deducing the effects of a policy by analogizing it to a single comparable situation whose effects are known. It might be called single-analogy deduction. We plan to illustrate that kind of analysis by attempting to determine the effects of various judicial-process changes that relate to plea bargaining (X_2), with regard to the effects on the likelihood and level of plea-bargaining settlements (Y) by analogizing plea bargaining to a no-fixed-price push-cart peddler transaction (X_1).

Deductive policy evaluation (pre-impact analysis) in a slightly more sophisticated form involves saying X_1 policy has been found to cause Y effect; X_2 policy has been found to cause Y_2 effect; X_3 policy is in the middle between X_1 and X_2, with regard to its relevant characteristics; and therefore we predict that X_3 policy will cause Y_3 effect, which is in the middle between Y_1 and Y_2. That kind of deductive policy evaluation involves deducing the effects of a policy by analogizing it to two comparable situations whose effects are known. It might be called double-analogy deduction. We plan to illustrate that kind of analysis by attempting to determine the effects on conviction rates (Y) of shifting from a 12-person to a 6-person jury (the X_3 policy) by analogizing jury decision-making to flipping 12 coins (X_1) and to bowling with 12 pins (X_2).

THE IMPACT OF JUDICIAL-PROCESS CHANGES ON PLEA-BARGAINING SETTLEMENTS

The essence of the criminal-justice process is not the trial stage, but rather the negotiation for a guilty plea between prosecutors and defense counsel. Therefore it is important in efficient planning of the criminal-justice system to be able to determine in advance how changes in the judicial system may directly or indirectly affect the likelihood or the level of plea-bargaining settlements. It is the purpose of this section to describe a simple model of the plea-bargaining process that may be useful in making such advance determinations and thereby allow for offsetting changes where it seems appropriate to do so.[3]

Plea Bargaining as a Buying and Selling Transaction

The model views the plea-bargaining process as being analogous to a buying and selling transaction in a market that has no fixed prices, like that of a pushcart peddler. The defense counsel or defendant is like a buyer seeking as low a price, charge, or sentence as possible. The prosecutor is like a seller seeking as high a price, charge, or sentence as possible within the constraints imposed by the criminal code and possibly his sense of equity. The defendant-buyer has in mind a rough notion of how high he is willing to go before breaking off negotiations and turning to the trial court as an alternative seller. Likewise, the prosecutor-seller has in mind a rough notion of how low he is willing to go before breaking off negotiations and in effect forcing the defendant into the trial alternative.

How high the defendant-buyer is willing to go depends on his perception of the probability of his being convicted and the sentence he is likely to receive if he is convicted. Likewise, how low the prosecutor-seller is willing to go also depends on his perception of the conviction probability and the likely sentence. By multiplying his perception of the conviction probability and the likely sentence, one can roughly obtain the expected value of going to trial for either the defendant or the prosecutor. Those expected values represent the upper bargaining limit of the defendant and the lower bargaining limit of the prosecutor before adjustments are made for other considerations. They are the outside limits in the sense that if the other side will not go that far, that limit is the expected value that can be achieved by turning to the trial alternative.

The defendant's upper limit, however, needs to be adjusted for such nonsentence goals as getting out of jail while awaiting trial, avoiding the cost of hiring an attorney, and waiving the due process safeguards associated with a jury trial. These nonsentence goals generally result in the defendant-buyer being willing to offer a bonus above his base price or unadjusted limit for early delivery of the product or resolution of the case. Likewise, the prosecutor's lower limit needs to be adjusted for such nonsentence goals as conserving his litigation resources, preserving his high conviction percentage, and waiving the use of the defendant as an example to others. Those nonsentence goals generally result in the prosecutor-seller being willing to offer a discount below his base price or unadjusted limit for early payment on the invoice or resolution of the case.

If both the defendant and the prosecutor have similar perceptions of the conviction probability and the likely sentence, then the defendant's upper limit would be about the same as the prosecutor's lower limit. If the defendant adds a bonus to his upper limit, and the prosecutor subtracts a discount, then they are likely to arrive at an agreement between the defendant's upper limit and the prosecutor's lower limit, where they both have a sense of having gained something over their outside limits. Any change in the judicial system is therefore likely to affect the likelihood or level of plea-bargaining settlements if the change affects their perceptions of the conviction probability or the likely sentence in a case, or if the change affects the defendant's bonus or the prosecutor's discount.

Relevant Judicial-Process Changes

A change that decreases the defendant's bonus factor (such as increased free counsel or pretrial release) will lower the defendant's adjusted bargaining limit without affecting the prosecutor's limit. This will have the effect of narrowing the room for settlement and the effect of lowering the level of the new settlement if one can still be reached, assuming that the settlement will still be roughly at the midpoint between the defendant's and the prosecutor's limits.

FIGURE 5.1

The Impact of Judicial Process Changes on Plea-Bargaining Settlements

Defense Counsel Strategy

1. Accept offer if less than perceived probability of conviction times sentence if convicted plus percent bonus to avoid litigation
2. Otherwise go to trial

Prosecutor's Strategy

1. Accept offer if greater than perceived probability of conviction times sentence if convicted minus percent discount to avoid litigation
2. Otherwise go to trial

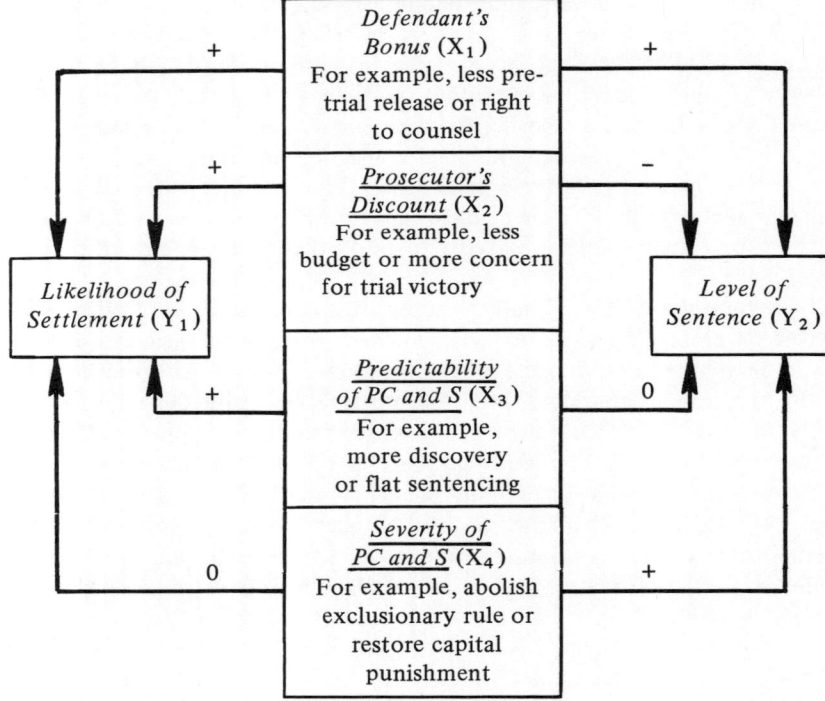

Meaning of Symbols:
+ means an increase in X causes an increase in Y, or a decrease in X causes a decrease in Y.

− means an increase in X causes a decrease in Y, or a decrease in X causes an increase in Y.

0 means X is not related to Y. All three types of relations assume other variables are held constant.

P.C. Probable Conviction.
S. Sentencing
Source: Compiled by the author.

The opposite occurs from a change that increases the defendant's bonus factor. A prosecutor who is aware that a change has occurred that decreases the defendant's bonus factor can, if he wants, offset the decreased settlements by offering better offers. He might especially want to do that if the decreased settlements add to his court congestion and thereby increase his desire to raise his discount factor.

A change that decreases the prosecutor's discount factor (such as more resources to the prosecutor thereby in effect lowering the cost of litigation) will raise the prosecutor's adjusted bargaining limit without directly affecting the defendant's limit (although more resources to the prosecutor may also affect the probability of conviction). This will have the effect of narrowing the room for settlement and the effect of increasing the level of the new settlement if one can still be reached. The opposite occurs from a change that increases the prosecutor's discount factor.

A change that improves the ability of one or both sides to predict more accurately the probability of conviction or the sentence upon conviction (such as pretrial discovery proceedings or flat sentencing) will have the effect of increasing the likelihood of settlements by decreasing misperceptions of their own bargaining limits by the respective parties. In the normal case, if both parties accurately perceive the probability of conviction and the sentence and thus have the same nonadjusted limits, then a settlement should be reached when the bonus factor raises the defendant's limit and the discount factor lowers the prosecutor's limit.

A change that increases the probability of conviction (such as more lenient admissibility of police-obtained evidence) or that increases sentencing payoffs (such as new mandatory minimum sentences) will have the effect of raising both the defendant's adjusted limit and the prosecutor's adjusted limit (if they both accurately perceive the effects of those judicial-system changes on the conviction probability and on sentencing) since their respective limits at least partly reflect the product of the perceived probability times the sentence that would be received if conviction occurs. The new limits will then still have as much room for settlement as before, but they will both be higher, thereby resulting in settlement at a higher level of charge or sentence. A change that decreases the probability of conviction or the sentencing payoffs will have the opposite effect.

Implications for Improving Plea Bargaining and the Judicial Process

The main implication this kind of analysis has for improving the plea-bargaining process is to provide a way of viewing the process so that one can better predict how judicial-system changes are likely to affect it. One can then try to make appropriate offsetting changes as a prosecutor, public defender, private defense counsel, court administrator, or judge, with regard to the offers or counteroffers of the prosecutor or defendant. "Appropriate," in this context, refers to seeking to preserve or change the status quo with regard to the percentage of cases that are settled through plea bargaining, the prosecutor's conviction rate, the public defender's litigation expenditures, or some other criteria.

One example of how the predictive model could be helpful in controlling the effects of judicial-process changes relates to the chain of effects produced by increasing the percentage of defendants who are released prior to trial. One would expect an increased release rate to result in a smaller county jail population, but the opposite might occur if one does not foresee the domino effect of an increased release rate. As mentioned, increasing pretrial release has the effect of decreasing the bonus that defendants are willing to offer in plea bargaining in order to obtain an early release from jail. To the extent that guilty pleas are thereby lessened, the backlog of cases and the length of time to process them may substantially increase. This could have the effect of increasing the length of time spent in pretrial detention by those defendants who do not qualify for pretrial release. As a result, the jail population may actually increase because its size is determined by the percent of defendants held in jail (which has gone down) and by the length of time the average detained defendant is held (which may go up to a more than offsetting degree). That selfdefeating chain of effects, however, can be avoided if the prosecutor and his assistants will improve the bargaining offers they make in order to preserve the previous likelihood of a settlement being reached, although now at a lower level. In other words, to preserve the previous settlement rate, the prosecutor will have to foresightfully offer a bigger discount to offset the average defendant's smaller bonus in light of the throes of trial and error, the prosecutor's intuitive bargaining sense, or the explicit model presented.

On a broader basis, this kind of analysis might also lead one to making policy recommendations with regard to how the plea-bargaining process can be made to result in settlements that better reflect the true probabilities of conviction and the true likely sentences. The process can come closer to that goal if three conditions are more prevalent in the criminal-justice system than they have been. First, the parties are as capable as possible of accurately perceiving the conviction probabilities and the likely sentences, which can be facilitated by better pretrial mutual-discovery procedures. Second, the defendant is not forced to offer an excessive bonus, which he otherwise might be (a) if he were being held in jail pending a distant trial, (b) if he could not afford an expensive lawyer and was not eligible for a free one, or (c) if he has a public defender who does not have the time or resources to take cases to trial where a trial will bring a lower likely sentence than plea bargaining will. Third, the prosecutor is not forced to offer an excessive discount, which he otherwise would be if he does not have the time or resources to take cases to trial where a trial will bring a higher likely sentence than plea bargaining will.

On a still broader level, this kind of analysis has implications for planning other aspects of the criminal- and civil-justice systems. The analysis emphasizes that people seek to maximize their respective satisfactions, and that in doing so they must often consider contingent events, such as the probability of rain (in a more general context) or the probability of conviction (in the criminal-justice context). Many aspects of the legal process involve diverse persons making decisions in light of contingent events like an arraignment judge deciding whether to release a defendant in light of the probability of his appearing in court, a personal-injury attorney deciding whether to accept a client in light of the probability of his establishing liability, or a would-be criminal deciding whether to commit a certain crime in light of the probability of his being caught. Although the subject matters are different, one can apply a similar decision-theory analysis in order to obtain insights into how those decisions would be affected by changes in the input variables that influence the decisional outcomes.[4]

THE IMPACT OF JURY SIZE ON THE PROBABILITY OF CONVICTION

Since *Williams v. Florida*[5] there has been considerable debate in the law review and social science literature concerning the impact of switching from a 12-person to a 6-person jury on the probability of an average defendant being convicted.[6] That debate may be quite relevant to the question of what is the optimum jury size since those who advocate 12-person juries often express a concern that 6-person juries will be substantially more likely to convict the average defendant and thus the innocent defendant as well, and those who advocate 6-person juries often express a concern that 12-person juries will be substantially less likely to convict the average defendant and thus the guilty defendant as well.

Empirical Comparisons

At first glance, one might think an appropriate way to determine the relation between jury size and conviction probability would be simply to compare the conviction rates in a state that uses 12-person juries with a state that uses 6-person juries. That approach is likely to be meaningless, however, because any differences we find in the conviction rates may be determined by differences in the characteristics of the law, the people, or the cases in the two states rather than differences in jury sizes.

As an alternative, one might suggest making before-and-after comparisons in a single state in order to control for those kinds of characteristics. If the conviction rate before was 64 percent with 12-person juries, the conviction rate after with 6-person juries might be substantially lower rather than higher, although most criminal attorneys would predict a higher conviction rate with 6-person juries. The conviction rate, however, might actually fall because of that prediction. This would be an example of a negatively fulfilling prophecy where the prediction ensures its failure. That is likely to occur by virtue of the fact that if defense attorneys predict a 6-person jury is more likely to convict, then they will be more likely to plea bargain their clients and to bring only their especially pro-defense cases before the new 6-person juries. Thus the nature of the new cases (not the change in the jury size), would cause the drop in the conviction rate, and there would be no accurate way to separate out those two potentially causal influences in such a before-and-after study.

As another alternative, one might suggest working with experimental juries, all of which would hear exactly the same case. Half of the juries would be 6-person juries, and half would be 12-person juries. Any differences between the two sets of juries could not be explained by saying they were hearing different cases or operating under different legal rules. People would also be randomly assigned to the two sets of juries so that the randomization process would tend to eliminate the explanation that people on the 12-person juries were different people than those on the 6-person juries. This experimental analysis, however, has the big defect that it in effect involves a sample of only one case. Whatever differences or nondifferences are found may be peculiar to that one case being very proprosecution, prodefense, prodivisive, or simply unrealistic, and the results may thus not be generalizable. What is needed is about 100 different trial cases on audio or video tape selected in such a way that 64 percent of them have resulted in unanimous convictions before 12-person juries and 36 percent in acquittals or hung juries. It would, however, probably be too expensive a research design to obtain and play 100 trials before a large set of 12-person juries and the same 100 trials before a large set of 6-person juries, especially if the experiment still lacks representative realism.

Deductive Comparisons

One remaining alternative is to try to determine the effects of different jury sizes by deducing conclusions from certain known facts and reasonable assumptions. One known fact is that the average 12-person jury convicts 64 percent of the time according to the University of Chicago jury research conducted by Harry Kalven and Hans Zeisel. Another known fact from that research is that the average juror votes to convict 68 percent of the time.[7] If jury voting were like flipping 12 independent coins, then we would expect the average juror to vote to convict 96 percent of the time. This is so since each coin would have to be unbalanced in the direction of coming up heads or conviction 96 percent of

DETERMINING THE IMPACT OF LEGAL POLICY CHANGES 99

the time in order to obtain 12 heads on 12 flips 64 percent of the time. In other words, only .96 (rather than any other number) multiplied by itself 12 times equals .64. On the other hand, jury voting may be like bowling, where all the pins tend to fall together if the evidence ball is well placed, or else none or less than all tend to fall if the evidence ball in effect goes in the gutter or away from the strike zone. If the bowling analogy applies, then we would expect each pin to have about a .64 propensity or 64 percent chance of falling over out of every 100 balls thrown at the pins.[8]

Since we know that the average juror has a .68 propensity to vote to convict, this in effect informs us that jury voting is much closer to the bowling analogy (.64 propensity) than the coin-flipping analogy (.96 propensity), but somewhere in between. We can determine where in between by simply thinking of the .58 as representing a weighted average between the bowling .64 and the coin-flipping .96. If the bowling .64 is a given a weight of 1.00, then the coin-flipping .96 must be given a weight of .13 for the .68 to be a weighted average in the formula .68 = [(1.00)(.64) + (.13)(.96)] / (1.00 + .13). This weight of .13 for the coin-flipping approach or model when the bowling approach has a weight of 1.00 will be useful in determining the probability of an average defendant being convicted with juries smaller than 12.

For example, with a jury of 6 persons, the bowling approach says the probability of a conviction is still .64 because either all the pins fall over 64 percent of the time, or less than all of the pins fall over the other 36 percent of the time. The coin-flipping approach, however, says that with a jury of 6 persons the probability of a conviction drops to .78, which is the same as the .96 propensity multiplied by itself 6 times rather than 12 times. Thus, if the bowling approach yields a probability of .64 and receives a weight of 1.00, and the coin-flipping approach yields a probability of .78 and receives a weight of .13, then the combined probability of a conviction with a 6-person jury would be .66, which is the same as [.64 + (.13)(.78)] / 1.13. This means that when moving from a 12-person to a 6-person jury, the probability of a conviction of the average defendant is likely to rise only 2 percentage points from 64 percent to 66 percent if all other relevant things are held constant besides jury size and the conviction probability.

The same simple but meaningful analysis can be applied to analyzing the effect of reducing the fraction required to convict from unanimity to 10/12 as was allowed in *Apodaca v. Oregon.*[9] The bowling approach says that with a 10/12 rule, the probability of a conviction is still .64 because the pins are collectively doing whatever happens to the average pin. If the average pin falls over, then all the pins fall over. If the average pin does not fall over, then all the pins do not fall over although they do not necessarily all stand up. The coin-flipping approach says that with a 10/12 rule, the probability of a conviction becomes .99 since the probability of exactly 12 out of 12 heads or conviction votes is .64 (with coins that individually have a .96 probability of coming up heads), and the probability of exactly 11 out of 12 heads is .29 with such a set of coins, and the probability of exactly 10 out of 12 heads is .06. Thus, the probability of at least 10 out of 12 heads or conviction votes is .99, which is the same as .64 + .29 + .06. Therefore, if the bowling approach yields a probability of .64 and receives a weight of 1.00, and the coin-flipping approach yields a probability of .99 and receives a weight of .13, then the combined probability of a conviction under a 10/12 rule would be .68, which is the same as [.64 + (.13)(.99)] / 1.13. This means that when moving from a 12/12 rule to a 10/12 rule, the probability of a conviction of the average defendant is likely to rise 4 percentage points from 64 percent to 68 percent if all other things are held constant, such as the type of cases and the nature of the jurors.

Significance of the Analysis

Adopting a 10/12 rule has more impact on increasing the probability of convicting an average defendant than adopting a 6/6 rule or a 6-person unanimous jury system. One might, however, say that neither change has much impact on conviction probabilities since they increase those probabilities by two and four percentage points respectively. On the other hand, one might say that an increase from .64 to .68 represents over a 6 percent increase since .04 divided by .64 equals .0625. A 6 percent increase in the conviction probability could mean a substantial and undesirable increase in the number of truly innocent defendants being convicted although we do not know how many innocent defendants go to a jury verdict out of the total number of jury verdicts. A 6 percent increase in the conviction probability could also mean a substantial and desirable decrease in the number of truly guilty defendants who are not convicted although we likewise do not know how many guilty defendants go to a jury verdict out of the total number of jury verdicts.

The same simple but meaningful analysis presented above can be applied to analyzing the effect of changing the jury size or the fraction required to convict on the number of errors likely to be made with regard to convicting the innocent or the number of errors likely to be made with regard to not convicting the guilty. Such an extension of the analysis requires that one be willing to make certain tentative assumptions about (1) the presence of innocent and guilty defendants in the jury decision-making process; (2) how much higher than .64 the probability is for convicting a truly guilty defendant; and (3) how much lower than .64 the probability is of convicting a truly innocent defendant. That extension could enable one to obtain insights with regard to arriving at an optimum jury size that will minimize the sum of both of the above-mentioned errors, where those errors are either weighted equally or with more weight to avoiding an error of convicting an innocent defendant.[10]

TABLE 5.1

The Impact of Jury Size on the Probability of Conviction

I. Basic symbols
   PAC = probability of an average defendant before an average jury being convicted—empirically equals .64 for a 12-person jury (shown to two decimal places).
   pac = probability of an average defendant receiving from an average juror a vote for conviction—empirically equals .677 for a juror (shown to three decimal places).
II. Implications of the coin-flipping analogy (independent probability model)
   PAC = (pac)^{NJ}
   .64 = (pac),^{12} which deductively means the coin-flipping pac is .964.
III. Implications of the bowling analogy (averaging model)
   PAC = pac
   .64 = pac, which deductively means the bowling pac is .640.
IV. Weighting and combining the two analogies
   Actual pac = [weight (coin-flipping pac) + (bowling pac)] / (weight + 1)
   .677 = [weight (.964) + (.640)] / (weight + 1), which deductively means the relative weight of the coin-flipping analogy to the bowling analogy is .13.
V. Applying the above to a six-person jury
   PAC = [weight (coin-flipping PAC) + (bowling PAC)] / (weight + 1)
   PAC = [.13 (.964)^6 + (.64)] / 1.13, which deductively means PAC with a 6-person jury is .66.
VI. Applying the above to a decision rule allowing two of twelve dissenters for a conviction
   PAC = [weight (coin-flipping PAC) + (bowling PAC)] / (weight + 1)
   PAC = [.13 (.99) + (.64)] / 1.13, which deductively means PAC with a 10/12 rule is .68.

Source: Compiled by the author.

One could also extend the coin flipping and bowling analogies to cover situations involving the determination of a third unknown probability from two or more prior probabilities. For example, if X_1 has a .70 probability of achieving Y in 10 attempts; X_2 has a .75 probability of achieving Y in 16 attempts; and Y was achieved at a .60 rate over the 50 sets of time periods or places used to arrive at the above .70 and .75; then what is the probability of achieving Y if we adopt both X_1 and X_2 policies (which are seldom if ever simultaneously adopted)? This is like saying black defendants received convictions in 7 out of

10 cases; indigent defendants received convictions in 12 out of 16 cases; and defendants in general received convictions in 30 out of 50 cases; then what is the probability of a black indigent defendant being convicted even though we have no data on black and indigent defendants combined. Deducing a combination probability from separate overlapping probabilities involves applying a fairly simple Bayesian probability formula.[11] With such a formula, one can deduce the probable effect of a combination of events that have not yet occurred together, or have done so too seldom for generalizing, or for which insufficient compiled data is available.

ADDITIONAL APPLICATIONS

Other Examples

Many other examples can be given of either the single-analogy deduction or the double-analogy deduction to determine the impact of a legal-policy change before the change occurs. The same kind of methodology can also be used to deduce a clearer understanding of decision making, as well as policy evaluation, in the legal process. The following syllogism is an example:

1. Among appellate-court judges (X_1), being a Democrat correlates positively with a tendency to vote in a liberal direction (the correlation is the Y effect).
2. Trial-court judges (X_2) differ from appellate-court judges (X_1) in the relevant direction of not having to write opinions justifying their decisions, and opinion writing decreases the ability of judges to inject their values into their decisions.
3. Therefore, trial-court judges (X_2) are even more likely to show a relation between being a Democrat and tending to vote in a liberal direction (Y) if all other things are held constant.

The first premise in this syllogism is based on inductive data from a large sample of judges.[12] The second premise is based on what seem to be obvious facts for which no data is needed. The conclusion is a deduction from the two premises. It represents another example of the single-analogy deduction in that trial-court judges are analogized to appellate-court judges the way plea bargaining was analogized to a pushcart sales transaction.

As a further simple example of the double-analogy deduction, one could use the following syllogism:

1. Interim-appointed judges (X_2) tend to be on the more conservative side of most types of cases (Y) when compared with elected judges (X_1) sitting on exactly the same cases on the same state supreme courts. (Interim-appointed judges are appointed to fill unexpired terms.)

2. Interim-appointed judges (X_2) are roughly in the middle with regard to their method of selection between elected judges (X_1) and purely appointed judges (X_3).
3. Therefore, purely appointed judges (X_3) are probably even more likely to be on the conservative side (Y) in a comparison with elected judges (X_1) if such a comparison could be made.

The first premise in this syllogism is based on inductive data from a large sample of judges controlling for party affiliation.[13] The second premise is a matter of definition. The conclusion is a deduction from the two premises. It represents a double-analogy deduction in that interim-appointed judges are analogized to elected judges and purely appointed judges the way jury decision making was analogized to flipping 12 coins and bowling with 12 pins.

Deduction is also important when one is attempting to test the validity of a causal model dealing with the relation between a policy and an effect. For example, if X policy has a +.40 relation with Z situation being present, Z has a +.30 relation with Y effect; then one would deduce that X would have a +.12 (or .40 times .30) relation with Y if X causes Z, which causes Y. If in spite of that deduction, X has -.25 relation with Y, then one should look for another causal model to explain the X to Y relation. Likewise if X and Y are suspected of being coeffects of Z, then one can logically deduce that the X to Y relation will go to zero when +X is compared with -X where all the units of analysis are +Z, or where all the units of analysis are -Z. If under those circumstances, the X to Y relation gets larger or remains the same rather than goes to zero, then that is a finding inconsistent with the syllogistic conclusion, thereby throwing doubt on the premise of a coeffects relation.

Deduction and Induction Combined

The plea-bargaining, jury decision-making, and judicial characteristics examples given above of deductive analysis are not designed to indicate that the deduction of conclusions from premises is in some sense more desirable than the induction of conclusions from many specific instances of persons, places, or things. On the contrary, any deductive model is improved by being based on inductive premises or on premises that are true by definition or that seem intuitively obvious. Thus, the jury model is dependent on the premise that 64 percent of the jury trials result in a conviction that is based on inducing from thousands of jury cases. Likewise, both of the above judicial characteristics syllogisms involve initial premises based on inducing or statistically inferring from a sample of judges. The plea-bargaining model is dependent on what seems to be a self-evident premise that the defendant wants to minimize his sentence and his costs of litigation and settlement, and that the prosecutor wants to maximize the sentence and minimize his costs of litigation and settlement. Likewise, both judicial characteristics syllogisms involve second premises based on self-evident or definitional notions.

It would also be desirable for all the conclusions to be empirically tested. Unfortunately, doing so may require a financially and morally expensive policy change that society might be unwilling to adopt simply to see if a deduced conclusion is empirically as well as logically valid. Also unfortunately, there may be no meaningful way to empirically test some deduced conclusions. For example, there seems to be no meaningful empirical way to test the effects of shifting from a 12-person jury to a 6-person jury as was discussed when dealing with empirical alternatives to the deductive jury model. Likewise, there is no way to get purely appointed judges and elected judges to sit on the same cases on the same courts. Nor is there any way to compare Democratic state trial-court judges with Republican trial-court judges hearing the same cases because they do not sit together en banc the way state supreme-court judges do, and their decisions are not readily available across the country.

Although it is unfortunate that not all deduced conclusions can be empirically tested, it is quite fortunate that social and political science is now reaching the stage of development where more conclusions can be deduced. As indicated, logically valid deduction involves deducing from empirically tested premises. As political science develops a greater body of tested knowledge, there simultaneously develops a greater body of premises for deducing relations that have not yet been empirically tested and that may be incapable of ever being fully empirically tested. The ability to deduce the Y effects from an X change is especially valuable where the X change is a governmental or legal policy, since the empirical approach may then be far too costly in monetary and other social costs. Deduction of policy effects from inductively derived premises and analogies holds substantial promise in future evaluation and impact research for both predicting and explaining results.

NOTES

1. On social science evaluation studies see Carol Weiss, *Policy Evaluation: Methods for Assessing Program Effectiveness* (Englewood Cliffs, N.J.: Prentice-Hall, 1972); and Stuart Nagel, ed., *Policy Studies and the Social Sciences* (Lexington, Mass.: D.C. Heath, 1975). On political science see Thomas Dye, ed., *The Measurement of Policy Impact* (Tallahassee: Florida State University, 1971); and Stuart Nagel, ed., *Policy Studies in America and Elsewhere* (Lexington, Mass.: D.C. Heath, 1975). On public law see Stephen Wasby, *The Impact of the United States Supreme Court Decisions* (New York: Oxford University Press, 1973).

2. Thomas Cook and Frank Scioli, eds., *Methodologies for Analyzing Public Policy* (Lexington, Mass.: D.C. Heath, 1975); Kenneth Dolbeare, ed., *Public Policy Evaluation* (Beverly Hills: Sage Publications, 1975); and James Caparaso and Leslie Roos, Jr., ed., *Quasi-Experimental Approaches: Testing Theory and Evaluating Policy* (Evanston, Ill.: Northwestern University Press, 1973).

3. For further detail concerning the plea-bargaining model that this article presents see Stuart Nagel and Marian Neef, "Plea Bargaining, Decision Theory, and Equilibrium Models," 51 *Indiana Law Journal* (Summer and Autumn 1976).

4. For further detail concerning the application of decision theory to the legal process see Gordon Tullock, *The Logic of the Law* (New York: Basic Books, 1971); Richard Posner, "An Economic Approach to Legal Procedure and Judicial Administration," *Journal of Legal Studies* 2 (1973): 399-458; William Landes, "An Economic Analysis of the Courts," *Journal of Law and Economics* 14 (1971): 61-197; American Bar Association Correctional Economics Center, *The Economics of Crime and Corrections: Bibliography* (Washington, D.C.: American Bar Association, 1974); Stuart Nagel and Marian Neef, *Operations Research Methods: Applied to Political Science and the Legal Process* (Beverly Hills: Sage Publications, 1976); and Stuart Nagel and Marian Neef, *Policy Optimizing Models and the Legal Process* (Lexington, Mass.: D.C. Heath, 1977).

5. In *Williams v. Florida*, 399 U.S. 78 (1970), the Supreme Court held that a jury of six persons satisfies the Sixth Amendment guarantee of trial by jury in criminal cases.

6. Richard Lempert, "Uncovering 'Nondiscernible' Differences: Empirical Research and the Jury-Size Cases," 13 *Michigan Law Review* 644 (1975); Hans Zeisel, ". . . And Then There Were None: The Diminution of the Federal Jury," 38 *University of Chicago Law Review* 710 (1971); Institute of Judicial Administration, *A Comparison of Six- and Twelve-Member Civil Juries in New Jersey Superior and County Courts* (New York: Institute of Judicial Administration, 1973); David Walbert, "The Effect of Jury Size on the Probability of Conviction: An Evaluation of *Williams v. Florida*," 22 *Case Western Law Review* 529 (1971); Alice Padawer-Singer and Allen Barton, "Interim Report: Experimental Study of Decision-Making in the 12- versus 6-Man Jury under Unanimous versus Nonunanimous Decisions" (New York: Columbia Bureau of Applied Social Research, 1975); and James Davis et al., "The Decision Processes of 6- and 12-Person Mock Juries Assigned Unanimous and 2/3 Majority Rules," 32 *Journal of Personality and Social Psychology* 1-14 (July, 1975).

7. The 64 percent conviction rate for 12-person juries is given in Harry Kalven and Hans Zeisel, *The American Jury* (Boston: Little, Brown, 1966), p. 56. The 68 percent proconviction voting rate for individual jurors is based on knowing—in an average sample of 100 cases—how many cases would involve unanimous convictions, unanimous acquittals, and hung juries. The breakdown of the votes for hung juries is given in Ibid., p. 460. According to the data, an average sample of 100 cases would involve 812 conviction votes out of 1,200 total votes for an average juror voting to convict 68 percent of the time.

8. For further detail on the deductive model presented here for determining the impact of jury size on conviction probability see Stuart Nagel and Marian Neef, "Using Deductive Modeling to Determine an Optimum Jury Size and Fraction Required to Convict," 1975 *Washington University Law Quarterly* no. 4.

9. *Apodaca v. Oregon*, 406 U.S. 404 (1972). On the same day in the case of *Johnson v. Louisiana*, 406 U.S. 356 (1972), the Court allowed the states to be able to convict by a decision of 9 out of 12 jurors.

10. For further detail on finding an optimum jury size, see the citation in note 8.

11. Frederick Mosteller, *Probability with Statistical Applications* (Reading: Addison-Wesley, 1961): 143-50; and Stuart Nagel, *The Legal Process from a Behavioral Perspective* (Homewood, Ill., 1969): 157-72. The answer to the probability deduction (given the hypothetical data) is .92, since .92 equals:

$$\frac{(30/50)\ (7/30)\ (12/30)}{(30/50)\ (7/30)\ (12/30) + (20/50)\ (3/20)\ (4/20)}$$

12. Stuart Nagel, "Political Party Affiliation and Judges' Decisions," *American Political Science Review* 55 (1961): 843-50.

13. Stuart Nagel, *Improving the Legal Process: Effects of Alternatives* (Lexington, Mass.: D.C. Heath, 1975), pp. 199-207.

CHAPTER

6

THE IMPLEMENTATION AND IMPACT OF
JUDICIAL POLICIES:
A HEURISTIC MODEL
Charles A. Johnson

Political scientists in recent years have extended their interest in political decision making and public policies to include the outcomes of and feedback resulting from those decisions and policies. The evaluation of public policy from this perspective has been variously termed impact analysis, evaluation research, and policy analysis. Regardless of the rubric under which the research is carried out, the critical question for the researchers is the same—"What happens after a public policy has been adopted?"

Judicial scholars have been in the forefront of the research examining the impact of public policies. During the past few decades, several monographs and readers, a text, and numerous articles have been written concerning the impact of judicial decisions.[1] There may be some question as to whether these research efforts have been cumulative, but there is no doubt that the reactions of several political actors to several judicial policies have been vigorously researched.

Though rich in empirical detail, it has been difficult to integrate the results of these studies to produce generalizations about impact phenomena. This problem, at least in part, is due to the lack of a general conceptual framework from which these studies might be viewed. Conceptual difficulties have been noted by several critics of impact analysis. A number of scholars have noted the confusion over and absence of any standard conceptualization of the term "impact" or "compliance" or "evasion." (Clark 1973; Wasby 1970). Other commentators have noted the bewildering array of political actors studied by judicial impact analysts and the problems of comparing these theoretical "apples and oranges."

I would like to thank Professor Bradley C. Canon of the University of Kentucky for his many helpful comments on an earlier draft of this chapter.

(Levine 1970). As Clark, Wasby, and other scholars have recognized, the development of theory in this area requires that impact phenomena be conceived more precisely and that actors engaged in implementing judicial decisions be functionally differentiated.

A HEURISTIC MODEL OF IMPACT PHENOMENA

This chapter proposes a conceptual model or framework of the impact phenomena that might be useful in organizing the research and theory in this area. It is not a theory of impact, rather it proposes a set of concepts that might provide the groundwork for further research and theory development. The model is presented diagramatically in Figure 6.1.

Two major conceptual components make up the model—populations and events within each population. The populations roughly correspond to the levels in impact discussed by Wasby (1970) and Levine (1970) except that a separate consumer population is identified. The events or behaviors within each population suggest that similar processes or events occur within the different populations, thus providing a basis for comparison. Considerations of the populations and events will follow in turn.*

The Interpreting Population.

For any appellate court decision, the political actor most often charged with the execution of the decision is a particular lower court—often a trial court. Beyond this immediate effect, in our common-law system many appellate-court decisions become policies to be used in deciding future cases. In a general sense, therefore, a superior court's policy affects all lower courts subject to its jurisdiction. This set of courts (and in some instances governmental officials such as attorneys general) might be termed the interpreting population. The interpreting population, as the name implies, responds to the policy decisions of a superior court by refining the policy announced by the superior court. Such refinements could have the effect of enlarging or limiting the original policy. This population, in other words, interprets the meaning of the policy and establishes the

---

*The populations identified in the model illustrated in Figure 6.1 are functionally identified. In the discussion of the model, except for the secondary population, populations will be referred to as being either superior or subordinate to each other. Attributing either position to a population will be based on a formal interpretation of the legal system as a hierarchical organization. The labels do not, however, imply the actual power of the populations or the relationships between the populations.

FIGURE 6.1

A Heuristic Model of the Implementation and Impact Process

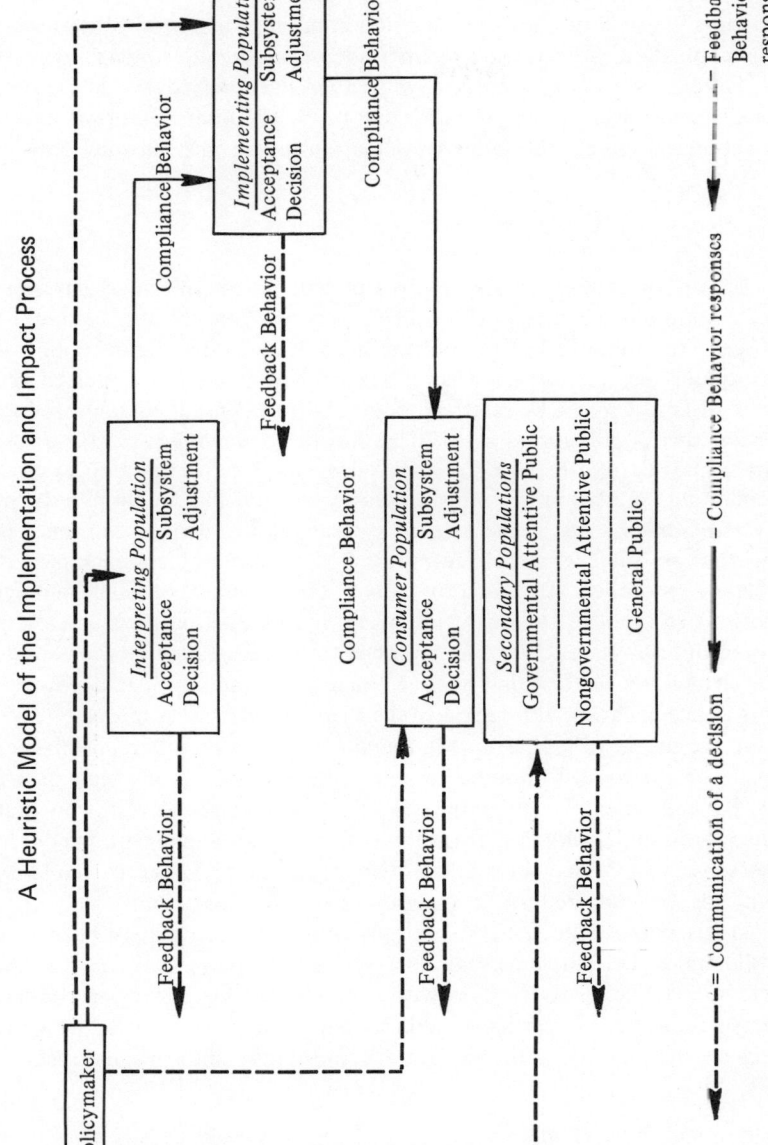

Source: Compiled by the author.

rules for questions not addressed in the original decision. As will be noted, all populations must "interpret" the decision in order to react to it. Interpretations of this population, however, are distinguished from the interpretations of others since theirs are viewed as authoritative in a legal sense by others in the political system. Hence, this population provides "official" interpretations of a court policy applicable to the subordinate populations under their jurisdiction.

The Implementing Population.

Lower courts theoretically apply a policy and the rules they develop only in cases coming before them. The policies resulting from the application of rules or official interpretations of the policies in addition to the original policy of the superior court may, however, affect a wider set of actors in the judicial system. This set of actors might be referred to as the implementing population. In most instances, this population is a set of authorities or members of the bar whose behavior may be reinforced or sanctioned by the interpreting population. The implementing population performs a policing or servicing function in the political system—that is, the application of system rules to various consumer populations that are subject to their authority. The most prominent examples of this population are police officials, prosecutors, public school officials, and certain administrative agencies. In many instances, the original policy and subsequent interpretations by lower courts are intended to set parameters on the behavior of the implementing population. A clear example of this involves decisions concerning police behavior with regard to the rights of criminal suspects.

A second set of participants in the implementing population is made up of members of the bar who do not possess political power in any legal or official sense. By and large, this subpopulation is composed of lawyers who practice before various judicial bodies. This subpopulation is an implementing population in the sense that it may insist that other participants follow or implement a certain rule promulgated by a superior court. The assertion of the rights of criminal suspects or the rights of citizens whose civil rights have been violated best illustrates the implementing role private attorneys play in the judicial process. Of course, as is the case with others in the implementing population, moves to implement a particular judicial policy may be rebuffed by an interpreting population whose decisions are authoritative and, in most cases, final.

The Consumer Population

Those for whom the policies are set forth by the court might be identified as the consumer population. This population is the set of individuals who would (or should) receive the benefits or disabilities of the political values allocated by the policy. In most instances this population will consist of individuals not affiliated with the government and whose rights are being protected from or limited by governmental action. Criminal suspects or students in newly desegregated schools, for example, are benefiting from judicial policies announced by the U.S. Supreme Court in *Miranda v. Arizona*, 384 U.S. 460 (1966), or *Brown v. Board of Education*, 347 U.S. 483 (1954). From another perspective, behavior may be limited and a consumer population may not benefit from a judicial policy. Not extending the right of jury trials to juveniles or requiring that corporations be split as a result of antitrust violations are illustrative of consumer populations benefiting in a negative sense from a judicial policy. From yet another perspective, members of a consumer population may either benefit or suffer limitations, depending on their attitudes toward the policy. School children who want to pray in public schools and those who do not are illustrative of this type of situation where some suffer limitations and others benefit.

The consumer population, depending on the policy involved, may include the entire population of the polity as with judicial decisions concerning general tax legislation. On the other hand, a very limited population may be involved, such as criminal suspects arrested by state authorities. Specification of this population may be troublesome for some judicial decisions, especially where the court is redistributing political values; reapportionment decisions are cases in point. In such cases, one could consider all individuals who benefit, positively or negatively, by the policy to be members of the consumer population. Establishing the parameters of this population may also pose problems if the policy affects a specific sector but supposedly is for the public good (for example, antitrust decisions).

The Secondary Population.

The populations dealt with thus far are those directly affected by the judicial policy or its implementation. Though not directly involved with the policy, certain other actors in the political system may respond to a judicial policy or its implementation. This response usually takes the form of some type of feedback behavior directed toward the original policymaker, one of the implementing populations, or the consumer population. This indirectly affected group might be termed the secondary population.

The secondary population may be divided into three subpopulations. First, there is a general population that includes those citizens who are not members of the consumer population. Second, there are the nongovernmental attentive publics that are generally more aware of a judicial policy and more concerned with, though not directly affected by, the policy. This subpopulation usually includes individuals related to the consumer population (for example, parents of bused school children), politically active individuals (political-party workers), and individuals associated with the media (newspaper editors). Finally, there are governmental attentive publics. This subpopulation includes governmental officials such as congressmen or executive officers who are not immediately affected by the decision. Though unaffected directly, some of the members of this latter subpopulation are occasionally in a position to officially support or sanction the original policymakers or those associated with the policy's implementation. This subpopulation is distinguished from other secondary subpopulations by the fact that they have direct, legitimate authority in the political system.

The basis of this classification of populations is primarily functional. We may, therefore, on different occasions find that particular individuals are members of different populations in different situations. For example, a state supreme-court justice may be a member of the interpreting population for U.S. Supreme Court decisions, but will be the original policymaker with regard to judicial policies within the state. When they are carrying out the orders of the judiciary, attorneys general may be members of the implementing population. On some occasions, however, they may be called upon to interpret a judicial decision and lay down guidelines for the state. In this instance they would be considered members of the interpreting population. This distinction is important when considering the influence of one population on another population or when comparing the relative impact of two different political actors in the impact process.

Implementing and Impact Behavior.

Several common concepts applicable to the impact process within each population are also identified in the model presented in Figure 6.1. These common concepts stress the similar processes or decision making occurring within different populations.

The first stage of the decision-making process for each population is the acceptance decision. As the name implies, at this initial stage, the original policy must be interpreted and accepted or rejected by the subordinate population. The concept basically concerns the psychological and attitudinal reactions of a population to a particular judicial decision.

Various issues may be involved in the acceptance decision. First, one must consider how the decision is interpreted by the population—that is, what the population's understanding of the decision is. Dolbeare and Hammond (1971), for example, concluded that understanding how a population interpreted a decision was critical to explaining the subsequent behavior of the population. Since a judicial decision rarely details the behavior required of a subordinate population and often does not anticipate the various circumstances in which the policy might be applied, interpretations of what is required by the court could be critical. It is, therefore, important for researchers to determine a population's understanding of a decision and what they believe is required of them by the decision before offering explanations of any other responses.

The attitudinal component of the acceptance decision may have several dimensions. While basically involving agreement-disagreement with a judicial policy, the intensity with which that attitude is held may also be important. Another dimension may be agreement-disagreement not with the policy, but with the fact that it was made by the judiciary. Some individuals may argue, for example, that while they agree with the substance of the U.S. Supreme Court's policy in *Roe v. Wade*, 410 U.S. 113 (1973), they do not believe national abortion policy should have been made by the judiciary.

Establishing the interpretation of a decision and a population's attitude toward it or toward the original policymaker may be difficult for the researcher since this involves essentially nonbehavioral reactions to the judicial policy. One of the responses that may be more readily apparent to the researcher is manifested in what is termed a subsystem adjustment. A subsystem adjustment within a population is a change in the normative and organizational structure of the population. The normative structure may involve formal norms and rules such as those of judicial procedure or those governing a school system. Informal norms are also included in this definition and may involve expectations within social or occupational groups, or patterns of behavior within a population (for example, a police department). Change in organizational structure might also be observed. Such changes could include the addition of new functions (for example, abortions for hospitals) or new sections to a department (such as public defender sections in local trial courts). The subsystem adjustments may influence the behavior of the adjusting population itself (for example, rules governing police behavior) or another population (for example, rules requiring legal assistance for indigent defendants).

The behavioral aspects of impact phenomena involve at least two components: compliance behavior and feedback behavior. Compliance behavior is that behavior directed toward the consumer populations in accordance with the policy or the interpretation and implementation of the policy. Compliance behavior specifically involves the compliance-noncompliance dimension of impact phenomena and, as such, is relevant to only the interpreting and implementing populations. The behavior may range from noncompliance where there is no change in behavior to full compliance where changes in behavior are made in accordance with the judicial policy.

Feedback behavior has been a familiar concept in political science for some time. Feedback behavior is conceived here as a behavioral response to a policy directed toward or received by a superior population. Feedback may also be directed toward or received by attentive publics in the secondary population. The purpose of feedback is usually to provide supports for or make demands upon other political decisionmakers in the political process concerning a particular judicial decision. For the framework outlined here, feedback means that populations may manifest some behavior (intentional or not) that influences others in the political process. Such behavior may be an important part of the impact of a judicial decision and hence must be considered in any impact analysis.

To summarize, each of the concepts described in this model tap one or more aspects of impact phenomena. Conceptions of impact phenomena in terms of these or similar concepts allow us to deal with the phenomena at an abstract level, thus enhancing the comparability of events and behavior across various sets of political actors. At the same time, the responses being examined and explained are more clearly identified. The merit of such distinctions is evidenced when two hypotheses about the relationship between perceived legitimacy of the court and the impact of the court's decisions are compared:

H_1: The greater the perceived legitimacy of the court, the greater the impact of the court's decisions.

H_2: For interpreting and implementing populations, the greater the perceived legitimacy of the court within the population, (a) the greater the likelihood the decisions will be positively accepted, (b) the more likely affected norms, rules, or policies will be changed to be consistent with the court's decision, (c) the greater the behavioral compliance with the decision, and (d) negative feedback to the court or others about the court decision will be less likely to come from the affected population.

Not only is the second hypothesis stated more clearly, it is more clearly testable. Importantly, the level of abstraction for the second hypothesis is roughly the same as the first general hypothesis. There is, in other words, a greater payoff in differentiating impact phenomena along the lines discussed here for both the specification of theory and the testing of hypotheses.

A REVIEW OF EXISTING RESEARCH

Ultimately, of course, the true test of a conceptual framework is whether it enables the researcher to move on to the tasks of theory development and empirical research. A conceptual framework may contribute to these tasks in at least two ways. First, such a framework may organize existing research to suggest where there are theoretical and empirical gaps in our knowledge. Such a review should also point to successful theory and research models used in past research. A second contribution to future efforts in this area may be to provide some fundamental concepts or reasonable theoretical boundaries for the development of theory and eventual research.

The following two sections build upon the model proposed here. Research on the various populations is reviewed and generalizations or questions are suggested. This review is followed by a discussion of the theory of impact analysis. In both of these sections the objective is to provide some direction and clarity to future research efforts.

The Interpreting Population.

Acceptance of superior-court decisions by subordinate courts involves lower court judges' agreement or disagreement with superior-court policies and their interpretations of those policies. Scholars have attempted to gauge acceptance decisions of this population by traditional methods of legal scholarship—studying the opinions of justices. Several political scientists have cited judicial opinions of lower-court judges (Vines 1964; Romans 1974; Canon 1975) and off-the-bench comments (Peltason 1961) to illustrate lower-court feelings about particular policies.

Direct and observable responses by lower courts to a superior-court policy are the subsystem adjustments made by these courts. Subsystem adjustments by courts involve changes in or the initiation of rules and norms regarding a particular policy. The subsystem adjustment may mean the reversal of rules where the previously used rule was declared unconstitutional (for example, the justiciability of reapportionment cases), the filling in of gaps left open by the superior court's decision (for example, are warrantless searches of automobiles legal in light of *Mapp v. Ohio*), or the development of rules that evade the thrust of a superior court's policy (such as school-desegregation decisions in the South during the 1950s). The study of subsystem adjustments is closely tied with the legal tradition of studying the judicial process. That is, the object of study is the policy as articulated in legal opinions. Inasmuch as these rules may be of consequence for cases in the future, for other lower-court decision making, and for the responses of other populations, the study of subsystem adjustments is important.

Policy decisions of the U.S. Supreme Court concerning school desegregation, reapportionment, and the rights of criminal suspects required or implied extensive changes in the rules governing judicial decision making. Systematic, quantitative studies of subsystem adjustments of lower courts in the desegregation and reapportionment cases have not been forthcoming. There have been, however, several traditional studies examining the changes of lower courts after the Supreme Court's desegregation order in *Brown v. Board of Education* (Blaustein and Ferguson 1957; Peltason 1961) and the reapportionment decisions of the Supreme Court (Dixon 1968).

Efforts to quantitatively examine subsystem adjustments by state supreme courts regarding criminal-justice policies may be found in Canon (1973) and Romans (1974). Canon examined state court actions concerning 16 legal questions presented by *Mapp v. Ohio*, while Romans studied liberal-conservative policies developed by state supreme courts prior to *Escobedo v. Illinois*, between *Escobedo* and *Miranda v. Arizona*, and after *Miranda*. Though more difficult to execute, studies of this latter type could lead to more systematic explanations of subsystem adjustments by testing hypotheses across several lower courts. Application of these methods to other issue areas would be useful.

Compliance behavior in the interpreting population involves the actual decisions and sanctions applied by lower courts with respect to the superior-court policy. Compliance may be of two types for this population—direct and indirect. Direct-compliance behavior involves the lower-court action after a case has been returned by an appellate court. Indirect-compliance behavior involves lower-court decisions applying the superior-court policies to other conflicts.

There have been a series of articles in law reviews presenting evidence concerning the extent of direct-compliance behavior for cases returned to lower courts by the U.S. Supreme Court. (*Harvard Law Review* 1942 and 1954; Beatty 1972). Unfortunately, all of these reports have dealt with only state court compliance. There is a clear need for research on direct-compliance behavior in lower federal courts.

Indirect compliance behavior has been studied at the lower federal-court level (Vines 1964; Peltason 1961) and at the state supreme-court level (Vines 1965; Beiser 1968). There have been few studies of compliance behavior by lower trial courts. Two notable exceptions concern compliance with *In Re Gault* (Lefstein et al. 1969; Canon and Kolson, 1971). Questionnaires or archival data in the form of lower-court files could be used to determine the extent of compliance behavior with various criminal-justice decisions of the U.S. Supreme Court. Such research would provide a broader empirical base for generalizations about compliance behavior by the interpreting population.

The study of feedback behavior by the interpreting population is virtually absent from the literature. The extent to which lower-court behavior is directed toward superior courts in an effort to persuade those courts to change policy is presently unknown. Subject courts could use direct legal channels through their decisions or the writing of opinions. Researchers could assume that such behavior constitutes feedback directed toward superior courts (see Canon 1975). While indirect channels of communication by lower courts might be more easily identified, there has been no research on feedback through such channels as law reviews or resolutions of legal meetings.

Occasionally nonjudicial populations are included in the interpreting population. This most often occurs when a legal officer such as an attorney general or district attorney issues an opinion interpreting a judicial policy. These interpretations usually have the force of law at least until challenged in court and are similar to subsystem adjustments discussed above. Krislov, one of the few scholars to study attorneys general as an interpreting population (1959), presents little evidence concerning the actual behavior of attorneys general. He does, however, present some theoretical arguments accounting for the general noncompliance and negative feedback behavior of Southern attorneys general concerning school desegregation.

The Implementing Population.

The implementing population has probably been the population most widely studied by the judicial-impact scholars. Court decisions in the areas of schoolhouse religion, criminal justice, and obscenity have provided readily identifiable sets of individuals who are charged with the implementation of policies that, in many instances, radically departed from policies prior to 1960. If we accept the proposition that different sets of individuals relevant to different policy areas are comparable, a few comments and rough generalizations might be advanced on the basis of this research.

Not surprisingly, acceptance of the Court's policies seems to be influenced by the implementing populations' attitudes toward the Supreme Court and toward the appropriateness of the Court policy in their situation. This observation is supported in the literature concerning public-school officials (Muir 1968; Johnson 1967; Reich 1970; Birkby 1966) and police officials (Skolnick 1966; Milner 1971). Some researchers have taken a step back in what appears to be a causal chain and have related acceptance decisions to the norms and values held in the organization and occasionally the community served by the population (Muir 1968; Johnson 1967; Dolbeare & Hammond 1971).

Organizational influences on acceptance decisions seem particularly pronounced in the instance of police officials and community norms in the instance of school officials. One might speculate that the reason for these varying influences is that in the case of the former relationship, technical policies about police procedure are involved and thus do not greatly concern community values or norms. In the instance of the latter relationship, symbolic policies are involved—religious practices. These symbolic policies are very much a part of the normative system of the community and, therefore, the influence of community norms on the impact of the policy is increased. This seems to suggest that acceptance decisions (and possibly compliance behavior) are related to organizational norms or community values are involved in the policy. If this is true, these variables constitute potentially powerful independent variables for predicting responses to court decisions.

Research on subsystem adjustments is not extensive for this population. Research has shown that most organizations or populations are officially or formally in compliance with the policy dictates of the Court (see, for example, Milner 1971; Way 1971; but see also Birkby 1966; Medalie et al. 1968). Those studies that examined policy changes found that in most instances policies changed in the direction of the court decision. Dolbeare and Hammond (1971), looking somewhat deeper into the question of policy changes, found that on many occasions policies were viewed as being in compliance with Court rulings when, in fact, this conclusion was based on a misreading of what the actual Court policy was. Their analysis suggests that the implementing populations make policy decisions on the basis of their interpretations of the court decisions. Perception and understanding of the decision could be critical variables in explaining variance in subsystem adjustments. The schoolhouse prayer studies also suggest that interpopulation communication of policy and subsystem adjustments is imprecise, if existent at all (Dolbeare and Hammond 1971; Birkby 1966). This could also result in an assertion of compliance with the Court decision when others in the organization were not adhering to the policy of either the Court or the organization.

A conclusion of virtually all studies of the implementing population was that compliance behavior was not generally consistent with the policy of the Court or even the subsystem adjustments to the Court decision. Again, attitudes toward the Supreme Court and toward the appropriateness of the Court policy in their particular situation seem to be important variables influencing compliance behavior. (Muir 1968; Johnson 1967; Reich 1970; Birkby 1966; Skolnick 1966; Milner 1971). Additionally, organization or community norms seem to play an important role in determining behavioral responses to court policies. A few researchers have suggested that the concept of a legal culture would be appropriate to summarize these norms and values. One dimension of this concept would probably be traditions and past behavior. (Canon 1975; Katz 1965; Reich 1970).

System-level variables may also play an important part in explaining compliance behavior. The system-level variable most consistently related to responses to court policy is region, particularly for religious decisions. (Canon 1974; Dolbeare and Hammond 1971). Regional influences may be a manifestation of cultural variations.

Very little has been done regarding feedback from the implementing population to other populations or decision makers in the political system. Feedback within a population seems minimal, either by design or organization of the population. Some have suggested that where there is little enthusiasm for the policy or subsystem adjustment, then enforcement of the policy within the population is minimal and feedback is either not attempted or not received when attempted (Dolbeare and Hammond 1971).

The relationship of the implementing population to other populations is an area where very little is known. Responses to interpreting populations, that is, lower courts, have not been studied in any systematic way. The rules made by the interpreting populations are applicable to the implementing population in a more direct organizational sense, yet we know little about this relationship. The few occasions where state courts are mentioned (for example, Milner 1971) give the impression that their policymaking or interpretations have very little impact on the implementing population.

Most of these remarks have been based on studies of only two implementing populations—police officers and school officials. It is granted that these two populations constitute major implementing populations in the political system. Nevertheless, other populations are potentially available for study, such as various officials in the criminal-justice system other than the police (for example, prosecutors, prison officials, and probation and parole officers) or state and federal administrative agencies. Additionally, there is virtually no research on the implementation of state or local judicial policies. Expanding research to different populations, different policies and different courts could lead to a better understanding of impact phenomena involving the implementing population.

The Consumer Population.

The consumer population is the set of individuals for whom the policy is developed by the initial policymakers. They gain or lose the government's services, benefits or protection as a result of the judicial decision. Political scientists, in analyzing the impact of judicial policies, have not generally considered this population. They have not considered, for example, important questions such as whether criminal behavior has changed because of the Supreme Court's criminal-justice decisions or whether desegregation rulings of the Court have affected the behavior of whites and blacks in desegregated and segregated settings.[2] Perhaps one reason for an avoidance of this research area has been that there is nothing here that is overtly "political." This population basically includes non-governmentally, non-politically involved individuals whose behavior might best be accounted for by sociologists or psychologists. Certainly, however, the analysis of the impact of public policy is not complete unless the set of individuals for whom the policy was originally made is examined to determine whether the policy affected their behavior and well-being. In contrast to the "normal" political science paradigm of how do various actors influence governmental decision making, in this instance the reverse would be asked—how does governmental decision making influence constituents?

The question of how the government affects its constituents involves at least two dimensions. First, assuming the consumer population is offered the governmental service, does the population avail itself of the service? For example, do criminal suspects use lawyers provided in the station house and do they remain silent after they receive the *Miranda* warnings? What are the factors that enter into these decisions? Of course, in certain situations, the consumer population may have no choice but to accept the consequences of a policy. Halting religious activities in a classroom may be an example—the children have no alternative to accepting the stopping of prayers led by the teacher.

A second dimension of the effect of governmental policies on consumer populations concerns what happens if the services are accepted or rejected. What happens, for example, if a suspect accepts an attorney in the station house or remains silent? Is his treatment in the judicial process any different from a suspect who did not accept the offer of an attorney or remain silent? This may be the ultimate question for policy analysis—what influence did the government program have on those for whom the policy was originated?

A few largely descriptive research efforts about this population can be found concerning the impact of desegregation on school children (Mayer et al. 1974) and the impact of criminal-justice decisions on criminal defendants (Casper 1971; Stover and Eckart 1973; Medalie et al. 1968). Each of the former studies present evidence of differing impacts within the relevant populations. Mayer et al., for example, presents evidence that school integration variously affects white and black students in terms of educational and social variables. Work such as that of Casper explores the use of the *Miranda* rights by suspects. The use of these rights and the reasons given by suspects or prisoners for their use or nonuse are reviewed, but specific hypotheses are not tested. From a slightly different perspective, the impact of reapportionment decisions on eventual policy outputs of the changed legislatures have also been examined (Hanson and Crew 1973).

Clearly, much research concerning the consumer population needs to be done. A variety of research methods could be used, a number of populations could be readily identified, and in many instances the initial data may be available in the form of trial outcomes, standardized tests of school children, or legislative enactments. Recent U.S. Supreme Court and state supreme-court decisions have provided different sets of consumer populations that might be examined.[3] Electoral and survey data could also be used to evaluate responses to certain decisions involving the general population as the consumer population, as is the case with the reapportionment decisions. At this point, even descriptive and speculative studies would be of considerable assistance in developing an understanding of the impact of judicial decisions on consumer populations.

The Secondary Population.

Political scientists have also been interested in the impact of judicial decisions on actors in the political system who are not immediately affected by the policy or its implementation. We have termed this set of actors the secondary population. This is a varied and diverse population whose composition varies with the policy being considered. Differentiation of this population along some very general dimensions may assist in our understanding of impact phenomena. Three subpopulations might be identified: the general public, a governmentally attentive public, and a non-governmentally attentive public.

There have been a series of studies of general public opinion regarding the Supreme Court and its activities. For the most part, the studies have concerned the public's attitude about the Court as a policymaker in our political system, not with any specific decision (Kessel 1966; Dolbeare 1967a, 1971; Murphy and Tanenhaus 1969). Additionally, the studies have avoided any mention of behavior by the respondents and only a few have dealt with the potentiality of behavioral responses to Court action (Kessel 1966; Dolbeare 1967a).

The studies of public opinion and the Supreme Court may be useful in the analysis of the impact process when one of two conditions is met: (1) when the analysis also includes analysis of the respondents' attitudes toward the Court or (2) when the analysis of public opinion allows us to infer factors that are important in the acceptance decisions of other populations of subpopulations. Unfortunately, few of the public-opinion studies meet either of these two conditions. The studies that do not meet either of these two criteria may, however, have relevance for other political scientists interested in the support of government institutions or public opinion generally.

The existence and identification of the members of an attentive public is difficult (see Devine 1970). They are usually defined as a set of individuals who are knowledgeable about and active in the political affairs of a relevant political system. Impact scholars have identified various sets of individuals in particular situations who appear to meet the general definition of an attentive public. In many instances, the researchers have referred to these individuals as community elites (Mayer 1974; Johnson 1967; Dolbeare and Hammond 1971). These studies argue that such elites are important in directing the community response to a court decision. More systematic evidence comparing different communities is needed before this proposition can be accepted. Another set of prominent studies of non-governmentally attentive publics consider media responses to judicial decision making (Johnson 1967 ; Nagel 1969). Existing research, however, has not demonstrated any influence of the media on the general public, elites, or any other population. Research is needed on not only responses to court decisions but also on the effects of such responses. Finally, there may be attentive publics for particular issues or court policies (for example, parents for busing decisions or Catholics for abortion decisions). These situationally attentive publics have not been examined by impact scholars.

The general public and attentive publics do not possess political authority to make binding political decisions except in elections. Governmentally attentive publics, however, do possess such authority. They can exercise this authority to frustrate judicial policies or to override such policies by statute or constitutional amendments, thus influencing the impact of judicial policies on any of the other populations.

The institution that is the most systematically studied in relation to the Supreme Court is the Congress. Specific reactions the Congress could make in response to a Court decision are presented in Murphy (1962). Few studies have been as specific as Murphy in analyzing congressional reactions to Court decisions; generally they consider only court-curbing actions or some type of negative reactions to the Court (Nagel 1969; Schmidhauser et al., 1971; Stumpf 1965). Comparison of these studies is tenuous because each employs a slightly different definition of what constitutes court-curbing activities, which in turn places parameters on the data they collect.

The studies of Stumpf and Schmidhauser examine congressional reactions to Court policies only in recent times. From our perspective they are interested less in congressional feedback than in congressional behavior or decision making regarding judicial policies. Nagel (1969), on the other hand, takes a historical view of Court-Congress relations and specifically considers congressional feedback to the Court and its effect on the Court's policymaking.

Research on the secondary populations involved in the impact process deal with diverse subpopulations. According to the model developed here, an important attribute of this population is the feedback behavior it directs toward other decision makers in the political system or populations in the impact process. Few of the research efforts contribute to our knowledge of this phenomenon. Even fewer of the analyses describe or explain reactions to feedback coming from this population. Greater attention could also be paid to other actors in the population such as chief executives or administrative agencies not immediately affected by a court decision.

The Impact of Lower-Court Policymaking.

The model that has been offered here has assumed that judicial policies will be made by appellate courts, primarily the U.S. Supreme Court. There are instances, however, when lower courts (those usually in the interpreting population) make original policies that are not appealed and have an impact on the political system within their jurisdiction. The impact of local courts has not been widely studied, however. Three studies are particularly relevant here (Dolbeare 1967b, 1969; Jacob 1969). These studies deal with only urban courts and each considers the urban court to be a part of the local political system involved in the allocation of political values. Opportunities for research in this area are virtually endless and with slight modification this model should be helpful in such research.

THEORY AND IMPACT PHENOMENA

Thus far a heuristic model for impact phenomena has been presented along with a review of some of the literature within the framework implied by that model. The model has been useful in organizing the research findings of impact scholars and in pointing to various areas where further research is needed. To this point, however, little has been said about theory and the impact of judicial decisions.

It should be clear, though it is worth restating, that the model discussed here is not a theory of impact. It is a heuristic model in the sense that it organizes both the phenomena with which we are concerned and the existing research about that phenomena. By so organizing the phenomena and existing research, we have introduced a few fundamental concepts that generally and abstractly describe actors, events, and behavior involved in the implementation and impact of judicial decisions. These concepts could contribute to the development of theory in this area of research by providing a more general basis for comparisons of data and by defining dependent variables that must be explained.

There are several theories of impact. By and large, most theories have not differentiated the concept of impact nor have they identified populations to which the theories apply. Nevertheless, many of those theories are not inconsistent with the model presented here. Those explanations of impact based on cognitive-dissonance theory seem to be directed toward what we have termed acceptance decisions (Muir 1968; Johnson 1967). Other scholars who have suggested economic decision-making explanations of impact seem to be concentrating on compliance behavior or possibly subsystem adjustments in the interpreting and implementing populations (Brown and Stover 1974; Rogers and Bullock 1972; Krislov 1965). From yet another perspective, a few scholars have suggested explanations based on various organizational theories where compliance behavior and possibly feedback behavior might be explained (Baum 1973; Wasby 1973).

There has not been sufficient research-testing hypotheses to determine the relative explanatory values of these and other theories of impact. Such evaluations might be more conclusive if comparable concepts and variables are used. For example, the relative explanatory power of organization theory as compared with utility theory might be more easily determined if tests were defined in terms of compliance behavior or subsystem adjustments in either the interpreting or implementing populations. By being specific, by setting parameters on empirical research, and by dealing with comparable theoretical concepts, reasonable explanations for impact phenomena should result and spurious explanations can be identified.

It is appropriate that this chapter end with some observations on the development of theories in this field. If we are to understand the impact of judicial decisions, it will not suffice to have a series of descriptions of the consequences of several different court decisions, no matter how complete or comprehensive. To assure a greater generalizability of research findings some theoretical groundwork must be provided by impact scholars.

In addition to the development of concise and meaningful theories of impact, there must be a greater effort to test the hypotheses derived from the theories. Attempts to refute or support a theory with empirical data represent the best means of evaluating that theory. In the impact research to date, there have been a number of studies that are wholly descriptive or that test only random hypotheses. Such research serves to inform future efforts in theory development, but it does not constitute a test of "theory." A few other research projects have been accompanied by post hoc explanations of the impact of a particular court decision. These also contribute to theory development, but should not be interpreted as theory testing.

Future researchers in the impact area should make some efforts toward the development of theories from which hypotheses might be derived and tested empirically. Differentiating impact phenomena would enhance such efforts by specifying both the actors and behavior covered by the theory. A basis for such differentiations has been suggested here.

NOTES

1. For a discussion of earlier works in impact analysis see Wasby (1970), Krislov et al. (1971), and Becker and Feeley (1973).
2. There have, however, been several reports of the effects of desegregation on the educational progress of school children that may have some application in this area. See, for example, Coleman (1966).
3. Such cases may include welfare-rights cases such as *Wyman v. James*, 400 U.S. 309 (1971); or *Shapiro v. Thompson*, 394 U.S. 618 (1969); or the abortion decision, *Roe v. Wade*, 410 U.S. 113 (1973).

REFERENCES

Baum, Lawrence. 1973. "An Organizational Theory of Judicial Impact." A paper delivered at the annual meeting of the Midwest Political Science Association, Chicago, 1973.
Beatty, J. K. 1972. "State Court Evasion of United States Supreme Court Mandates During the Last Decade of the Warren Court." 2 *Valparaiso University Law Review* 260.
Beiser, Theodore L. 1968. "A Comparative Analysis of State and Federal Judicial Behavior: The Reapportionment Cases." 62 *American Political Science Review* 788.
Birkby, Robert H. 1966. "The Supreme Court and the Bible Belt: Tennessee Reaction to the 'Schempp' Decision." 10 *Midwest Journal of Political Science* 304.
Blaustein, Albert P., and Clarence C. Ferguson, Jr. 1957. *Desegregation and The Law*. New Brunswick, N.J.: Rutgers University Press.
Brown, Don W., and Robert V. Stover. 1974. "An Economic Approach to Compliance with Court Decisions." A paper delivered at the annual meeting of the American Political Science Association, Chicago, 1974.
Canon, Bradley C. 1975. "Organizational Contumacy in the Transmission of Judicial Policies: The *Mapp, Escobedo, Miranda* and *Gault* Cases." 20 *Villanova Law Review* 50.

―――. 1974. "Taking Advantage of a Quasi-Experimental Situation: The Impact of *Mapp v. Ohio.*" A paper delivered at the annual meeting of the American Political Science Association, Chicago, 1974.

―――. 1973. "Reactions of State Supreme Courts to a U.S. Supreme Court Civil Liberties Decision." 8 *Law and Society Review* 109.

Canon, Bradley C., and Kenneth Kolson. 1971. "Rural Compliance with *Gault*: Kentucky, A Case Study." 10 *Journal of Family Law* 300.

Casper, Jonathan D. 1971. "Did You Have a Lawyer When You Went to Court? No, I Had a Public Defender." In *Criminal Justice: Law and Politics*, ed. George F. Cole, pp. 236-47. Belmont, Calif.: Duxbury Press, 1971.

Clark, R. H. 1973. "The Impact Study: A Friendly Evaluation of the State of the Art." A paper delivered before the annual meeting of the Midwest Political Science Association, Chicago, 1973.

Coleman, James. 1966. *Equality of Educational Opportunity*. Washington, D.C.: Government Printing Office.

Devine, Donald. 1970. *The Attentive Public*. Chicago: Rand McNally.

Dixon, Robert G. 1968. *Democratic Representation: Reapportionment in Law and Politics*. New York: Oxford University Press.

Dolbeare, Kenneth M. 1969. "The Federal District Courts and Urban Public Policy: An Exploratory Study (1960-1967)." In *Frontiers of Judicial Research*, eds. J. Grossman and J. Tanenhaus, pp. 373-404. New York: John Wiley, 1969.

―――. 1967a. "The Public Views the Supreme Court." In *Law, Politics, and the Federal Courts*, ed. Herbert Jacob, pp. 194-212. Boston: Little, Brown, 1967.

―――. 1967b. *Trial Courts in Urban Politics*. New York: John Wiley and Sons.

Dolbeare, Kenneth M., and Phillip E. Hammond. 1971. *The School Prayer Decisions: From Court Policy to Local Practice*. Chicago: The University of Chicago Press.

Hanson, Rodger A., and Robert E. Crew. 1973. "The Policy Impact of Reapportionment." 8 *Law and Society Review* 69.

Harvard Law Review. 1954. "Evasion of Supreme Court Mandates in Cases Remanded to State Courts since 1941." 67 *Harvard Law Review* 1251.

―――. 1942. "Final Disposition of State Court Decisions Reversed and Remanded by the Supreme Court, October Term 1931, to October Term, 1941." 55 *Harvard Law Review* 1347.

Jacob, Herbert. 1969. *Debtors in Court: The Consumption of Government Services*. Chicago: Rand McNally.

Johnson, Richard. 1967. *The Dynamics of Compliance*. Evanston: Northwestern University Press.

Katz, Ellis. 1965. "Patterns of Compliance With the *Schempp* Decision." 14 *Journal of Public Law* 396.

Kessel, John H. 1966. "Public Perceptions of the Supreme Court." 10 *Midwest Journal of Political Science* 75.

Krislov, Samuel. 1965. *The Supreme Court in the Political Process*. New York: Macmillan.

―――. 1959. "Constituency v. Constitutionalism: The Desegregation Issue and Tensions and Aspirations of Southern Attorneys General." 3 *Midwest Journal of Political Science* 75.

Krislov, Samuel; Keith O. Boyum; Jerry N. Clark; Roger C. Shaefer; and Susan O. White, eds. 1971. *Compliance and the Law*. Beverly Hills: Sage Publications.

Lefstein, Norman; Vaughan Stapleton; and Lee Teitelbaum. 1969. "In Search of Juvenile Justice: *Gault* and Its Implementation." 3 *Law and Society Review* 491.

Levine, James P. 1970. "Methodological Concerns in Studying Supreme Court Efficacy." 4 *Law and Society Review* 583.

Mayer, Robert R.; Charles E. King; Anne Borders-Patterson; James S. McCullough. 1974. *The Impact of School Desegregation in a Southern City: A Case Study in the Analysis of Educational Policy.* Lexington, Mass.: D.C. Heath.

Medalie, Richard J.; Leonard Zeitz; and Paul Alexander. 1968. "Custodial Police Interrogation in Our Nation's Capital: The Attempt to Implement Miranda." 66 *Michigan Law Review* 1347.

Milner, Neal. 1971. *The Court and Local Law Enforcement: The Political Impact of Miranda.* Beverly Hills: Sage Publications.

Muir, William K., Jr. 1967. *Prayer in the Public Schools: Law and Attitude Change.* Chicago: University of Chicago Press.

Murphy, Walter. 1962. *Congress and the Court.* Chicago: University of Chicago Press.

Murphy, Walter, and Joseph Tanenhaus. 1969. "Public Opinion and the United States Supreme Court: Mapping of Some Prerequisites for Court Legitimation of Regime Changes." In *Frontiers of Judicial Research*, eds. J. Grossman and Tanenhaus, pp. 273-303. New York: John Wiley and Sons, 1969.

Nagel, Stuart S. 1969. *The Legal Process From a Behavioral Perspective.* Homewood, Ill.: Dorsey Press.

Peltason, Jack L. 1961. *Fifty-eight Lonely Men: Federal Judges and School Desegregation.* New York: Harcourt, Brace and World.

Reich, Donald R. 1970. "Schoolhouse Religion and the Supreme Court: A Report on Attitudes of Teachers and Principals and on School Practices in Wisconsin and Ohio." 23 *Journal of Legal Education* 123.

Rodgers, Harrell R., and Charles S. Bullock, III. 1972. *Law and Social Change: Civil Rights Laws and Their Consequences.* New York: McGraw-Hill.

Romans, Neil. 1974. "The Role of State Supreme Courts in Judicial Policy Making: *Escobedo, Miranda* and the Use of Judicial Impact Analysis." 27 *Western Political Quarterly* 38.

Schmidhauser, John R.; Larry L. Berg; and Albert Melone. 1971. "The Impact of Judicial Decisions: New Dimensions in Supreme Court-Congressional Relations," *Washington University Law Quarterly* 209.

Skolnick, Jerome H. 1966. *Justice Without Trial.* New York: John Wiley and Sons.

Stover, Robert V., and Dennis R. Eckart. 1973. "The Indigent's Right to Counsel: How Much Does It Help?" A paper delivered at the annual meeting of the Midwest Political Science Association, Chicago, 1973.

Stumpf, Harry P. 1965. "Congressional Response to Supreme Court Rulings: The Interaction of Law and Politics." 14 *Journal of Politics* 337.

Vines, Kenneth W. 1965. "Southern State Supreme Courts and Race Relations." 18 *Western Political Quarterly* 5.

_____. 1964. "Federal District Judges and Race Relations in the South." 26 *Journal of Politics* 337.

Wasby, Stephen L. 1973. "The Communication of the Supreme Court's Criminal Procedure Decisions: A Preliminary Mapping." 18 *Villanova Law Review* 1086.

_____. 1970. *The Impact of the United States Supreme Court: Some Perspectives.* Homewood, Ill.: Dorsey Press.

Way, Frank, Jr. 1968. "Survey Research on Judicial Decisions: The Prayer and Bible Reading Cases." 21 *Western Political Quarterly* 189.

CHAPTER 7

JUDICIAL IMPACT AS A FORM OF POLICY IMPLEMENTATION
Lawrence Baum

JUDICIAL IMPACT AND THE IMPLEMENTATION MODEL

The impact of court decisions constitutes a relatively recent concern in the field of public law, but by now it has become a central interest for students of the judicial process. Over the last two decades social scientists and legal scholars interested in the effects of judicial decisions have produced an extensive and valuable literature on this subject.[1]

The body of literature on judicial impact varies widely in its concerns. Indeed, the general label "judicial impact" may be unfortunate, for it places under a single heading political phenomena as diverse as judicial treatment of cases remanded from higher courts and public perceptions of Supreme Court decisions.[2] Analytically, it is more useful to examine particular types of impact than to discuss decisional impact as a general phenomenon. The type of impact that has received the greatest attention from scholars is the response of lower courts and administrative agencies to Supreme Court decisions.[3] It is this process and the literature concerned with it that this chapter will examine.*

---

*In the remainder of this paper, the terms "judicial impact" and "impact" will refer to this specific type of impact.

The author would like to thank John Gardiner, Jerry Goldman, William Jenkins, and Stephen Wasby for their helpful comments on an earlier draft of this chapter.

Judicial and administrative response to Supreme Court decisions might be conceptualized in a variety of ways. Explicitly or implicitly, most scholars who study this process have conceived of it as a species of legal compliance. Supreme Court rulings on legal questions are seen as forms of law that impinge on the policy making activities of subordinate officials, law that these officials may obey or disobey. The empirical questions probed by scholars generally are framed in terms of whether policy makers "comply with" a newly issued Supreme Court ukase by changing practices that conflict with it.[4]

Some scholars may have adopted a compliance perspective as a matter of convenience, without considering its implications. However, others have used this perspective deliberately as a means to link judicial impact with related political and social processes and with the products of research on these processes. Samuel Krislov and his colleagues employed compliance as a concept to encompass judicial impact and other phenomena such as the learning of social norms and the deterrent effect of legal sanctions.[5] Robert Stover and Don Brown have developed a theoretical approach to the analysis of compliance with law that they apply to court decisions as well as other forms of "law."[6]

The insights achieved by scholars like Stover and Brown indicate the utility of what might be called the "compliance model" of judicial impact. Like any other model, however, it imposes a limited and distorted view of reality on those who employ it. In this respect, the compliance model has three significant weaknesses.

The first lies in its conception of court decisions as a kind of binding law. Except where direct court orders are issued to policymakers, this conception is misleading. The duty of judges and administrators to follow rules of law laid down by the Supreme Court in cases in which they did not participate is an ambiguous one,[7] and one should not equate this duty with citizens' obligations to refrain from behavior proscribed by criminal statutes.[8] Certainly this equation increases the danger that the complexity of response to court decisions will be oversimplified into an obedience-disobedience dichotomy.

Second, the compliance model tends to exclude from consideration one very important kind of judicial influence. Much of an appellate court's policy leadership is exercised through the establishment of decisional trends that signal its inclination without creating explicit rules of law. A federal court of appeals, for instance, may invalidate a series of patents and thereby signal a "hard line" on patent validity to the district judges in its circuit.[9] Clearly the concept of compliance bears little relationship to this kind of leadership; this is one reason that students of judicial impact have devoted little attention to the influence of decisional trends on lower-court judges and legally oriented administrators. This lack of interest in an important kind of appellate influence is unfortunate.

Finally, it is difficult to examine with the compliance model certain response to court decisions that is not easily defined as "compliant" or "noncompliant." Behavior designed to evade a ruling, but not clearly inconsistent with it, becomes the source of definitional problems.[10] Similarly, a policymaker's willingness to go beyond the requirements of a ruling to facilitate its success through supportive action[11] is difficult to analyze in terms of compliance.

These weaknesses hardly render the compliance model useless. Because they exist, however, there is a need for alternative models with which to analyze judicial impact. Of the alternatives that might be offered, perhaps the most promising is a model based on a conception of response to court decisions as a form of policy implementation.[12]

The implementation model differs from the compliance model in a fundamental way. From an implementation perspective, judges and administrators are seen as policymakers whose responsibilities may include the implementation of particular court decisions.* The task of implementation is not a legal obligation but an action requested by a policymaking agency that stands higher in the legal structure. The central question for analysis then is not whether officials "obey" a decision but simply how they respond to it.

A conception of judicial impact as implementation has its own limitations.† However, the broad perspective associated with this conception seems to fit the complexity of response to court decisions more easily than does the narrower compliance model, and it does not share the major weaknesses of that model. Moreover, use of the implementation model stresses the linkage between response to court decisions and other forms of policy implementation, and it suggests the mutual relevance of the literature on judicial impact and the body of literature on implementation as a general process. Certainly this model merits consideration as a perspective from which to analyze judicial impact.

An implementation conception has been implicit in some scholarly work on Supreme Court impact. For instance, Martin Shapiro's studies of the Court's relationships with administrative agencies have the flavor of an implementation perspective.[13] However, the implementation model has received little explicit use as a means to analyze response to court decisions and to relate judicial impact to other forms of implementation.

In an earlier paper, I employed the implementation model as a basis for one theoretical analysis of judicial impact.[14] In this chapter, I wish to examine

---

*The implementation perspective discussed here is based upon conceptions of implementation contained in the public-policy literature, to be discussed in the next section of this article.

†The compliance model may be criticized for oversimplifying the process of response to court decisions, but its simplicity facilitates analysis in some respects. The relative complexity of an implementation conception creates some roadblocks to systematic analysis of impact as a dependent variable.

the literature on judicial impact as a literature about policy implementation and to assess its contribution to the understanding of implementation. This examination will begin with a brief discussion of the literature on implementation in the field of policy analysis. Then, the existing literature on judicial impact will be evaluated in terms of its contribution to policy analysis. Finally, I will offer some suggestions concerning future directions that students of judicial impact might take to increase that contribution and to improve our understanding of judicial impact as a specific form of implementation.

THE STUDY OF POLICY IMPLEMENTATION

Like other broad concepts in political science, the concept of policy implementation does not admit to an easy or universally satisfactory definition. For our purposes, implementation may be defined as the relevant actions and inactions of public officials who have responsibility to achieve objectives contained in previously enacted policies.[15] Thus, implementation includes such processes as the administration of Medicare by the Department of Health, Education and Welfare; the spending of federal education grants by local school districts; and the application by trial judges of appellate rulings on the rights of criminal defendants. Defined in this way, the concept of implementation encompasses rather well the kinds of behavior that have been studied by scholars interested in judicial and administrative response to Supreme Court decisions.

Policy implementation as such has become a subject of explicit scholarly interest only recently. However, there exists a long tradition of research implicitly concerned with implementation processes. This research includes the classic case studies by Philip Selznick on the Tennessee Valley Authority and those of Herbert Kaufman on the Forest Service,[16] as well as studies of bureaucratic behavior, such as Marver Bernstein's book on the independent regulatory agencies.[17]

Explicit interest in the process of policy implementation has grown out of the developing field of public-policy analysis.[18] Spurred in part by problems of implementation in recent federal programs, students of public policy have given increased attention to the implementation process. A new wave of empirical studies has been undertaken, primarily on federal social programs. Among these studies are Derthick's books on the "new towns" and public-assistance programs, several works on federal aid to education, and the Pressman-Wildavsky study of the Economic Development Administration.[19] Scholars are also beginning to discuss implementation in general terms; the most notable contributions to this discussion thus far are the papers by Van Meter and Van Horn.[20]

The literature on policy implementation has contributed to the understanding of public policymaking in several respects. It has underlined the role of implementation in the policymaking process and shown the need to consider the implementation process in the design and evaluation of policy innovations. The literature also has increased our understanding of aspects of implementation such as intergovernmental relations in state implementation of federal programs.

Perhaps the most important contribution of this literature for students of judicial impact is the evidence it provides concerning difficulties in the implementation of legislative policies and the sources of these difficulties. Students of the judicial process frequently seem to assume that problems of ineffective implementation are unique to the courts and that they stem from courts' special characteristics as policymakers.[21] The implementation literature indicates the fallacy in this view by showing the ubiquity of implementation problems. Moreover, one may infer from this literature that difficulties in implementation arise for similar reasons in judicial and nonjudicial arenas.[22] Confronted with the implementation literature, students of judicial impact are obliged to seek explanations of their findings at a higher level of generality.

The literature on policy implementation does suffer from some significant limitations, two of which are particularly relevant to our concerns. First, relatively little progress has been made in theory building. Few scholars have attempted to develop general propositions about the implementation process, and empirical studies tend to be rather atheoretical.[23] If a general understanding of policy implementation is to be furthered, more attention must be devoted to theoretical work.

Second, the recent implementation literature has dealt with a limited range of implementation situations. Perhaps most notably, research has focused almost exclusively on the administrative implementation of legislative policies. The roles of the courts as enactors[24] and as implementors[25] of policy have been studied hardly at all, and few scholars have perceived the relevance of the judicial-impact literature to their own work on policy implementation.[26]

Despite these limitations, as suggested, the implementation literature has much to offer to students of judicial impact. In the next section, the nexus between the two fields of study will be examined from the other side; our concern will be with the contribution of the judicial-impact literature to the study of policy implementation.

THE JUDICIAL-IMPACT LITERATURE

The literature on judicial impact has been the subject of much critical analysis.[27] In this section, that literature will be assessed specifically in terms of its contribution to the understanding of policy implementation. This assessment will provide a basis for some recommendations for future directions in the study of judicial impact.

Empirical Research: Describing the Impact Process

Descriptive empirical research on judicial impact has varied considerably in its quality. Much of this research gives too little attention to the methodological requisites for determination of decisional impact;[28] as a result, its findings must be discounted. However, there also exists a significant body of empirical studies that provides well-founded conclusions about the effects of Supreme Court decisions.[29]

The findings of these studies constitute a valuable resource for scholars interested in policy implementation, particularly in the development of inductive theories of implementation. The research on judicial impact is especially valuable for scholars in the field of public policy because their own work has dealt so little with this form of implementation. Moreover, the best studies of judicial impact can serve as useful methodological models for the study of policy implementation.

Empirical work on judicial impact, then, has much to contribute. However, the utility of this literature for an understanding of policy implementation is limited by its focus on a narrow range of judicial decisions as objects of study. This narrowness of focus has several aspects that merit consideration.

First and most obvious is an interest almost solely in the U.S. Supreme Court as a source of enactments. The field of impact studies is the most notable vestige of the traditional public-law emphasis on the highest court in the land; very little research has been done on responses to decisions of other courts.[30] This emphasis on the Supreme Court has limited the scope of our knowledge about implementation patterns in two ways. First, we have learned little about the significance of the identity of the enacting court as an independent variable in the implementation process. Moreover, we have missed opportunities to ascertain and to explain the effects of judicial decisions through comparisons among jurisdictions whose courts have adopted different positions in a particular area of law.

Second, impact research has continued to focus on civil-liberties decisions, to the near exclusion of decisions in other policy areas. Even the Supreme Court devotes a large portion of its energies to fields of economic policy such as antitrust and taxation,[31] yet the impact of its work in these fields has been virtually ignored.[32] One unfortunate effect of this emphasis is an absence of literature on specialized courts and regulatory agencies as implementors of judicial policies.

Third, as has been noted, the use of a compliance perspective has led researchers to study the impact of judicial rules of law rather than of decisional trends. Decisional trends represent a particularly interesting subject to examine because judges and administrators have no obligation to follow trends of decision in a superior court; willingness to follow these trends must come from other motivations. It is unfortunate that so little research has been done on this kind of policy leadership.[33]

Finally, the preponderance of empirical research concerns decisions that demand major policy changes from judges and administrators, the kinds of decisions to which the greatest resistance might be expected. Little attention has been given to the implementation of decisions that reinforce the preexisting inclinations of most affected policymakers, such as the Burger Court decisions limiting the force of *Mapp* and *Miranda*.[34] Nor have researchers investigated the impact of decisions relatively trivial in their import, decisions to which judges and administrators might be indifferent. As a result, the picture of implementation processes that emerges from studies of judicial impact is based on a highly unrepresentative sample of situations.

The dominant subject matter of empirical research on judicial impact is analogous to the focus of recent research on implementation in the field of public policy. In both cases, scholars have dealt primarily with dramatic new policies adopted by the highest level of government, policies that place heavy demands upon implementing agencies. This coincidence of focus limits the ability of the judicial-impact literature to expand the range of vision of students of policy implementation. In this respect the impact literature has far to go to achieve its full potential.

Theory-Building: Explaining the Implementation Process

The earliest students of judicial impact gave little consideration to the building of theories to explain response to Supreme Court decisions. Over the past decade, however, interest in theory development has burgeoned in this field. Several scholars have offered inventories of variables with which to explain variation in response to decisions.[35] Others have elaborated insightful theoretical schemes based upon sociological conceptions of power, psychological conceptions of cognitive dissonance, and economic conceptions of utility.[36]

As we would expect, theories of impact generally grow from a conception of response to judicial decisions as a form of legal compliance.[37] Despite this orientation, these theories are applicable to the study of implementation because they seek to explain behavior with which students of implementation also are concerned. The dependent variable labeled "compliance" may be translated as the extent to which implementors carry out enacted policies, probably the most important dependent variable for those interested in the implementation process.

The compliance orientation of these theories does tend to limit the scope of their explanatory schemes. Most important, theories of impact often seem to assume that implementors always will be capable of carrying out enacted policies.[38] But these theories may be adapted to make them more comprehensive, and they provide a good base for further theory development. Certainly they represent a considerable resource on which students of implementation may draw in building theoretical schemes.

Unfortunately, students of judicial impact have done little testing of these theories. Some empirical studies offer useful explanations of their findings,[39] but very few studies have attempted systematically to test general theoretical propositions about response to court decisions.[40] The gap between the theoretical literature and the atheoretical empirical work in this field is striking.

The lack of theory-testing in this field has retarded our understanding of the variables that have been posited as influencing the implementation of decisions. The significance of some variables, like the policy preferences of judges and administrators, is assumed almost universally. The roles of others, such as the legitimacy of the Supreme Court,[41] are disputed. But in neither case can we offer extensive systematic evidence to students of implementation. This fact represents a serious weakness in the impact literature, one that limits significantly our knowledge about the implementation process.

The assessment of the judicial-impact literature that grows out of the discussion in this section is a mixed one. This literature provides a wealth of empirical studies that are particularly valuable in the development of theories about implementation processes and that can serve as methodological models for studies of implementation. Moreover, the literature on impact offers some good explanatory schemes that can serve as bases for the building of theories of implementation. On the negative side, the scope of empirical studies has been unfortunately narrow, and the theoretical propositions advanced by students of judicial impact remain largely untested. The contribution of the impact literature to an understanding of policy implementation is considerable, but this contribution could be much more extensive. In the final section of this chapter, some prescriptions concerning future directions in the study of judicial impact as policy implementation will be offered.

FUTURE DIRECTIONS IN THE STUDY OF JUDICIAL IMPACT

The preceding discussion of the literature on judicial impact leads directly to two prescriptions for future work in this field. The first prescription, to expand the subject matter of empirical research, is a relatively simple one. Scholars profitably could turn their attention to decisions of courts below the Supreme Court, to non-civil liberties decisions, to the impact of courts' decisional trends, and to decisions that do not demand major policy changes from implementors.

These shifts in focus entail significant costs because they require scholars to take on some difficult tasks. Thus, to study the decisions of courts other than the Supreme Court will require careful investigation to locate appropriate decisions to study. To expand the substantive concerns of impact studies beyond civil liberties, scholars will have to work in areas of law and policy with which they are relatively unfamiliar. But these costs will be more than compensated by an expansion in the breadth of our knowledge about the implementation of court decisions and thus in our ability to map the process of response to decisions.

In their selection of subject matter, students of judicial impact could perform an important service with one further expansion of their interest—to the implementation of nonjudicial policies. The failure of students of public policy analysis to venture into the judicial arena for studies of implementation has been noted. Given that fact, scholars in the field of judicial politics could usefully undertake comparative studies of response to judicial and nonjudicial policies in the same fields of activity. Students of "legal" policy areas, particularly Rodgers and Bullock, have done valuable work of this type.[42] But much more of this kind of research needs to be done, with an emphasis on probing similarities and differences between the implementation of judicial and nonjudicial policies. The findings of such studies should be particularly useful for those interested in understanding courts in comparison with other policymaking institutions.

The second prescription, to engage in concerted testing of theory, requires more careful consideration. The dearth of theory-testing in studies of judicial impact reflects the fact that certain characteristics of the implementation process complicate the testing of hypotheses. The behavior to be characterized is usually collective rather than individual. Implementation is a continuing process rather than a single discrete act. Implementation behavior as a dependent variable and some significant independent variables defy easy operationalization.

These characteristics are not unique to policy implementation but are common in the forms of institutional behavior studied by social scientists. Moreover, they are far from insuperable. Students of complex organizations, who face similar methodological problems, have ameliorated their effects by developing techniques to overcome them.[43] Multiple indicators for complex variables and multiple data sources are utilized; systematic qualitative analysis is employed where data are not susceptible to quantitative analysis. These techniques are applicable to the study of policy implementation, and the success with which they are used makes it clear that meaningful testing of propositions about response to judicial decisions is possible.

We should not expect that concerted testing of major hypotheses would settle questions about the forces that shape the implementation process. Even in the study of voting behavior, where methodological problems are far more limited, major questions concerning the voting decision remain unsettled despite a massive commitment of scholarly resources to theory development.[44] However, systematic theory-testing would allow more precise judgments about the variables that determine response to enacted policies. For instance, our understanding of institutional legitimacy as a variable would be enhanced by direct analysis of its relationship with implementors' behavior. The findings of such research would be invaluable for the understanding of implementation in the judicial arena and of implementation in general.

The prescriptions that have been offered in this section represent means to enhance the contribution of a field of scholarship that already has accomplished much. This accomplishment lies not only in satisfying scholarly curiosity but also in helping to meet judges' need for feedback about the effects of judicial policies.[45] Even more can be accomplished in the future, however, if scholars work to transcend the limitations that have characterized the study of judicial impact thus far.

As this chapter has suggested, a conception of judicial impact as a form of policy implementation provides one useful model on which future research on impact can be based. If judicial and administrative response to court decisions is seen as a process similar to the implementation processes studied in the field of public policy, the work done in these two areas can be used to strengthen each other. Moreover, the goal of improving understanding of the policy-implementation process can serve as a general benchmark against which work concerning judicial impact can be assessed. In this, as in other areas of judicial politics, students of the courts could do no better than to conceive their work as a contribution to the understanding of public policymaking.

NOTES

1. The best summary of the literature remains Stephen L. Wasby, *The Impact of the Supreme Court: Some Perspectives* (Homewood, Ill.: Dorsey Press, 1970). See also Martin Shapiro, "The Impact of the Supreme Court," *Journal of Legal Education* 23 (1970): 77-89; and Kenneth M. Dolbeare, "The Impacts of Public Policy," in *Political Science Annual*, vol. 5, ed. Cornelius P. Cotter (Indianapolis: Bobbs-Merrill, 1974), pp. 97-102.

2. See, respectively, Jerry K. Beatty, "State Court Evasion of United States Supreme Court Mandates," *Valparaiso University Law Review* 6 (1972): 260-85; and Gregory Casey, "Popular Perceptions of Supreme Court Rulings," *American Politics Quarterly* 4 (1976): 3-45.

3. The most popular subjects of impact studies of this type have been lower-court and administrative response to the desegregation decisions, police and lower-court response to criminal procedure decisions, and public-school response to decisions on school religious practices. See, respectively, J. W. Peltason, *Fifty-Eight Lonely Men: Southern Federal Judges and School Desegregation*, 2nd ed. (Urbana: University of Illinois Press, 1971); Neal Milner, *The Court and Local Law Enforcement: The Impact of Miranda* (Beverly Hills: Sage Publications, 1971); and Kenneth M. Dolbeare and Phillip E. Hammond, *The School Prayer Decisions: From Court Policy to Local Practice* (Chicago: University of Chicago Press, 1971).

4. See, for instance, Ellis Katz, "Patterns of Compliance with the *Schempp* Decision," *Journal of Public Law* 14 (1965): 396-408; and Michael J. Petrick, "The Supreme Court and Authority Acceptance," *Western Political Quarterly* 21 (1968): 5-19.

5. Jerry N. Clark, Keith O. Boyum, Samuel Krislov, and Roger C. Shaefer, "Compliance, Obedience, and Revolt: An Overview," in *Compliance and the Law: A Multi-*

Disciplinary Approach, ed. Samuel Krislov et al. (Beverly Hills: Sage Publications, 1971), pp. 9-32.

6. Robert V. Stover and Don W. Brown, "Understanding Compliance and Noncompliance with Law: The Contributions of Utility Theory," *Social Science Quarterly* 56 (1975): 363-75. See also Stuart S. Nagel, "Causes and Effects of Constitutional Compliance," in *Nomos XII: Political and Legal Obligation*, ed. J. Roland Pennock and John W. Chapman (New York: Atherton Press, 1970), pp. 219-28.

7. Arthur S. Miller and Alan W. Scheflin, "The Power of the Supreme Court in the Age of the Positive State: A Preliminary Excursus," 1967 *Duke Law Journal* (April, 1967): 289-92.

8. This equation is more reasonable on the level of perceived obligation. The judge's acceptance of an obligation to follow a relevant appellate directive may be as strong as the citizen's acceptance of an obligation to obey the prohibitions of criminal statutes. See Marvin Schick, *Learned Hand's Court* (Baltimore: Johns Hopkins Press, 1970), p. 167; and Austin Sarat, "Support for the Legal System," *American Politics Quarterly* 3 (1975): 3-24. However, it probably distorts reality to conceive of an official's unwillingness to apply a court-made rule of law to another case as disobedience of the law.

9. See John L. Young, "Obviousness in the Eighth Circuit," *St. Louis University Law Journal* 14 (1970): 672-85.

10. There is a useful discussion of these definitional problems in Wasby, op. cit., pp. 30-32.

11. An example would be efforts of police departments to communicate appellate decisions to officers and to educate them in the desirability of these decisions. On communication of the Supreme Court's decisions to police, see Stephen L. Wasby, "The Communication of the Supreme Court's Criminal Procedure Decisions: A Preliminary Mapping," *Villanova Law Review* 18 (1973): 1086-118.

12. Another alternative model is one that views impact in terms of communication and diffusion of innovation. See Stephen L. Wasby, "The United States Supreme Court's Impact: Broadening Our Focus," *Notre Dame Lawyer* 49 (1974): 1028-36. Another possible alternative, more diffuse in orientation, views impact as a stage in the functioning of an Eastonian political system. See Sheldon Goldman and Thomas P. Jahnige, *The Federal Courts as a Political System*, 2d ed. (New York: Harper and Row, 1976), pp. 237-78.

13. Martin Shapiro, *The Supreme Court and Administrative Agencies* (New York: Free Press, 1968). An implementation perspective is also found in the work of Bradley Canon, especially "Reactions of State Supreme Courts to a U.S. Supreme Court Civil Liberties Decision," *Law and Society Review* 8 (1973): 109-34. Some hints of this perspective appear in several other studies of judicial impact.

14. Lawrence Baum, "Implementation of Judicial Decisions: An Organizational Analysis," *American Politics Quarterly* 4 (1976): 86-114.

15. For other conceptions and definitions of implementation, see Donald S. Van Meter and Carl E. Van Horn, "The Policy Implementation Process: A Conceptual Framework," *Administration and Society* 6 (1975): 447; Douglas R. Bunker, "Policy Sciences Perspectives on Implementation Processes," *Policy Sciences* 3 (1972): 72; and Jeffrey L. Pressman and Aaron Wildavsky, *Implementation* (Berkeley: University of California Press, 1973), p. xiv.

16. Philip Selznick, *TVA and the Grass Roots: A Study in the Sociology of Formal Organization* (Berkeley: University of California Press, 1953); Herbert Kaufman, *The Forest Ranger: A Study in Administrative Behavior* (Baltimore: Johns Hopkins Press, 1960).

17. Marver H. Bernstein, *Regulating Business by Independent Commission* (Princeton: Princeton University Press, 1955). In addition, much of the best work in organization theory takes as its subject the behavior of public policy-implementing agencies. See, for

instance, Peter M. Blau, *The Dynamics of Bureaucracy: A Study of Interpersonal Relationships in Two Government Agencies* (Chicago: University of Chicago Press, 1955).

18. For discussions of this field and examples of work that fall within it, see Austin Ranney, ed., *Political Science and Public Policy* (Chicago: Markham Publishing Company, 1968); and James E. Anderson, *Public Policy-Making* (New York: Praeger, 1975).

19. Martha Derthick, *New Towns In-Town: Why a Federal Program Failed* (Washington, D.C.: The Urban Institute, 1972); Derthick, *The Influence of Federal Grants: Public Assistance in Massachusetts* (Cambridge, Mass.: Harvard University Press, 1970); Stephen K. Bailey and Edith K. Mosher, *ESEA: The Office of Education Administers a Law* (Syracuse: Syracuse University Press, 1968); Jerome T. Murphy, *State Education Agencies and Discretionary Funds* (Lexington, Mass.: D.C. Heath, 1974); Pressman and Wildavsky, op. cit.

20. Van Meter and Van Horn, op. cit.; Carl E. Van Horn and Donald S. Van Meter, "The Implementation of Intergovernmental Policy," in *Public Policy-Making in a Federal System*, ed. Charles O. Jones and Robert Thomas (Beverly Hills: Sage Publications, 1976). See also Bunker, op. cit.; and Thomas B. Smith, "The Policy Implementation Process," *Policy Sciences* 4 (1973): 197-209.

21. The fact that this is not the case was underlined early in the study of judicial impact by Walter Murphy. See Walter F. Murphy, "Lower Court Checks on Supreme Court Power," *American Political Science Review* 53 (1959): 1017.

22. See, for instance, Neal Gross, Joseph B. Giacquinta, and Marilyn Bernstein, *Implementing Organizational Innovations* (New York: Basic Books, 1971); and Walter Williams, *Social Policy Research and Analysis: The Experience in the Federal Social Agencies* (New York: American Elsevier, 1971).

23. A general theoretical framework is offered in Van Meter and Van Horn, op. cit., and a few empirical studies provide theoretical perspectives. See Jerome Murphy, op. cit., pp. 118-27.

24. The term "enactors" is used to refer to the roles of courts as adopters of new policies that then require implementation by lower courts and/or administrative agencies.

25. There is an extensive and useful literature on judicial implementation of legislative enactments, produced primarily by legal scholars, which apparently has not come to the attention of students of public policy. See, for instance, Edwin M. Lemert, *Social Action and Legal Change: Revolution Within the Juvenile Courts* (Chicago: Aldine, 1970); Barbara Yngvesson and Patricia Hennessey, "Small Claims, Complex Disputes: A Review of the Small Claims Literature," *Law and Society Review* 9 (1975): 219-74; and Marilyn M. Mosier and Richard A. Soble, "Modern Legislation, Metropolitan Court, Miniscule Results: A Study of Detroit's Landlord-Tenant Court," *Journal of Law Reform* 7 (1973): 8-70. More broadly, the whole body of literature on trial-court behavior is concerned with a species of policy implementation.

26. But see Van Meter and Van Horn, op. cit., pp. 456-57.

27. Wasby, *Impact of the Supreme Court*; Shapiro, "Impact of the Supreme Court"; Glendon Schubert, "Judicial Process and Behavior, 1963-1971," in *Political Science Annual*, vol. 3, ed. James A. Robinson (Indianapolis: Bobbs-Merrill, 1972), pp. 166-74.

28. On these requisites, see Richard Lempert, "Strategies of Research Design in the Legal Impact Study," *Law and Society Review* 1 (1966): 111-32; and James P. Levine, "Methodological Concerns in Studying Supreme Court Efficacy," *Law and Society Review* 4 (1970): 583-611. Also relevant is Donald T. Campbell, "Reforms as Experiments," *American Psychologist* 24 (1969): 409-29.

29. See, for instance, Neal Milner, *The Court and Local Law Enforcement: The Impact of Miranda* (Beverly Hills: Sage Publications, 1971).

30. Some research on lower-court impact does exist. For instance, there is a concern with the impact of state supreme-court policies in James P. Levine, "Constitutional Law and

Obscene Literature: An Investigation of Bookseller Censorship Practices," in *The Impact of Supreme Court Decisions*, 2d ed., eds. Theodore L. Becker and Malcolm M. Feeley (New York: Oxford University Press, 1973), pp. 119-38. Administrative response to decisions of the federal courts of appeals is discussed in Daniel J. Fiorino, "Judicial-Administrative Interaction in Regulatory Policy Making: The Case of the Federal Power Commission." Paper delivered at annual meeting of the American Political Science Association, San Francisco, September 2-5, 1975.

31. See, for example, the case analyses and statistical materials in "The Supreme Court, 1974 Term," *Harvard Law Review* 89 (1975): 202-11, 234-74, 279-81.

32. See the discussion of the field of economic regulation in Wasby, *Impact of the Supreme Court*, pp. 103-16.

33. One valuable analysis of the implementation of decisional trends is found in Shapiro, *Supreme Court and Administrative Agencies*, pp. 143-226.

34. *Mapp v. Ohio*, 367 U.S. 643 (1961); *Miranda v. Arizona*, 384 U.S. 436 (1966). One useful study of the impact of the Burger Court decisions deals, unfortunately for our interest, with the response of those policymakers who were unfavorable to the new decisions. Donald E. Wilkes, Jr., "The New Federalism in Criminal Procedure: State Court Evasion of the Burger Court," *Kentucky Law Journal* 62 (1974): 421-51. I have discussed a policy question on which the Supreme Court's decisions reinforced preexisting inclinations of lower-court judges in "The Federal Courts and Patent Validity: An Analysis of the Record," *Journal of the Patent Office Society* 56 (1974): 758-87.

35. See, for instance, Wasby, *Impact of the Supreme Court*, pp. 42-56; and Joel B. Grossman, "The Supreme Court and Social Change," *American Behavioral Scientist* 13 (1970): 545-46.

36. See, respectively, Richard M. Johnson, *The Dynamics of Compliance* (Evanston: Northwestern University Press, 1967), Chapter 2; William K. Muir, *Prayer in the Public Schools: Law and Attitude Change* (Chicago: University of Chicago Press, 1967); and Stover and Brown, op. cit.

37. Stover and Brown, op. cit.; Johnson, op. cit.; Samuel Krislov, *The Supreme Court in the Political Process* (New York: Macmillan, 1965), pp. 134-39.

38. The one outstanding exception is Stover and Brown, op. cit.

39. See, for instance, Robert Birkby, "The Supreme Court and the Bible Belt: Tennessee Reaction to the 'Schempp' Decision," *Midwest Journal of Political Science* 10 (1966): 304-19; Edward N. Beiser, "A Comparative Analysis of State and Federal Judicial Behavior: The Reapportionment Cases," *American Political Science Review* 62 (1968): 788-95; and Milner, op. cit.

40. One significant exception is Canon, op. cit., which tests some general propositions about judicial impact.

41. Petrick, op. cit.; James P. Levine and Theodore Becker, "Toward and Beyond a Theory of Supreme Court Impact," *American Behavioral Scientist* 13 (1970): 561-62.

42. Harrell R. Rodgers, Jr., and Charles S. Bullock, III, *Law and Social Change: Civil Rights Laws and Their Consequences* (New York: McGraw-Hill, 1972). See also Chapter 10 of this volume.

43. On methodologies for the analysis of organizational behavior, useful sources include Peter M. Blau, "The Comparative Study of Organizations," *Industrial and Labor Relations Review* 18 (1965): 323-38; James S. Coleman, "Relational Analysis: The Study of Social Organizations with Survey Methods," *Human Organization* 17 (1958-59): 28-36; Allan Barton, "Organizational Measurement and Its Bearing on the Study of College Environments," in *Readings on Modern Organizations*, ed. Amitai Etzioni (New York: Prentice-Hall, 1969), pp. 259-90; and James L. Price, *Handbook of Organizational Measurement* (Lexington, Mass.: D.C. Heath and Company, 1972).

44. See Richard G. Niemi and Herbert F. Weisberg, eds., *Controversies in American Voting Behavior* (San Francisco: W. H. Freeman, 1976).

45. See, for instance, Bradley C. Canon, "Is the Exclusionary Rule in Failing Health? Some New Data and a Plea Against a Precipitous Conclusion," *Kentucky Law Journal* 62 (1974): 681-730.

CHAPTER
8

WHEN COURTS SHOULD MAKE POLICY: AN INSTITUTIONAL APPROACH
Lief H. Carter

In 1857 the Supreme Court, in *Dred Scott v. Sandford*, invalidated the legal basis on which claims for Negro equality rested.* The decision helped precipitate a civil war. In 1954 the Supreme Court voided officially sponsored segregation in public schools in *Brown v. Board of Education*. In 1974 federal courts held that the president of the United States was not beyond the reach of the legal process. *Brown* changed both our schools and the way we think about racial policy and racial justice. *United States v. Nixon* may have been a necessary condition for the first nonelectoral toppling of an executive regime in the United States. In each of these cases the Court made policy. Judges interpreted the Constitution and therefore made decisions that, but for the unpredictable process of constitutional amendment, escaped formal political review. In practical terms the judicial judgment displaced the judgments of elected policymakers.[1]

The public policy work of the courts is truly immense. In the decade of the 1970s the courts have thus far:

1. Erected a constitutional barrier to governmental prohibitions on abortions in the first trimester of pregnancy (*Roe v. Wade*, 1973).

---

*An alphabetical list of the cases cited follows the body of this chapter, in addition to the footnotes.

Particular thanks go to Professor Jerry Goldman, Northwestern University, for his comments on an earlier draft of this chapter.

2. Denied those attacked in newspaper editorials a right to editorial space for rebuttal (*Miami Herald Publishing Co. v. Tornillo*, 1974).

3. Blocked administration of existing capital-punishment statutes (*Furman v. Georgia*, 1972).

4. Set minimum standards for operation of state mental hospitals (*Wyatt v. Stickney*, 1972).[2]

5. Ordered that widowered fathers of minors receive the same social security benefits as widowed mothers now receive (*Weinberger v. Wiesenfeld*, 1975).

6. Held that unless a student's presence in school poses a physical threat to others, schools must not temporarily suspend students without some form of notice and hearing (*Goss v. Lopez*, 1975).

7. Set standards for delegate selection to political conventions.[3]

8. Ruled that developing communities, that is, those communities "in the path of inevitable future residential, commercial, and industrial demand and growth," may not zone so as to exclude the construction of low-cost housing (*Southern Burlington NAACP v. Township of Mt. Laurel*, 1975).

Collectively these cases illustrate the breadth of judicial policymaking in matters that directly affect large numbers of people and that indirectly can affect us all. We should not avoid the responsibility of evaluating the quality of these policies.

This chapter seeks first to clarify how we think about judicial policymaking through constitutional interpretation. The next section suggests that we can profitably ask four kinds of questions about the role and work of courts. The analysis will focus on the U.S. Supreme Court; but by implication it can apply to state supreme courts and, to the extent law, procedure, and judicial creativity allow discretionary policy choices, to lower courts as well. The chapter's heart, its remaining four sections, elaborates the last of these four questions, the "institutional approach." The institutional approach holds that we can match the informational, technological, and political characteristics of various policy problems with the institutional characteristics of courts and thereby determine when courts should or should not proceed to make or influence policy. This approach hopefully provides some practical guidance to the enlightened judge who recognizes that judges inevitably make policy and who would like guidance as to where judges may do so effectively.

FOUR TYPES OF QUESTIONS ABOUT JUDICIAL POLICYMAKING

It is judicial review itself—the authority of judicial officials to make final public policy through constitutional interpretation—consistent with democratic theory? So stated, this first question aids the exploration of the nature of democracy, if for no other reason than that it calls for a precise definition of democracy. But cases do not frequently raise this problem today, and from the policy evaluator's perspective, this question contributes little to judicial assessment for the rather practical reason that judicial review has entrenched itself in both professional and popular expectations of the courts and the political process. From the policy perspective, this question either resolves into a gerrymandered definition of democracy that in turn accommodates judicial review, or an admission that democracy is not always desirable, or an assertion that "it all depends."[4]

The second set of questions asks: Have the courts responded wisely to a given problem? Did a court in a given instance adopt empirically sound assumptions? (For example, does segregated education impose identifiable social, psychological, and economic costs on black students?) Has a court's solution produced the intended consequences? (Has reapportionment equalized the voice of competing political interests in the legislative process?) Does the new policy survive the test of cost/benefit analysis when compared to other policy approaches? (Has the absence of capital punishment affected the incidence of one or more categories of crime?) Political scientists and economists deem themselves particularly capable of answering this second set of questions. Malcolm Feeley has indicated how difficult the evaluative task here is but we shall continue to attempt policy evaluations of this sort, with varying success, because the consequences of admitting that one cannot tell wise from unwise policies is, to say the least, politically and professionally demoralizing.[5]

Answers to the third set of questions appear more commonly in the writings of scholars of constitutional law. While they have not refrained from attempting answers to the second kind of question, they tend to prefer to formulate evaluative questions somewhat differently. The third category of questions thus includes: What is the nature and quality of the legal reasoning that produces a policy judgment? How carefully does the decision follow or distinguish potentially applicable precedent? Does a decision follow from the assumptions that it purports to (or implies it must) make? The question can overlap type two, for reasoning about assumptions often leads to a concern for policy. But lawyers still tend to think about policy in logical-positivist rather than empirical terms. In party, lawyers need to do so in order to convert judicial decisions into predictions of hypothetical judicial rulings upon the related but not identical legal problems of their clients. Additionally, the tradition of constitutional scholarship in the United States has produced a theory of judicial legitimacy. The theory states that our willingness to acknowledge the authority of courts to make policy and our willingness to abide by judicial results hinges on the preservation of neutral and impartial principles and reasoning so that decisions will be formulated in such a way as to apply equally to opposing political factions. Since illogical reasoning inevitably raises the suspicion that the court in that instance sought a partisan result, craftsmanlike reasoning in all matters becomes essential.[6]

All three of these question types have provoked an extensive literature, which we need not document further here. From the perspective of a Supreme Court Justice, however, these questions do not provide a satisfactory purchase on an important practical decision. The problem appears in its starkest form when a U.S. Supreme Court justice must decide whether to hear a case, whether to vote for or against granting a petition for certiorari, whether to vote for or against the dismissal of an appeal. The justice in this instance will almost surely assume that democratic theory poses no automatic bar to judicial policymaking, and he will not give that question serious thought. He almost surely would like to give questions two and three serious consideration, but he can not.[7] Question two requires post hoc analysis of the consequences of a policy in action. At the initial review stage the justice might be able to predict the consequences of policy alternatives with some success, even though he does not have the data in hand. The problem is that at this stage he cannot predict which policy alternative the Court will adopt. He has not heard the evidence. He can predict neither his own vote nor that of the majority. Similarly he will not know how successfully he or his brethren will articulate their reasons for their conclusion. A great many other strategic choices may intervene to influence the final legal product.[8] But in the face of these uncertainties he must nevertheless decide whether to proceed. We are not far from Justice Louis Brandeis' frequently quoted assertion that, "The most important thing we do is not doing."

While courts may make policy simply by negating the policy choices of other governmental actors, in practice they often make policy in more explicit ways. The reasons advanced to support a nullification may narrow the range of remaining policy choices, as did even the amorphous *Furman v. Georgia*. The specific remedy that a court may order for a constitutional abuse, for example, school busing to reduce school segregation, is even more explicit. At times the courts have openly promulgated general policy, for example, *Miranda v. Arizona* (1966). In short, judges should anticipate that intrusion (even intrusions that uphold constitutional validity of policy) can have tangible and sensitive policy consequences.

Thus the fourth set of questions searches for indicators of the capacity of courts to respond to problems effectively. We may assess effectiveness both in isolation and in comparison with the institutional characteristics of other policymaking bodies. These indicators necessarily attempt to point the way to conclusions about the degree of fit between the characteristics of problems and the characteristics of institutions that can cope with them. To illustrate, this approach would ask whether the circumstances in which the problem of school segregation was raised in the early 1950s were such as to make the courts an appropriate place to initiate a policy response. The approach would not assess the quality or the impact of *Brown* itself. Similarly this method would ask whether the issue of equalization of public-school finance raised in *San Antonio Independent School District v. Rodriguez* (1973) is more or less appropriately suited to judicially created responses than was school desegregation or was the specification of proper policy toward pornography in *Roth v. United States* (1957).

Three final points before proceeding further. First, finding a fit between problem and institution is not in any sense an end; it is a means to some decidedly unmysterious ends that policymakers in many institutions presumably share, namely that policies accord with fundamental, widely shared beliefs about acceptable governmental action, that the policy selected in a given case carry some plausible hope of alleviating the problem, and that promulgation and implementation of policy will not destroy the position and authority of the policy's source.

Second, the following two sections seek primarily to present a way of thinking about the judicial policymaking function. The reader will not misconstrue the author's intentions if he or she perceives considerable support in what follows for the work of the Supreme Court in the last quarter century. I may, however, misapply my own evaluative format. I would only hope that readers unhappy with the substantive conclusions offered here will try to rebut them in terms of the method of inquiry proposed here before rejecting the method altogether.

Finally, the following analysis does not mean to downgrade the importance of seeking answers to questions of the second and third type mentioned above. I would argue that these two questions matter more because the answer to the institutional question, when courts should make policy, suggests that courts have in the last quarter century generally chosen policy domains wisely and that determining the quality of this activism therefore becomes the first order of evaluative business.

INDICATORS OF INSTITUTIONAL POLICY EFFECTIVENESS

This section lists in the abstract the characteristics of institutions, public or private, that determine their qualifications for and their ability to formulate policy effectively. The remaining sections then apply these indicators to the judiciary. For convenience, I refer to policymaking institutions in the abstract as PMIs.

The first indicator is surprisingly straightforward. It states that the members of a PMI should be familiar with the language through which a policy problem expresses itself and they should have gained, through training and experience in the field, some understanding about the cause-and-effect beliefs that define the existence of a problem in the first place. Perhaps this indicator at bottom only restates the familiar advantages of a division of labor. No person or group can command all knowledge. For the sake of wise decision making, all people and groups specialize to a degree. The simplicity of this observation should not, however, cloud the main point that policy problems emerge and are expressed through different languages that we cannot all understand. Some problems are defined through the language of econometrics, others through the vocabulary of game theory, and others through the language of statistical expression. Some matching between the skills of PMI members and the problem language is therefore essential if we are to meet the objective of effective policymaking. (We shall therefore distinguish in the next section those policies that traditionally express themselves through legal language from those that do not, and argue that the distinction is a valuable one in the evaluation of judicial policymaking.

The second indicator is really a corollary of the first. It examines whether, regardless of the skills of members of a given PMI, any other PMI is equally or better prepared to proceed, and whether alternative policy sources, even if they may be better equipped technically to proceed, will in fact do so. It is, for example, plausible to justify governmental intervention in the area of automobile safety not because the government included the most skilled technicians but because of ample evidence that the PMI that included the best technicians, the auto industry itself, was disinclined to make policy at all.

Obviously past experience with a problem area builds the kind of problem familiarity we desire. While it constitutes bootstrapping to argue that a PMI should enter a policy field because in doing so it will develop experience in the area, it is quite another matter to justify present policymaking activity on the basis of received experience, even if the PMI initially developed its experience by unwarranted policy fiat.

The third indicator is a bit more complicated. A PMI whose members possess the capacity to make sense of a problem technically does not thereby automatically possess a guaranteed access to the full range of information about (a) causal conditions underlying the problem; (b) all proposed solutions; (c) the consequences, direct or indirect, of all policy choices; (d) the targets and strategies for successful implementation of a policy choice (for example, strategies for winning compliance with new policy choices). The third indicator therefore requires that the PMI be structured in such a way as to have reliable access to information that bears on these requirements of policy. The fourth indicator is the comparative corollary of the third.

The fifth indicator and its corollary, the sixth, are closely related to the third and fourth. Policy initiation will generate new and unanticipated information that should feed back into refinements of rules and decisions in a policy field. We must also therefore ask whether a PMI is structured to reformulate policy when new information emerges from implementation efforts. One of the most important features that problems possess differentially, and which institutions must match in order to deal with problems successfully, is the nature of the time period within which this feedback and reformulation must occur. Warfare and diplomatic negotiations, indeed bargaining of all kinds, involve very rapid exchanges of information and alterations of position on the basis of such information. Often the problem is such that successful policy can only emerge from rapid exchanges among many institutions, both public and private. The best example of such a process recently occurred in the efforts to avoid default by New York City on a portion of its bonded indebtedness. At the other extreme exist policies where virtually no feedback and reevaluation can occur after the initial policy choice is made. The very recent decision to provide nationwide immunizations against a possible outbreak of swine-type influenza, anticipated to begin at the end of 1976, illustrates the category. Cost/benefit information may be gathered and evaluated exhaustively as the initial decision is formulated. Simulation and controlled experimentation designed to estimate infectiousness of the virus may yield some estimates of the policy's expected success; but once the order to innoculate the nation is issued, feedback will occur only at the lowest technical level.

One more indicator (plus its comparative corollary) remains. In a world where values conflict, where different interests define right and wrong differentially and therefore evaluate policies not simply in terms of their effectiveness but also in terms of the moral and symbolic qualities of both means and ends, the indicators specified above cannot fully answer the question of when an institution should make policy. They do not insure either political accountability or institutional survival. We must therefore inquire into the content of public belief systems concerning both the problem and the authority and competence of PMIs. Is there wide public identification or acknowledgment of the existence of a problem, or is the existence of a problem and its seriousness acknowledged only by immediately affected interests? Do mass publics believe that the present policy is in some way inadequate or is there widespread support for the existing state of affairs? Conversely, will mass publics ignore policy initiatives regardless of their content? (Where belief in the existence of a problem and awareness of policy response to it is confined to the interests immediately affected by it, the technical and informational criteria probably suffice, for the immediate interests presumably will possess the competence to assess the policy response in these terms.) Do those who acknowledge the existence of a problem agree in their perceptions of the problem? Do they agree that the problem is a failure to meet a widely desired end, or does the problem lie in the inability to specify desired objectives in the first place? Do affected publics perceive the processes of specifying either means or ends as requiring extensive empirical information sifting, or is the problem perceived as requiring choices among competing norms?

Where those who identify the existence of a problem also agree about the character of the problem, that is, that it is normative or empirical or that the policy conflict concerns either means choices or ends choices, then a PMI may proceed so long as the public believes its authority and competence match the problem. In other words, a PMI may proceed as long as it is perceived capable of empirical evaluation on the one hand or capable of philosophical deductions on the other (and in some instances, of course, a combination of the two). But where widespread conflict exists about the existence or character of a problem, then a PMI should proceed only if it is perceived capable of reconciling conflict. The reconciliation of conflict will occur through bargaining and compromise, and a PMI should proceed only when the public perceives it capable of doing so.

To summarize, three kinds of indicators (each with a comparative corollary) help assess proper and improper institutional policy activity. The first (indicators one and two) we might call indicators of technical competence, the second (three through six), indicators of effective information processing, and the third (seven and eight) indicators of political acceptability. A PMI must be able to claim that the processes by which it defines the desirability of ends and by which it selects means to ends are at least as likely to meet publicly defined standards of acceptability as are those of other PMIs.

JUDICIAL POLICY EFFECTIVENESS

How do these indicators translate into assessments of judicial policy making? How can the enlightened justice apply them to the decisions he must make? Courts will, on the basis of the first indicator, appropriately address problems that arise out of the legal system itself, particularly the administration of the legal system, and that have traditionally been expressed through the language of law. Additionally, past judicial action can partially influence current judicial competence. The process of deciding will increase the technical and informational competence of judges in the problem area. Judicial attempts at policy implementation may increase judicial capacity to identify needed policy modifications.

The preceding paragraph suggests a tendency for expansion of judicial policy activity, but perhaps the most important implication of these indicators for courts as for all PMIs is that the indicators will support different conclusions at different times as policy moves generate new information and as political conditions and public values change. For example, the characteristics of the policy problems that coalesce in the word "integration" are vastly different in 1977 from the characteristics of the problem when the Supreme Court made its first policy moves. In 1954 virtually no evidence supported the proposition that state or national PMIs other than the Court would act, but the strain between the practice of segregation and our political philosophy was very great. In 1954 no national bureaucratic machinery existed to gather, sift, plan, or enforce desegregation policies. In the absence of data and experience, the issue was properly perceived in essentially normative or philosophical terms. The configuration and implications of the data since generated by the Court's choices is vastly different today.[9] Secondary policy changes, in employment practices and residential patterns, have occurred that complicate the process of planning, to say nothing of the impact of demographic changes. Most important, voting changes and other changes in the configuration of political power in many jurisdictions make the adjustment of competing interests through bargaining more likely to occur. In short, we now perceive the problem as empirically more complex. Policy assumptions are more susceptible to empirical falsification. The conflict over the empirical and normative components of the problem, that is, both whether previously accepted ends are desirable and whether alternative means to ends will work, have increased so that the process of conflict adjustment becomes increasingly important in defining the desirability of policy. Dramatic extensions of judicial policy in the area are therefore less warranted than were its initial moves because legislatures, and other electorally oriented governmental units, are better structured to generate acceptable compromises of values and because they are more likely to hear the voices of various interests in fact than they were in 1954.

FURTHER ILLUSTRATIONS: FIVE EASY CASES AND THREE DIFFICULT CHOICES

Judicial history provides examples of instances where, on the basis of the indicators, we can confidently conclude that judicial-policy activism either is or is not appropriate. This history also reveals that these indicators do not make all choices simple ones for the courts.

Reapportionment.

Reasonable men can easily disagree in their selection of the policy area best suited to judicial intervention, but a very powerful case exists for judicial intervention in legislative malapportionment. Only this problem by its own terms makes a policy solution from other branches of government unreliable (*Baker v. Carr*, 1962). The legislature's inclination not to act, as Tennessee had failed to do for decades, was the problem! Furthermore, the Court could expect (and did in fact receive) broad support from the general public on the issue because it couched specific policy choices in terms of a philosophically powerful and empirically unfalsifiable set of assertions about means-ends relationships. While students of the political process criticized several of the Court's specific policy assumptions, the Court faced virtually no threat that empirical evidence would establish clear costs flowing from judicial intervention. It was, in other words, easy for the Court to maintain that the conditions it challenged served no rational purpose and attempts to alleviate them would inevitably move closer to the attainment of undisputedly desirable ends. Such a conclusion does not require that we approve each and every reapportionment decision. In all probability the courts insisted on excessive mathematical exactness in the late 1960s. But in a sense this only raises the final reason for supporting judicial policy-making in this area, for the combination of the timing of elections and the availability of new census information is such that litigation can successfully lead to the restructuring of policy on the basis of experience gained through its administration, for example, modifications in the requirement for mathematical exactness which the Court has in fact made.[10]

Criminal Procedure.

Admittedly judges had not gained detailed familiarity with the subtleties of malapportionment by virtue of their training and experience in law. To the extent specific policy choices proved inadequate in the reapportionment area, the indicator of technical competence may supply the explanation. In the area of criminal procedure, on the other hand, this indicator provides a powerful justification for continuing judicial activity. These problems arise out of the administration of the legal system itself. At bottom they involve the capacity of the legal system to do its job, to attain its own values. To take the most obvious example in the field, there is probably no body of policymakers whose experience better equips them to understand the importance of legal counsel in trial than lawyers and judges who review the transcripts of trials where counsel was absent (*Gideon v Wainwright*, 1963). Similarly the Fifth Amendment concern for coerced confessions represents in part a desire to improve the quality of fact-finding in trial. Fourth Amendment issues of search and seizure raise a different issue, for an illegally conducted search may produce evidence probative of guilt at trial. But two other characteristics of this problem justify judicial action. The goal of avoiding excessive police power is widely shared and deeply rooted in the American philosophical tradition. More important, neither law enforcement bodies nor legislatures could reliably be expected to move in this field. The organizational incentives of police departments push in the other direction, and the victims of illegal searches and seizure from neither a numerically large nor politically legitimate interest group of the sort capable of moving a legislature to action.[11] Finally, like reapportionment and unlike warfare or diplomacy, litigation occurs over a timespan that matches the development of information by which policy can be refined.

Substantive Due Process.

To switch to a policy area where the indicators point to judicial abstention, beginning in the late nineteenth century the Supreme Court invalidated much state regulation of the economy, legislation involving regulation of prices, wages, and hours of work. And federal legislation succumbed as well, culminating in the rejection of New Deal policies in the mid-1930s. While the judiciary lacked experiential and linguistic familiarity with these problems, the political indicators cut most forcefully against judicial policy intrusions in this field. The substantive due process issues contrast nicely with reapportionment. While the courts did lack complete technical competence to deal with reapportionment, the political indicators and all comparative corollaries indicated that judicial action was nevertheless defensible. These indicators cut in the opposite direction regarding substantive due process. While the Court treated the issue normatively, the debate over economic policy was to a large extent both distributive and empirical. The problem involved the configuration of power and wealth in the community. The stakes were high, and by every indication competing points of view, some backed by money and status and others by votes, advanced themselves in public debate and before legislatures. Finally, the courts took in this period an empirically falsifiable (and abundantly falsified) position. The Spencerian philosophy on which the Court based its reasoning required perfect competition in economic matters. The philosophy did not accommodate the reality that uncontrolled private power led to monopoly of economic power and in the process destroyed its own premise. In contrast, the normative proposition that legislative apportionment by population furthers democracy is (although analytically suspect) not empirically falsifiable.

Prayers in Public Schools.

The Court's significant rulings regarding prayer in public schools, stretching from *McCollum v. Board of Education* in 1948 to *School District v. Schempp* in 1963, have not received universal acclaim by any means. Advocates of school prayer have made serious attempts to change the policy through constitutional amendment. These attempts have been deflected only because formal religious organizations have not uniformly opposed the Court and because school prayers have tended to persist in those parts of the country where intense pressures for prayers persist.[12] Nevertheless the bulk of the indicators justify judicial intervention. Of the four policy problems thus far covered, the school prayer issue is most thoroughly normative. No experimental empirical findings are likely to establish a convincing linkage between the forbidden prayers and the attainment of undisputed policy goals. The issue is not, therefore, one where extended legislative or bureaucratic investigations would likely produce meaningful policy-related information. At the same time the problem falls squarely within the framework of First Amendment values, the separation of church and state. The empirical information required by the policymaking process involves only the limited question of whether the activities in question carry substantial religious content in fact, and litigation can effectively sift information on this point. With respect to the likelihood that other PMIs will intrude, the issue closely resembles criminal procedure. Those the undisputed goal seeks to protect are unlikely to possess resources sufficient to place the issue on legislative or bureaucratic agendas.

Legal Challenge to the Bombing of Cambodia.

Holtzman v. Schlesinger (1974) did not directly challenge strategic or tactical decisions in the conduct of the war in Indochina. To the extent the challenge rested on the failure to follow constitutionally specified procedures for the declaration of war, the case would seem to fall well within the Court's acknowledged area of technical competence. However, at least two characteristics of the policy situation surrounding the war made judicial abstention wise. First, the Court had virtually no control over the processes of implementation. Second, as in most foreign-policy matters, the courts have no routinized access to information concerning international negotiations and agreements. The Court cannot therefore easily predict how its decisions will influence the substance of policy strategies already being negotiated nor can it predict how the precedent of judicial intrusion will change the assumptions under which future negotiations are conducted.

Abortion.

In some respects the problem addressed in the 1973 abortion decision, the first of our three "difficult choices," resembles the school prayer problem. Existing policy affected a minority with a limited capacity to force policy reevaluation through the normal political process. But abortion and school prayer diverge on several critical dimensions. The separation of church and state carries a rich symbolic baggage deriving both from our political history (or rather from what many people perceive to be our political history) and from the constitutional preeminence of the First Amendment. In the abortion case, however, the legal and political traditions are less clear. Indeed, the state of the law on which the Court based the abortion finding was as shadowy as the penumbra of rights that the Court created in *Griswold v. Connecticut* in 1965. Additionally, the abortion issue raises empirical issues of a very different kind from those embedded in the prayer controversy. To the extent the issue forces the Court to reason about the beginning of life, changes in medical technology that allow the sustaining of life *ex utero* may invalidate the court's position.

The Death Penalty.

The result (since no clear majority opinion emerged we can hardly call it a decision) in *Furman v. Georgia* created a state of law that now makes further judicial policy action mandatory. If we read the result as holding arbitrary and capricious administration of the death penalty inconsistent with the Eighth Amendment, then refinements in state policies to meet the requirement must be assessed, or the Court must dismiss the requirement altogether. That process is, of course, now under way. But was judicial intrusion wise at all? As in abortion policy, the Court cannot invoke a clear historical or constitutional norm. Both history and our constitutional tradition seem rather to assume the appropriateness of the death penalty without serious question. Moreover, the empirical consequences of the death penalty on widely desired policy goals, that is, the control of crime, has not been resolved. It may never be resolved, but the problem is that the public perceives the linkage between the death penalty and crime control as an empirical one. Worse, the Court's policy itself may shoulder the blame for the inability to refine the linkage because such determinations require comparative data. Furthermore, the issue is a bargainable one, with opponents of the death penalty presumably willing to accept very narrow limits, for example, for the killing of policemen or prison guards, to the penalty. Finally, by intruding in this area the Court risks running counter to intense and broad retributive feelings that could in highly publicized future cases subject the Court to extreme and unpredictable criticism. Perhaps the fairest conclusion is that *Furman* represents a wise policy choice in an area in which very few wise or defensible policy choices are available. More aggressive policies might reveal more clearly the dangers.

Some Concluding Thoughts on Racial Policy.

The courts have not yet satisfactorily resolved a sensitive issue of racial policy, the propriety of preferential admission of minorities to educational and other public programs through which limited resources are distributed selectively to the public. *DeFunis v. Odegaard* (1974), which the Court dismissed as moot, raised the problem. Sooner or later the Court will have to decide whether to substitute national constitutional standards for the individual policy decisions of program administrators.

Justice Douglas' dissent from the finding of mootness in *DeFunis* raised two separate issues. The contrast between them provides a convenient summary of this essay's argument. The first point asks whether it is proper for governmental units with no history of racially antagonistic policies to confer benefits preferentially upon people on the basis of their membership in a racial class that has been previously disadvantaged. Douglas answered the question confidentially in the negative, but it is not the content of his answer that matters for our purposes. In fact, just as the Court's eagerness to duck the question would suggest, the problem poses a real dilemma in judicial policymaking that our indicators can only highlight. The issue is fundamentally a philosophical one. The propriety of policy will not be hammered out in legislative debates and statutory compromises. It is difficult to see why racial preferences should be acceptable in Seattle but not New Orleans. Decisions either allowing or prohibiting the use of race as a decisional criterion will not require extensive implementation effort. Extensive monitoring or planning to refine the policy through implementation would not be necessary.[13] Public policy in many settings other than university admissions offices would benefit from a coherent answer to this question since other plans hinge on it. But, like abortion and the death penalty, the Court cannot defend its authority to resolve the matter on the basis of a powerful political tradition comparable to the First Amendment tradition authorizing policies dealing with expression and religion. In fact, public feelings regarding the desirability of quotas seem clearly hostile to the concept. Large segments of the public may perceive themselves directly affected by policy responses. If the Court chooses to make national policy on this matter, it must do so with great care.

Fortunately (if only because it produces an unambiguous conclusion for this section), we can dispatch Douglas' second point more quickly. Here Douglas challenged the predictive validity of the Law School Admissions Test and hence its constitutional acceptability. This conclusion rests on technical assumptions that are neither linguistically nor experientially a routine of judicial decision making. (The statistical reasoning in *Furman* was equally suspect.) The possibility therefore exists that the Court will make policy erroneously, will make policy based on assumptions and conclusions that will be falsified conclusively. More important, the Court is not the only PMI capable of or motivated to answer the question. Both the Educational Testing Service and the nation's law schools presumably seek the most accurate predictors of performance. To the extent present predictors seem inadequate, reliably better information will emerge only through the familiar processes of experimentation. And experiments are hard to undertake, especially by law schools, when they are illegal.

CONCLUSION

These difficult choices reveal, not surprisingly, that the indicators do not necessarily simplify a judge's life. The indicators will in some instances simply cancel each other out. But can judges use them at all? Can judges facing the discretionary decision whether to proceed to formal hearing of a case ever know what they need to know to make these indicators meaningful? Not always, of course, and never with complete foresight. But judges can in some instances make rough but plausible answers to at least these questions:

Does the case raise problems that men with legal training and experience have any special competence to analyze?

Is this case likely to receive wide or narrow press coverage? Will it likely become a general campaign issue? Will virtually any available policy choice offend widespread political values and interests?

Are other PMIs currently actively attempting to deal with this policy issue, or is the policy issue presented to the court tangential or unrelated to issues on current electoral and/or bureaucratic agendas?

To what extent will the public perceive the issue as necessarily embodying values ingrained in both popular political philosophy and constitutional doctrine—freedom of speech and religion, due process of law—such that the courts may claim moral competence to make policy? To what extent, conversely, does the court run the risk of resolving normatively what is widely believed to be empirical, hence the risk of being perceived factually wrong?

The list is, hopefully, not exhaustive. Rough answers to such questions should, at least in the long run, advance the twin goals of wise policy and judicial legitimacy more effectively than no answers at all.

TABLE OF CASES

Baker v. Carr, 369 U.S. 186 (1962).
Brown v. Board of Education of Topeka, 347 U.S. 483 (1954).
De Funis v. Odegaard, 94 Sup.Ct. 1704 (1974).
Dred Scott v. Sandford, 60 U.S. 393 (1857).
Furman v. Georgia, 408 U.S. 238 (1972).
Gideon v. Wainwright, 372 U.S. 335 (1963).
Goss v. Lopez, 419 U.S. 565 (1975).
Griswold v. Connecticut, 381 U.S. 479 (1965).
Holtzman v. Schlesinger, 414 U.S. 1304 (1974).
McCollum v. Board of Education, 333 U.S. 203 (1948).
Miami Herald Publishing Co. v. Tornillo, 418 U.S. 241 (1974).
Miranda v. Arizona, 384 U.S. 436 (1966).
Roe v. Wade, 410 U.S. 113 (1973).
Roth v. United States, 354 U.S. 476 (1957).
San Antonio Independent School District v. Rodriguez, 93 Sup.Ct. 1278 (1973).
School District v. Schempp, 374 U.S. 203 (1963).
Southern Burlington NAACP v. Township of Mt. Laurel, 67 N.J. 151 (1975) at 160, appeal dismissed 96 Sup.Ct. 18 (1975).
United States v. Nixon, 418 U.S. 683 (1974).
Weinberger v. Wiesenfeld, 420 U.S. 636 (1975).
Wyatt v. Stickney, 344 F.Supp. 373 (1972).

NOTES

1. Courts of course make policy when they amplify common law. Courts now wrestle, for example, with the question of tort liability of psychiatrists who fail to warn those whom their patients state an intent to injure, for example, *Tarasoff v. Board of Regents*, 529 P.2d 553 (1974). And courts also make policy when they give concrete meaning to statutory language. In both areas, however, legislatures can alter judicial policy in the normal course of legislative business. We shall therefore confine the concept of judicial policymaking here to the realm of constitutional interpretation where the courts in the name of the Constitution nullify the policy choices of other policymakers. I therefore exclude from consideration those cases of judicial nullification, often "on technicalities," that do not restrict the ability of other governmental units to pursue their substantive policy objectives.
2. See also "A Judge in the Line of Fire," *The Atlanta Journal and Constitution Magazine*, October 12, 1975, p. 6 ff, discussing the career of Alabama Federal District Court Judge Frank M. Johnson and noting his more recent ruling prohibiting further prison admissions, on Eighth Amendment grounds, until their numbers have been reduced to the maximum design capacity of the unit.
3. See "Comment: Judicial Intervention in Political Party Disputes," *UCLA Law Review* 22 (1975): 622-53.
4. Clifton McCleskey, "Judicial Review in a Democracy: A Dissenting Opinion," *Houston Law Review* 3 (1966): 354-66.
5. See Malcolm Feeley and Theodore Becker, *The Impact of Supreme Court Decisions* (New York: Oxford University Press, 1973).
6. See the opinion of J. Brandeis in *Ashwander v. TVA*, 297 U.S. 288 (1936); Herbert Wechsler, *Principles, Politics, and Fundamental Law* (Cambridge: Harvard University Press, 1961); Alexander M. Bickel, *The Supreme Court and the Idea of Progress* (New York: Harper and Row, 1970).
7. The U.S. Supreme Court justice (or his clerk) no doubt finds the criteria expressed in the Court's Rule 19 regarding the granting of certiorari dispositive in many cases. Rule 19 does not dispose of all cases, but it does provide a partial answer to when courts should make policy that we do not further address here.
8. Walter Murphy, *Elements of Judicial Strategy* (Chicago: University of Chicago Press, 1964). Murphy has reviewed many of the strategic choices so elegantly that we hardly need to review them here. The decision whether to proceed is of course a strategic choice also, but our approach does not derive from the perspective of a judge seeking to advance his personal policy preferences but from the perspective of a judge concerned primarily with preserving the court's ability to protect its political position and to make and implement specific policy choices wisely. The reader should bear in mind, however, that judges will make the kinds of choices described here often in conditions of highly imperfect information and in considerable uncertainty about the probability to attach to each alternative outcome.
9. See, for example, Christopher Jencks, *Inequality* (New York: Basic Books, 1972).
10. See *Mahan v. Howell*, 93 Sup. Ct. 979 (1973).
11. Those suspected or accused of crime have never formed a potent lobby. Convicted prisoners are perhaps the least potent of all. As the late Earl Long reportedly said in response to suggestions to improve the deplorable conditions in the Louisiana prison named for an African nation, "There ain't any votes in Angola."
12. See Kenneth M. Dolbeare and Phillip E. Hammond, *The School Prayer Decisions* (Chicago: University of Chicago Press, 1971).

13. The intricate empirical complexities of the school finance equalization issue, raised in *San Antonio Independent School District v. Rodriguez* (1973), far exceeded those of either school desegregation or reapportionment. I have considerable doubt that the Court could have successfully articulated convincing national standards for dealing with this difficulty, and the task of supervising implementation in this area would have proved messy. Judicial abstention on institutional grounds in this case was probably prudent.

CHAPTER

9

SCHOOL DESEGREGATION:
A COST/BENEFIT
LONGITUDINAL ANALYSIS
Harrell R. Rodgers, Jr.
Charles S. Bullock, III

In a momentous 1954 decision the United States Supreme Court ordered southern schools desegregated "with all deliberate speed."[1] Almost in unanimity southern citizens and officials vowed that the order would never be implemented. Governor Griffin of Georgia reflected the southern mood when he pledged: "Come hell or high water races will not be mixed in Georgia schools."[2] More circumspectly the governor of Virginia promised to "use every legal means at my command to continue segregated schools."[3] But George Wallace became the principal spokesman for the "never" philosophy of the South with his defiant challenge: "I draw the line in the dust and toss the gauntlet before the feet of tyranny and I say segregation now, segregation tomorrow, segregation forever."[4] Recent history records the extreme recalcitrance of the South toward the Court's directive,[5] but by the early 1970s dual schools in the South had generally been replaced with unitary systems.[6]

Numerous studies reveal that laws and court decisions frequently are not implemented, even when there is no organized opposition.[7] Yet in the face of very considerable opposition, school desegregation was achieved in the South. The purpose of this chapter is to determine why. We pursue the answer to this question by investigating the factors associated with local compliance with school desegregation edicts in 31 Georgia school districts. Our study period

---

This chapter originally appeared in the April 1976 issue of the *American Politics Quarterly* and is reprinted by permission of the authors and Sage Publications, Inc. It is based on research made possible under Grants GS-38157 and GS-38158 from the National Science Foundation. This chapter is part of an ongoing stream of research in which we are alternating the authors' names to indicate that the studies are in every way joint efforts.

extends from the 1965-66 school year to 1973-74. Our major goal is to glean insight into the factors that influenced school officials to obey the law.[8] This orientation allows us to contribute theoretically and empirically to the increasingly sophisticated literature on individual compliance behavior.[9] Additionally, these findings will enhance understanding of the conditions that must prevail if a law is to accomplish its stated goals.

Two reasons prompted study of the implementation of school desegregation policy as a vehicle for understanding the ability of law to promote social change. First, it provided an opportunity to select communities for analysis in which law has led to various degrees of change. This facilitates identification and evaluation of factors critical in achieving various levels of school desegregation.[10] Second, because of widespread public opposition, insight into this area will advance our understanding of the problem of achieving social change under unfavorable conditions. Indeed school desegregation has been surrounded by as much controversy as any contemporary law. Measured by time, energy, and resources invested, progress in school desegregation has certainly been the most difficult of all civil rights objectives.[11]

RESEARCH DESIGN FOR THE MEASUREMENT AND EXPLANATION OF CHANGE

The 31 districts were chosen to insure the presence of maximum variation in progress and in conflict over the desegregation process. All Georgia districts were divided into six categories that reflected the degree of coercion necessary to achieve compliance.[12] On the basis of perceived accessibility, districts were chosen from each of these categories.[13] In each district personal interviews were conducted with past and present school officials (that is, superintendents, assistant superintendents, principals, assistant principals, and school-board members), local newspaper editors, and others identified as important in making or influencing school policy. The total was 250 and included both black and white respondents. The bulk of the interviews were conducted during the summer of 1973.[14]

The information gathered from local interviews was supplemented with and checked against articles in local newspapers, information obtained from the files of the Office for Civil Rights (OCR) of the Department of Health, Education and Welfare (HEW), personal interviews with OCR and Department of Justice officials, and census data.

Measuring Change—The Dependent Variable

Our immediate goals are to: (1) measure desegregation change over time (1965-66 to 1973-74); and (2) isolate those variables associated with change.

These objectives require a dependent variable that shows the amount of school desegregation annually in each district. The simplest method of doing this would have been to use the figures released by HEW each year and examine the annual proportion of black students attending majority-white schools. This percentage, however, lacks reliability since it would not account for the varying number of black students in each district. Obviously if in one district 10 percent of the student population is black and in another the black/white ratio is 50/50, a 10 percentage point change in each district in the number of black students attending school with whites could not be interpreted in the same way.[15]

The alternative chosen from several indexes considered and tested overcomes this problem and meets our needs extremely well.[16] The index of dissimilarity shows the discrepancy between the racial composition of all schools in a system and the racial mix of students attending public schools in the district. The standard of comparison is the percentage of black students in the public schools and the extent to which each school deviates from this percentage. Since HEW and the Department of Justice's compliance standards after 1968 were based on the ratio of black to white students in each school, the index is excellent for our analysis. For each school in the district the formula yields the absolute difference between the ratio of white students in a given school to total whites in the district and black students in the school to total blacks in the district. For the entire district the formula is computed:

$$\tfrac{1}{2} \sum_i |w_i/W - n_i/N|$$

where:

w_i = the white students in ith schools
n_i - the black students in ith schools.

For each year the index reveals the minimal percentage of minority students in the district who would have to change schools to achieve racial balance in all schools. The index ranges from 0 for complete racial balance to 100 for total racial isolation. For example, an index of 60 indicates that at least 60 percent of the black students in the public schools would have to be shifted before all schools in the district have the same percentages of black and white pupils.

Indexes of dissimilarity (Ds) were computed for each of our districts beginning with the 1965-66 school year and ending with 1973-74 (see Table 9.1). The Ds yield three important insights, First, by 1973-74 most of the districts were desegregated. A D index of 20 or below usually indicated maximum desegregation, or a close approximation.[17] Thus, unitary systems had been achieved in 23 of our districts by 1973-74. Three other districts had scores of 24 to 35, indicating only moderate segregation problems. Two of our districts had Ds above 40, indicating rather serious segregation problems, and 3 others were still heavily segregated (Ds of 60 or above). The five districts with serious segregation problems (Ds above 40) are located in urban areas and three have majority-black student populations.

Second, dual schools were eliminated in most districts within a two-year span. Twenty districts achieved racial balance in 1970 (Ds below 20) and five did so in 1969. Only one district was balanced as early as 1966 and two made progress very late (1972 and 1973).

Third, elimination of dual schools usually came in one or two drastic moves. Thirteen districts shifted from Ds of 90+ in one year to Ds of 24 or lower the next year. Four other districts with D 80 in one year eliminated dual schools the next year and another substantially reduced isolation (the D dropped from 83 in 1969 to 36 in 1970). Of the other districts that have desegregated, change usually occurred in one or two shifts of 30 to 40 points in the D index. Although gradual changes did occur in some of the districts (2 to 10 points change here and there), none eliminated its dual schools incrementally. Every district that was racially balanced by 1973-74 experienced major shifts.

Theoretical Framework

Conceptualizing compliance behavior in terms of utility theory facilitates the identification of those variables that could have influenced decision maker compliance with desegregation edicts. An underlying assumption of most compliance research, and one we believe warranted, is that individual compliance behavior can best be understood as the product of a cost-benefit calculus.[18] This theory stipulates that the average citizen frequently seeks to maximize his utilities by taking those compliance actions that yield the most pleasure and the least pain.[19] Thus citizens obey most laws because they perceive that the utilities of compliance outweigh the utilities of noncompliance. However, when citizens perceive that the utilities of the situation favor disobedience, they break the law. The individual's values and expectations (that is, perceptions about the positive and negative fulfillment of values) determine how he calculates the net pleasure/pain that he expects to result from a particular act. To understand compliance, therefore, we must understand the range of factors that enter into a calculation.

We can say that an individual will violate a particular law when he perceives that the utilities of noncompliance are greater than the utilities of compliance.[20] Symbolically this can be expressed

$$N_p > C_p$$

where:

TABLE 9.1

Desegregation Changes: Indexes of Dissimilarity

District	1965	1966	1967	1968	1969	1970	1971	1972	1973
Americus City	099	097	096	097	095	024	017	010	004
Atkinson	100	100	100	100	100	006	008	004	006
Atlanta City	098	098	097	095	093	086	083	081	079
Baker	095	085	094	093	093	002	012	013	000
Buford City	100	100	100	100	056	002	007	005	007
Clinch	096	092	090	058	042	011	009	004	006
Coffee	099	094	091	057	023	022	010	013	014
Decatur City	094	082	067	059	066	052	052	053	041
DeKalb	100	100	083	081	070	072	069	070	078
Dodge	099	098	093	060	056	006	008	010	011
Dougherty	097	093	092	092	092	075	064	063	063
Elbert	099	099	093	092	093	021	022	022	012
Gainsville City	100	098	097	085	012	009	009	011	016
Greene	100	100	099	099	096	015	015	009	012
Griffin-Spaulding	098	095	093	081	060	021	025	029	030
Hancock	099	097	098	098	094	087	083	082	024

Jeff Davis	099	090	087	087	084	002	004	005	003
Jefferson City	019	019	003	024	015	014	013	008	008
Lee	100	098	097	097	097	005	004	003	007
Lincoln	100	100	099	099	099	023	005	010	001
Madison	098	082	076	076	076	029	031	033	035
McDuffie	100	100	099	098	097	011	010	010	010
Miller	100	100	100	100	100	004	006	003	002
Mitchell	100	099	098	098	098	006	000	002	002
Morgan County	100	100	100	098	096	007	003	005	003
Oconee	099	093	085	076	006	003	002	004	005
Richmond	099	098	096	095	090	079	072	041	043
Rockdale	097	094	090	082	005	008	008	005	004
Taylor	100	100	100	100	100	007	017	017	016
Tift	100	098	095	083	083	036	036	006	008
Wilkes	099	099	098	094	099	004	003	004	002

Source: Compiled by the author.

N_p = the utility of breaking the law
C_p = the utility of obeying the law

Both N_p and C_p have subunits. N consists of the sum of the expected benefits of noncompliance minus the costs of noncompliance, and C is the sum of the expected benefits of compliance minus the costs of compliance. Therefore we would expect noncompliance with a particular law when:[21]

$$B_n - Co_n > B_c - Co_c$$

where:

B_n = a positive value denoting the expected benefits of committing violation n.
Co_n = a negative value denoting the expected costs of n.
B_c = a positive value denoting the expected benefits of compliance.
Co_c = a negative value denoting the expected costs of noncompliance.

The value of the terms in the formula vary with each compliance situation. For example, for a particular law B_n might involve financial gain, expected power and prestige, or simply convenience. Co_n might include the perceived certainty of formal or informal sanctions, or internal pressures such as one's sense of self-condemnation. B_c could consist of maintaining personal esteem financial gains, or receiving the esteem of others. Co_c could be considerable inconvenience, ostracism, or increased responsibilities.

This shows the range of considerations that are involved in a compliance decision. While the average person typically lacks the information (or even the inclination at times) necessary to make perfect calculations (for example, the chance of punishment is often unknown), and while his values will vary over time, utility theory directs our attention to the type of vectors that should influence compliance behavior.

If we want to understand school officials' desegregation decisions, therefore, cost/benefit theory would lead to an examination of factors that influenced decision makers' perceptions of the utilities of compliance.

Independent Variables

Our selection of independent variables reflects those factors that could have produced desegregation changes. If a factor was constant over time, it could not have directly influenced change. Therefore we do not examine here variables such as districts' racial and economic characteristics. These and a number of decision-maker attitudinal variables frequently proved to be important threshold variables but their direct impact was negligible.[22] The independent variables selected for analysis, however, varied significantly over time and could have accounted directly for changes in school desegregation. We did not investigate the direct impact of a number of decision-maker attitudinal variables because our research design did not allow us to code attitude by year. Our resources did allow us to code the independent variables considered by year.

Coercion

Previous studies provide considerable insight into the factors that generally determine how decision makers evaluate the cost/benefits of a law. For this study the most obvious vector suggested by extant literature is coercion. Studies demonstrate quite clearly that unpopular laws will usually not be obeyed unless they are vigorously enforced.[23] For example, Milner speculated that one reason the Supreme Court's decision in the *Miranda* case was not implemented by the police in the four cities he studied was that enforcement was lacking.[24] Similarly, Dolbeare and Hammond concluded that prayers continued in public schools in part because of the lack of an enforcement agency.[25] Wirt[26] and Rodgers and Bullock[27] concluded that compliance with various civil rights laws was proportionate to the quality of enforcement efforts by the federal government. These findings seem quite logical for our study since it seems clear that desegregation would not have resulted without coercion. As one school official said: "All-black schools would not have been eliminated in the South without pressure—not in my lifetime." Thus:

H1: Progress in school desegregation was influenced by federal coercion.

To test this hypothesis a yearly coercion index was generated for each district that reflects simply whether significant federal coercion was present.[28] We know that the degree of federal coercion needed to eliminate dual schools varied according to certain district characteristics.[29] Our concern here, however, is not with the degree of coercion necessary to produce change but with the more basic question of whether coercion preceded change; and, if so, the relative importance of coercion compared to other variables.

Black Activism

A second independent variable that might have influenced yearly changes in school desegregation is the degree of pressure within the community for compliance with the law. At least three major studies have concluded that the impact of a law is significantly determined by the cohesiveness, activity, and resources of those who would benefit from compliance.[30] These studies found that organization and agitation raise the costs of noncompliance by putting pressure on recalcitrant officials. However, a study by Kirby and Crain concluded that civil rights demonstrations were not associated with school desegregation in northern communities.[31] Kirby and Crain's study may not be comparable to ours since little federal pressure to desegregate was applied in the communities they studied. At the time of their analysis the courts had yet to adequately spell out the obligations of northern districts.[32] Thus:

> H2: Progress in school desegregation was associated with black pressure for compliance.

Black activism in a district was considered to be present if in a particular year demonstrations occurred, or group pressure tactics were employed.[33]

Organized White Opposition to Desegregation

While previous studies indicate that decision makers normally retain ample jurisdiction and authority when responding to compliance demands to make their decisions reflect (at least partially) their personal inclinations, several studies have found officials' compliance behavior somewhat constrained by public opinion or constituent pressures.[34] It is reasonable to expect that school officials, like other decision makers, are sometimes constrained by their constituents' attitudes toward, and actions in response to, certain issues. This might be particularly likely when a highly emotional issue such as school desegregation is involved. If local whites strongly opposed desegregation and were organized to thwart the process, this might raise considerably the costs of compliance. However, Kirby and Crain reported that white opposition to desegregation was ineffective in the northern communities they studied.[35] We are ambivalent about whether Kirby and Crain's findings are applicable to our data. Our communities tended to be rural and Kirby and Crain's were urban. In rural areas we would expect public officials to be more isolated and vulnerable to pressure. Also in our communities the intensity of opposition seemed greater than in the communities studied by Kirby and Crain. Still, our interviews indicate that organized opposition to desegregation may have occurred too late to significantly influence desegregation. Thus, admitting uncertainty, we test the hypothesis that:

> H3: Progress in school desegregation was not impeded by organized white opposition.

The yearly index for white opposition measured organized activities such as demonstrations, planned mass attendance by large numbers of hostile whites at school board meetings, petitions, and other lobbying activities.[36]

Private Schools

A number of school officials stated that the establishment of a private, segregated school in their district aided progress in school desegregation.[37] Their reasoning was that the private, segregated school drew off the children of the most vocal and active white racists in the district, making it easier for officials to comply with the law. Thus:

> H4: The establishment of a private, segregated school was associated with progress in school desegregation.

This index reflects the establishment of a school specifically for the purpose of providing a refuge for the children of white parents who did not want their children to attend schools with blacks.[38]

Superintendent Change

School superintendents frequently played a key role in desegregation decisions. They were the local decision makers most often in contact with federal officials and they frequently set the meed for desegregation negotiations. A change in a district school superintendent, therefore, could have a considerable impact on desegregation, either positive or negative. In some districts which had long held out on desegregation, the superintendent was frequently the leader of the segregationist forces. In fact, in several of the 11 districts in which school superintendents resigned between 1967 and 1970, the ex-superintendent became head of the newly established private, segregationist school in the community. Thus, resistance to desegregation might be reduced to some extent if the district obtained a new superintendent. The new superintendent might be under pressure from constituents but usually he was younger than his predecessor and often more liberal in his racial attitudes. Additionally, the new superintendent might feel no need to continue resistance for the purpose of defending past recalcitrance.[39]

However, in several other communities the superintendent was literally run out of town by rabid segregationists because his loyalty to segregation and dedication to resistance were questioned. Therefore, in these communities the new superintendent would undoubtedly be an individual who could be trusted to resist desegregation as long and as vigorously as possible.

Our data suggest that the former situation was more common than the latter.[40] Therefore, again admitting uncertainty, we test the proposition that:

> H5: School superintendent change was associated with progress in school desegregation.

Methodology

Two data-analysis techniques were employed. Pearson's r was used to determine the simple correlation between each independent variable and the dependent variable. In addition, multiple regression was employed to determine whether the independent variables account for a significant proportion of the statistical variance in school desegregation. For each school year the lagged independent variables were correlated and regressed against the index of dissimilarity.[41]

RESEARCH FINDINGS

Coercion

As Table 9.2 shows, the analysis reveals little significance for the independent variables except for 1970-71. Before and after this school year there was too little variance in desegregation levels for significant relationships to emerge. However for 1970-71, the year of major change, the analysis is quite insightful. The simple correlation for coercion was .71, indicating a very significant role for this variable. It seems clear that without coercion, major change would not have occurred. Still, the analysis reveals that the mere presence of coercion in any particular year was not necessarily sufficient to produce major change. By 1967 the districts were under pressure to achieve some desegregation but 25 of the districts still had Ds of 90 or above. Thus it usually took several years of pressure, and in many instances several degrees of pressure, to achieve significant desegregation.[42] Thus, in 1968-69 and 1969-70 coercion correlated positively (indicating segregation rather than desegregation) with the Ds because generally only token changes were occurring.

Black Activity

Contrary to our expectations, black activity proved to be an indication of segregation rather than desegregation. Consistent with Kirby and Crain's analysis, blacks seemed to have become active when their district was slow to desegregate but their activities did not produce the desired change. The correlations for black activity were -.06 in 1968-69, -.24 in 1969-70, and -.79 in 1970-71. The significant correlations for the latter two years are negative, indicating that segregation remained rather high in districts in which blacks were the most active.

The explanation for the persistence of segregation in districts in which blacks were most active varies according to whether the district was rural or

TABLE 9.2

Correlates of Desegregation Change: 1967-68 to 1970-71

SCHOOL YEAR	SIMPLE r
1967-68	
Coercion	.15
Black Pressure	-.07
White Opposition	-.07
Private Schools	.01
1968-69	
Coercion	-.36
Black Pressure	-.06
White Opposition	.07
Private Schools	-.20
1969-70	
Coercion	-.17
Black Pressure	-.24
White Opposition	.07
Private Schools	.02
Superintendent Change	-.09
1970-71	
Coercion	.71
Black Pressure	-.79
White Opposition	-.11
Private Schools	-.34
Superintendent Change	-.28

Note: All signs were reversed to make positive correlations indicate desegregation and negative signs indicate segregation.
Source: Compiled by the author.

urban. Four of the eight districts in which black activity occurred were rural. In these districts (some of our most recalcitrant), whites had such a firm grip on power that they could simply ignore black demands. Kirby and Crain additionally concluded that:

> One reason why civil rights activity has little impact is that the nonviolent demonstration is not a strong coercive device. Since they can really do little financial or other harm there is little reason for the

school administrators not to ignore a sit-in, street demonstration or boycott.[43]

We suspect that Kirby and Crain are only half right. Nonviolent demonstrations were very effective in promoting black enfranchisement and in bringing down the barriers to public accommodations because they provoked federal intervention.[44] However, in these communities black activity neither stimulated much publicity nor increased federal aid for efforts to achieve desegregation; thus local blacks were left isolated and impotent.

The situation in the four urban districts was somewhat different. In these districts blacks filed private suits against the schools. When private suits were filed, HEW and the Department of Justice, in keeping with their usual policy in Georgia, discontinued supervision of these districts and left the matter to the plaintiffs. At the time of the decision in the private suits, the Supreme Court had not rendered the *Swann* decision[45] and therefore cross-district busing was not required in court orders desegregating these large urban districts. Thus even though these districts came into compliance with final court orders by 1970-71, the orders allowed considerable segregation to remain. Less populous rural districts that desegregated before *Swann* had such small student populations that the only feasible plans for establishing unitary schools necessitated complete desegregation. This was not true in urban areas and since the desegregation orders of these districts have not been updated to require complete racial balance, the districts remain both in compliance and considerably segregated. In the final analysis, then, black activity was the agent of the change in the urban districts but these activities did not produce racial balance in all schools.

One finding from the Kirby and Crain analysis is not supported here. They concluded that an additional reason that civil rights demonstrations were ineffective was that demonstrations created a backlash among white elites.[46] However, at the aggregate level we found no relationship between black activity in a district and the attitudes of white elites.[47]

White Opposition

Hypothesis 3 proved correct. Organized white opposition occurred in only nine communities, coming chiefly in 1969-70 and 1970-71. The correlations for the four school years shown in Table 9.2 (the strongest correlation being -.11 for 1970-71) indicate that white opposition had a negligible impact on desegregation. Organized opposition seems to have occurred when desegregation began or was imminent. Before it became obvious that desegregation was about to occur, whites apparently saw no need to demonstrably oppose the process since school officials were successfully thwarting federal objectives. By the time whites did organize, it was a rearguard action just before or after dual schools were eliminated. The tardiness of organized opposition rendered it futile.

This does not mean, of course, that unorganized white opposition to desegregation did not play a role over the years in slowing desegregation. The in-depth interviews indicated that decision makers almost universally perceived public resistance to desegregation and were concerned about it. At the very least this resistance reinforced the opposition of many of the school officials and in some instances it undoubtedly restricted their compliance activities. White resistance, therefore, was at least in part responsible for school officials delaying desegregation until federal pressure became compelling. But only after school officials made obvious plans to comply did organized opposition occur. These activities simply occurred too late.

Once dual schools were abolished and it became apparent that white opposition could not resurrect the status quo ante, opposition quickly subsided. Since 1971 there has been little organized opposition by whites in the communities studied.

Private Schools

Excluding three urban areas,[48] 17 districts established private, segregated schools. The interviews revealed that private schools were frequently established in districts that were the most resistant to change, and that they were organized and supported by parents who did not want their children to attend desegregated schools. We hypothesized that establishment of these schools contributes to progress in school desegregation. The analysis did not support this expectation. The simple correlation between private schools and desegregation was -.20 in 1968-69, .02 in 1969-70, and -.34 in 1970-71. The negative correlations for two of the three years indicates that private schools were associated with segregation rather than desegregation. Private schools, in other words, most frequently indicated a highly resistant district.

The in-depth interviews yielded insight into why the correlation between private schools and segregation is not stronger. In some districts the private schools were established after the district had agreed to dismantle its dual schools. Thus, in these communities private, segregated schools were established too late to have any real impact on desegregation.

Superintendent Change

For the 1970-71 academic year, the analysis seems modestly to support hypothesis 5. The correlation between superintendent change and desegregation is .28. The positive correlation indicates that districts that obtained a new superintendent in 1969 desegregated the next fall. The correlation indicates that changing a superintendent can be important in determining desegregation progress although this condition is much less significant than coercion.

Multivariate Analysis

The regression results are consistent with the bivariate analysis. Like the correlation analysis, the regression is insightful only for the 1970-71 academic year when 20 districts desegregated. The regression for that year revealed that coercion and superintendent change were the only significant factors associated with desegregation, with coercion being extremely important (beta = .70). If we removed from our sample the four districts that desegregated pursuant to private suits rather than federal pressure, the significance of coercion is even more dramatic. In 1970-71, the simple r for coercion was .76, and the beta was .78. In 1970-71, coercion alone accounted for 58.5 percent of the variance in desegregation change in nonprivate suit districts. Thus coercion was by far the most significant single factor in producing school desegregation.

The beta for superintendent change was .26. When coercion and superintendent change are combined, the multiple r is .75, accounting for .57 percent of the variance in school desegregation in all the districts for 1970-71.

SUMMARY AND CONCLUSIONS

Our findings yield support for a cost/benefit theory of compliance. School officials generally obeyed desegregation edicts only when the costs of noncompliance became high enough to outweigh other considerations. Change primarily occurred when federal coercion created pressures severe enough to compel desegregation. As one of our respondents said: "We did just enough to stay out of jail. That's why segregation lasted so long." Black activity in rural areas was incapable of producing desegregation, but black actions in urban districts resulted in court orders requiring desegregation. However, because of the timing and the size of the districts involved, the court orders allowed the urban districts to comply and yet remain highly segregated.

Organized white opposition to desegregation occurred too late to seriously delay the elimination of dual schools. Even though local whites typically opposed desegregation, they usually failed to organize until after their district was committed to a final desegregation plan. This meant that whites had to try to reverse a decision rather than prevent one, which was more than they could do.

We hypothesized that the establishment of a private, segregated school in a district would promote desegregation. This hypothesis proved incorrect. Private schools frequently indicated considerable opposition to compliance and tended to be associated with segregation rather than desegregation.

A change in school superintendents in a community seemed to have a modest impact on desegregation. The removal of superintendents who had a personal, psychological stake in segregation and their replacement with individuals who evaluated the costs of desegregation as less severe made desegregation somewhat easier.

In the final analysis, the major point emphasized by the research is that coercion may be extremely critical to obtaining compliance with certain types of laws.[49] In our districts, compliance with the *Brown* decision finally occurred 16 or so years after the Supreme Court ruled de jure segregation to be unconstitutional. Without federal coercion, de jure segregation would undoubtedly still prevail in most of our districts and in most of the South.

NOTES

1. *Brown v. Board of Education of Topeka*, 347 U.S. 483 (1954).
2. Quoted in Benjamin Muse, *Ten Years of Prelude: The Story of Integration Since the Supreme Court's 1954 Decision* (New York: Viking Press, 1964), p. 24.
3. Ibid.
4. Quoted in "Federal Enforcement of School Desegregation," *Report of the United States Commission on Civil Rights*, September 11, 1969, p. 2.
5. The literature is considerable here but for a review see Harrell R. Rodgers, Jr. and Charles S. Bullock, III, *Law and Social Change: Civil Rights Laws and Their Consequences* (New York: McGraw-Hill, 1972), pp. 69-111.
6. In *Alexander v. Holmes County*, 396 U.S. 19 (1969), the Supreme Court required de jure systems to immediately terminate dual school systems based on race and operate only unitary school systems. They defined a unitary system as one "Within which no person is to be effectively excluded from any school because of race or color."
7. For examples, see Neal Milner, *The Court and Local Law Enforcement: The Impact of Miranda* (Beverly Hills: Sage Publications, 1971); Frederick Wirt, *Politics of Southern Equality: Law and Social Change in a Mississippi County* (Chicago: Aldine, 1970); Kenneth Dolbeare and Phillip Hammond, *The School Prayer Decisions: From Court Policy to Local Practice* (Chicago: University of Chicago Press, 1971).
8. By compliance we mean overt behavior that is in accord with the law. See Don W. Brown and Robert V. Stover, "An Economic Approach to Compliance with Court Decisions," paper presented at the annual meeting of the American Political Science Association, Chicago, August 29-September 2, 1974.
9. See the studies cited in note 7 and Kenneth Dolbeare, "The Supreme Court and the States: From Abstract Doctrine to Local Behavioral Conformity," in Theodore L. Becker, ed., *The Impact of Supreme Court Decisions* (New York: Oxford University Press, 1969), pp. 206-13; Joel B. Grossman and Mary H. Grossman, eds., *Law and Change in Modern America* (Pacific Palisades, Calif.: Goodyear, 1971), pp. 1-10; H. Frank Way, "Survey Research on Judicial Decisions: The Prayer and Bible Reading Cases," *Western Political Quarterly* 21 (June 1968): 187-205; Gordon M. Patric, "The Impact of a Court Decision: Aftermath of the McCollum Case," *Journal of Public Law* 6 (Fall 1965): 455-63; Frank

Sorauf, "Zorach v. Clauson: The Impact of a Supreme Court Decision," *American Political Science Review* 53 (September 1959): 777-91; Robert H. Birkby, "The Supreme Court and the Bible Belt: Tennessee Reaction to the 'Schempp' Decision," *Midwest Journal of Political Science* 10 (August 1966): 304-15; Ellis Katz, "Patterns of Compliance with the Schempp Decision," *Journal of Public Law* 14 (Fall 1965): 396-408.

10. While building on earlier research we have sought to improve on it in three ways. First, we have made certain that there is variance in our dependent variable. Second, we included enough units of analysis to allow for hypotheses formulation and testing. Third, our research has a theoretical orientation and is tested with multivariate statistics.

11. See Rodgers and Bullock, op. cit., pp. 69-111.

12. The compliance categories were: (1) voluntary compliance; (2) Justice Department enforcement of Title VI; (3) private litigation; (4) loss of federal funds but state funds not threatened; (5) threatened loss of state funds; and (6) loss of federal funds and threatened loss of state funds.

13. We pondered long on how to select the school districts. Ideally we would have preferred to draw a random sample of districts based on one of the independent variables. However, it was essential to our research design that our sample include a significant number of districts that represented each of six compliance categories. Dividing the districts by compliance categories and then drawing a random sample would not have suffice because there would have been too few districts in some of the categories. Consequently we purposefully selected districts that represented each compliance category with an eye toward the geographical location of the district, its overall desegregation experience, and perceived accessibility.

14. To accommodate work and vacation schedules we had to conduct some of the local interviews as late as May 1974.

15. We computed another index formulated by Farley and Taeuber known as the index of replacement. After testing it against the index of dissimilarity it was rejected because it allows less variance than does the index of dissimilarity (the former ranges from 0 to 50 while the latter ranges from 0 to 100). Both the index of dissimilarity and the replacement index are explained in Reynolds Farley and Alma F. Taeuber, "Racial Segregation in the Public Schools," *American Journal of Sociology* 79 (May 1974): 893-98. We also considered and rejected two other familiar measures of change because they are also based on assumptions that are unacceptable for school desegregation. The first was a measure of relative change represented by the formula where:

T_1 = Percentage of school desegregation achieved at Time 1
T_2 = Percentage of school desegregation achieved at Time 2
M = Maximum possible desegregation: 100 percent

This formula also distorted our data. For example, if a district changed from 20 to 40 percent desegregation from one year to the next, the formula would show a 25 percent change. However, if a district changed from 50 to 70 percent desegregation, it would show a 40 percent change. This formula, in other words, contains the opposite bias of the relative change formula. That is, the assumption is that change is hardest when progress in school desegregation is already high. Obviously this is an assumption that is frequently not correct. Additionally the formula makes no distinction between the number of blacks in school districts and it contains perhaps an unrealistic assumption—that districts are required by law to achieve 100 percent desegregation.

16. Ibid.

17. A district could achieve or approach maximum desegregation and not score 0 on the index because of unequal distributions of students by race at various age levels. For example, at the high-school level, white students frequently outnumbered blacks because of higher dropout rates for blacks. If the ratio of black to white students in a district was 50-50 at the elementary level and 40-60 at the high school level, the D index would exceed 0 even

if maximum desegregation had been achieved. The index is also modestly affected by sexual segregation in some districts, and the number of schools for each grade level in a district (for example, one high school versus six elementary schools).

18. See Robert V. Stover and Don W. Brown, "Understanding Compliance and Noncompliance with Law: The Contribution of Utility Theory," *Social Science Quarterly* 56 (1975): 363-75, mimeographed; Gary S. Becker, "Crime and Punishment: An Economic Approach," *Journal of Political Economy* 16 (March-April 1968): 160-217; George J. Stigler, "The Optimum Enforcement of Law," *Journal of Political Economy* 18 (May-June 1970): 526-36.

19. The literature suggests that citizens obey many laws without subjecting them to evaluation. However, a variety of circumstances lead citizens to evaluate laws. See the concept of the "Zone of Indifference" in Chester I. Barnard, *The Functions of the Executive* (Cambridge, Mass.: Harvard University Press, 1938), pp. 167-70.

20. This formulation is taken from Stover and Brown, "Understanding Compliance and Noncompliance." See also Stover and Brown, "An Economic Approach to Compliance."

21. This formulation is taken from Stover and Brown but we have altered the formula slightly.

22. This analysis is carried out in Charles S. Bullock, III and Harrell R. Rodgers, Jr., "Coercion To Compliance: Southern School Districts and School Desegregation Guidelines," mimeographed.

23. See Malcolm Feeley, "Coercion and Compliance: A New Look at an Old Problem," *Law and Society Review* 4 (May 1970): 505-19.

24. Milner, op. cit., pp. 48-68.

25. Dolbeare and Hammond, op. cit., p. 8.

26. Wirt, op. cit., pp. 281-92.

27. Rodgers and Bullock, *Law and Social Change*, pp. 192-202.

28. This variable was coded 1 for no pressure and 5 if any meaningful pressure was being placed on the district. Signs of pressure were on-site visits by HEW, notification of an HEW hearing, a court suit or court order, an HEW threat of fund termination, a termination of federal funds, or a threat to terminate state funds. Information for this variable was obtained from the in-depth interviews. School officials' perceptions were checked against reports of federal activity in local newspapers and summaries of HEW and Department of Justice activity in each community.

29. See Charles S. Bullock, III and Harrell R. Rodgers, Jr., "Coercion to Compliance."

30. Milner, op. cit., pp. 65-68; Wirt, op. cit., p. 283; Rodgers and Bullock, *Law and Social Change*, pp. 185-91.

31. David J. Kirby and Robert L. Crain, "The Functions of Conflict: School Desegregation in 91 Cities," *Social Science Quarterly* 55 (September 1974): 487.

32. See Harrell R. Rodgers, Jr., "The Supreme Court and School Desegregation: Twenty Years Later," *Political Science Quarterly* 89 (Winter 1974-75): 763-75.

33. This variable was coded 1 for no pressure; 3 for minor activities, such as small meetings or complaints to school officials; and 5 if a lawsuit was filed, demonstrations held, or group pressure tactics were employed.

34. Dolbeare and Hammond, op. cit., p. 7; Wirt, op. cit., pp. 282-83; Rodgers and Bullock, *Law and Social Change*, pp. 189-92.

35. Kirby and Crain, op. cit., p. 490.

36. This variable was coded 1 for no pressure; 3 for minor activities such as complaints to school officials (by letter or phone); and 5 for demonstrations, petitions, mass attendance at school-board meetings, and so forth.

37. Because the D index measures the racial mix of students in the public schools it would be possible to have simultaneously white flight and increases in desegregation.

38. This variable was coded 1 for no private school; 3 for one or more private schools with a minor enrollment (under 200 students); and 5 for private schools with 200 or more students.

39. Psychologists point out that most people have a strong need to be correct. Thus, once decision makers decide not to obey a law or decide that a law is invalid, they may resist ever obeying the law because this would be an admission that their earlier behavior was wrong. See Charles A. Kiesler and Sara B. Kiesler, *Conformity* (Cambridge, Mass.: Addison-Wesley, 1969), pp. 42-44.

40. This variable was coded 1 for superintendent change and 5 for no change.

41. A standard lag factor of one year was used.

42. See Bullock and Rodgers, "Coercion to Compliance."

43. Kirby and Crain, op. cit., p. 487.

44. See Charles S. Bullock, III and Harrell R. Rodgers, Jr., *Racial Equality in America: In Search of an Unfulfilled Goal* (Pacific Palisades, Calif.: Goodyear, 1975), pp. 15-51.

45. *Swann v. Charlotte-Mecklenburg Board of Education*, 402 U.S. 1 (1971).

46. Kirby and Crain, op. cit., p. 489.

47. We tapped elite attitudes toward desegregation with four measures. None of these variables correlated significantly with black activity. The questions were: (1) What are your personal preferences on school desegregation? (2) Have they changed over the years? (3) Basically, do you believe integration has improved or hurt the achievement of students in your schools? (4) Has it had any effect on race relations?

48. These areas long had private schools and thus it was unnecessary for parents in these areas to develop new ones.

49. We are not suggesting that manipulating coercion would produce compliance with all laws. Still, with civil rights laws and many other public policies we believe the evidence supports the efficacy of coercion. However, we suspect that law is an inappropriate vehicle for pursuing many of the policy goals it is currently used for; and, therefore, increased coercion would be useless. The policy goals implicit in many of the laws designed to punish victimless crimes are basically unattainable (for example, discouraging homosexuality). Additionally, law cannot be effective if its goals are unrealistic. For example, short of some drastic measure such as mass execution of criminals, even very severe penalties for crime will be unlikely to promote substantial crime reductions. For some people, those who are discriminated against, unemployed, and suppressed, crime is frequently their most viable economic alternative. Thus until the conditions that spawn crime are eradicated, even highly coercive laws can play only a limited role. Last, we are sensitive to the fact that some degree of coercion could be incompatible with democratic freedoms. In the extreme case it could become tyranny. Our focus, however, is on public policies designed to ensure fundamental rights that are sometimes subverted by recalcitrant minorities (often entrenched elites). Here we believe coercion is efficacious and compatible with democratic freedoms.

CHAPTER
10
THE POLITICS AND ECONOMICS OF PHARMACEUTICAL REGULATION
David Seidman

"If thalidomide cured leukemia, it would be on the market today," or so a Food and Drug Administration lawyer told me.* The claim is surely correct. But thalidomide is only a sedative, and an army of deformed babies is too high a price for the bit of calm that thalidomide might produce. That price would be worth risking, however, for a sure-fire cure of a fatal disease.

The decision to approve or prohibit the marketing of a drug is often a difficult one, because no drug is perfectly safe if it is powerful enough to be useful. Aspirin, for example, "has been said or shown to interfere with platelet function, to cause allergic reactions in the sensitive, to induce exfoliation of renal epithelial cells, to initiate gastric and to exacerbate duodenal ulcer, and to aggravate liver disease under certain circumstances," and is known to cause gastric bleeding in normal use (Ingelfinger 1974, p. 1197). The decision to approve turns on the balance of the possible benefits and the risks to health and even life. Assessing the balance is difficult, because neither the risks nor the benefits can be known precisely, and in any case must be evaluated in terms of values that cannot easily be stated or quantified and that may not be consensual.

Since 1962, policy in the United States, roughly speaking, has been to allow marketing of only those pharmaceuticals demonstrated to be safe and effective. The pattern of implementation of this policy by the Food and Drug

---

*This statement and others in this chapter are from interviews conducted with various officials in Washington. While not all interviewees cared whether their statements remained anonymous, all quotations from these interviews will be anonymous here.

The views expressed in this chapter are those of the author and are not necessarily those of the Social Science Research Council.

Administration (FDA) is, of course, not fully specified by law: the FDA both writes the regulations called for in legislation and has discretion within those regulations. The legislated policy and the pattern of FDA implementation are likely to have effects going well beyond the availability of any particular drugs: FDA decisions on marketing become part of the costs of developing new drugs. Criticism of both the policy and the FDA's actions is common. There are, in broad outline, two schools of critical thought. One holds that drugs are too readily approved for marketing. The other holds that drugs are too readily rejected. There is, unfortunately, no obvious way to decide who is right.

There have been several attempts to evaluate the impact of the policy and its implementation. This chapter examines these evaluations and their exceedingly chilly reception by the policy community. This is, then, a case study of the politics of policy evaluation.

I begin with a brief overview of the drug market and the regulatory structure and then discuss dilemmas inherent in this kind of regulation. Following this, I turn to the alternative approaches to evaluation and then discuss the interplay of evaluators and institutions, which I have called the politics of evaluation. Only prescription drugs will be considered. Though some of the questions are identical, over-the-counter drugs will be ignored.

THE REGULATORY CONTEXT

Understanding of the politics of evaluation depends, at least in part, upon some familiarity with the nature of the market for pharmaceuticals and of the regulatory structure.

The Market for Pharmaceuticals

The ultimate consumer of pharmaceuticals, the patient, does not fit the classical model of the free-market consumer because, incompetent himself to evaluate pharmaceuticals, he leaves the choice of a product to the doctor. The patient-consumer is therefore not sovereign. Rather, the doctor's preferences, willingness to run risks, and information produce the fact that "... for practical purposes, fully informed patient participation in the selection and use of prescription drugs is an illusory goal" (Merrill 1973, p. 8).

Though he makes the choices, the doctor does not bear the financial and other costs of taking the drugs. He is insulated from the consequences of his actions, and may therefore not have the consumer's normal incentive to be well informed. Without conducting large controlled experiments, he will not learn greatly from experience. The professional literature is too vast for anyone to master. Typically, the doctor relies heavily upon information provided by the drug manufacturer.

The manufacturer's incentive to provide information is strong: sales depend upon it. Vast quantities are therefore provided to the doctors (U.S. Congress 1972, pp. 54-59; Applied Management Sciences 1974). But there is far less incentive to provide accurate information, or to care whether the drugs sold do the patient any good (U.S. Congress 1972, pp. 59-70). Thus manufacturers generally make more extensive promotion claims but provide less information about potential hazards when selling their drugs in Latin America than they do in the more tightly regulated markets of the United States (Silverman 1976). Doctors and patients cannot independently check the manufacturer's information, at least in the short run. The word may eventually get around, but within broad limits, manufacturers are free from the consequences of providing misinformation, except such consequences as may be provided by regulators. Liability law is only a weak supplement to market incentives: "Current theories of liability offer uncertain prospects of recovery against a manufacturer of prescription drugs" (Merrill 1973, p. 49).

The market, then, is imperfect, even perverse. Regulation, therefore, polices the market, and in particular is aimed at the problems created by poor information.

Pre-1962 Regulation

The Food and Drugs Act of 1906 (34 Stat. 768) first regulated a drug market that was chaotic and dangerous (Adams 1905). The Food, Drug, and Cosmetic Act of 1938 (52 Stat. 1040; see Toulmin 1963) created something resembling the present regulatory structure. Under it, manufacturers had to file a New Drug Application (NDA) with the FDA presenting evidence that the drug was safe for use under certain specified conditions. The FDA had 60 days in which to reject the application (there were very limited grounds for rejection). Unless rejected, the NDA became "effective," and the drug could be marketed. (Actually, it was the entry of a "new drug" into interstate commerce which the NDA governed.)

In order that the drug could be tested before marketing, there was an exemption to these requirements for investigations by "qualified" investigators. These tests—including those on human subjects—were, for all practical purposes, unsupervised by the FDA or anyone else.

The act speaks only of safety, but safety is closely linked to the effectiveness of a drug, so the FDA in principle took effectiveness into account in considering the NDA. FDA Commissioner Larrick explained the pre-1962 FDA approach in testimony given in 1964:

> Basically drugs have certain degrees of toxicity. If we had used the term "safety" in the dictionary definition, we would have taken

nitroglycerin off the market, sulfanilamide off the market, and drugs of the value of insulin off the market. It was obvious to us as administrators that was not what Congress intended. So taking what we thought was the legislative history of this section into account, we then announced to the world . . . that in dealing with lifesaving drugs we would have to consider whether a drug was effective in considering safety. [U.S. Congress 1964-44, Part I, p. 185; see also Sellers and Grundstein 1940, pp. 95-96 and n. 119, for an early semiofficial statement of this position.]

Attention to effectiveness was, however, limited: the FDA could not require evidence of effectiveness in an NDA.

The system, then, allowed widespread use of a drug—for investigational purposes—with virtually no government controls, required some evidence that the drug was safe before it could be marketed, and almost totally ignored the drug after marketing approval was given. The consumer, the patient, therefore had some reasonable assurance that the drugs he bought had, at one point in their history, been shown, on the basis of some evidence, not to be strikingly unsafe. There was less assurance that the drug was useful. And there was no assurance of anything in the case of drugs that the consumer did not buy but, rather, was given by a doctor conducting an informal bit of research with an "investigational" drug.

Thalidomide

This regulatory structure kept thalidomide off the market in the United States, thereby preventing the sort of tragedy that occurred elsewhere (Mintz 1967; Harris 1964). But the American experience with thalidomide was unsettling anyway. Disaster was prevented through a combination of luck and the sort of dedication and courage that any system would be unwise to assume as typical. (President Kennedy awarded a gold medal for distinguished government service to Dr. Frances O. Kelsey, the FDA medical officer who blocked the marketing of thalidomide on the grounds that the testing had been inadequate.) Furthermore, thalidomide was widely distributed and used under the investigational exemption. According to the FDA, "2,528,412 'experimental' thalidomide tablets, and 'lesser quantities of liquids and powders containing the drug' had been distributed" to 1,267 physicians. At least 19,822 patients had received thalidomide. Of these, 624 were reported as pregnant: "10 deformed babies were born to American women who had obtained thalidomide from domestic sources and taken it in the critical first trimester of pregnancy" (Mintz 1967, pp. 260-61). Physicians were under no legal obligation to inform those patients took the drug that it was experimental.

The thalidomide incident (along with other events) suggested at least four conclusions: First, that the regulatory structure allowed somewhat precipitous "investigational" use of drugs in humans: the potential of tests conducted on animals was rarely exhausted. Second, such investigational use was, at least in some cases, extremely casual. Third, the evidence upon which the FDA relied in considering NDAs was often weak: much of it amounted to testimonials, rather than careful studies. Fourth, the procedure for considering NDAs was not well-designed either to allow detailed consideration of the evidence by FDA medical officers or to allow the FDA to resist industry pressures for approval of drugs. The Kefauver-Harris Drug Amendments of 1962 (76 Stat. 780) and the implementing regulations altered the regulatory structure to take account of these points and others.

Post-1962 Regulation

Premarketing requirements under the 1962 amendments and implementing regulations are considerably more elaborate. The sequence of events is roughly as follows.

A new substance (or a new use for an old one) is invented. Various studies of safety and efficacy are carried out in the laboratory, without the use of human subjects. Then, in order to receive permission for human testing (actually permission to introduce the drug into interstate commerce for the purpose of human tests), the manufacturer must file with the FDA a "Notice of Claimed Exemption for a New Drug" (IND) (21 USC 355(i); 21 CFR 312.1). This document details the testing already done and sets out the plan for subsequent testing, including information about the investigators. The proposed tests must be "adequate," and they are subject to elaborate rules, including one requiring consent of the subjects. The FDA has the power to prevent the IND from becoming effective. Once the IND becomes effective, the tests that will later provide the basis for an NDA may begin. This elaboration of testing is a crucial addition to the regulatory structure.

Following testing in the IND phase, the manufacturer submits an NDA. Another crucial difference between the old and the new system is found here: the tests must not merely demonstrate that the drug is safe, but must also provide "substantial evidence that the drug will have the effect it purports or is represented to have under the conditions of use prescribed, recommended, or suggested . . . ," where "'substantial evidence' means evidence consisting of adequate and well-controlled investigations, including clinical investigations, by experts qualified by scientific training and experience to evaluate the effectiveness of the drug involved . . ." (21 USC 355(d)). This can be interpreted as a requirement of experimentation involving the highest standards of design and analysis. (Achieving this standard is difficult: a statistical consultant to the FDA told me that if the highest standards were applied, none of the tests he examines would pass. It is notoriously difficult to carry out a perfect experiment outside the laboratory.) Testing for safety is now considerably more elaborate than it once was. Testing for effectiveness is elaborate and new.

In principle, only when safety and efficacy have been established according to these rigorous standards is an NDA approved and the drug released for marketing.* Even if the standards are applied with something less than full rigor, the cost in time and money of developing a new drug and bringing it to market can be very high:

> The impact of these requirements on a drug maker was considerable. For example, a Parke-Davis official reported that when the company first marketed a particular epinephrine preparation in 1938, all it had to submit was a 27-page report concerned primarily with safety. In 1948, when it introduced a new expectorant, only a 73-page report was required. Another new drug marketed in 1958 needed a 430-page submission. But in 1962, when Parke-Davis requested FDA approval of its contraceptive Norlestrin, it had to present a report amounting to 12,370 pages. And in 1968, when approval was requested for its new anesthetic Ketamine, the required documents totaled slightly more than 72,000 pages in 167 volumes. [Silverman and Lee 1974, p. 119, citing Scandusk 1969.]

It is in large measure these costs that raise the question of protection and overprotection.

Protection and Overprotection: The Dilemmas of Regulation

The present regulatory structure for new drugs is designed to protect the public in two ways. First, it is to prevent physical harm by keeping "unsafe" drugs off the market. Second, it is to prevent the physical harm that may result from taking ineffective drugs—a harm that may occur simply because effective drugs would have cured the disease—and the economic harm of spending money on drugs that do no good. But these worthy aims cannot be achieved without some costs. The cost of bringing a drug to market has been substantially increased by the new testing requirements. Unless manufacturers absorb all this new cost, much of it is presumably recovered through the market, which means

---

*If a drug is intended for long-term use, showing that it is safe for such use may take decades. FDA has therefore devised a sort of halfway house for important drugs of this kind (21 CFR 310.303). Levodopa and methadone are currently in this position (21 CFR 310.304).

higher prices. It may be that these costs cannot be recovered in the case of drugs with a relatively small potential market (Cooper 1973, p. 23). If the cost of developing new drugs has increased, standard economic theory would suggest that there is, in consequence, less development.

There are also costs in time. If nothing else, the requirement of more extensive testing (and the resulting need for more consideration by the FDA) should serve to delay the introduction of new drugs onto the market. This is not surprising: many who supported the 1962 amendments felt that drugs were being brought onto the market entirely too quickly. However, suppose a safe and effective new drug is developed. The period during which it is being tested is a period in which its therapeutic benefits are not generally available. As an American Medical Association spokesman said, "it is entirely possible that more lives could be lost by keeping a valuable drug off the market during extensive clinical trials than would be saved by gaining a precise knowledge of the exact type and incidence of all side effects" (U.S. Congress 1964-66, Part I, p. 224).

One final potential cost should be mentioned. Under the present regulatory structure, it is almost always the case that a drug is either not permitted on the market, or else it is permitted on the market with almost no controls over its use (by doctors). We enforce, so to speak, an all-or-none choice.* But the effects of drugs do not fit a similar model. Drugs may help some individuals while injuring others. The individual doctor, exercising care and judgment (as he sometimes does not), may be able to determine that what is generally a dangerous drug is in fact not so dangerous to his particular patient. Thus even if a drug is generally unsafe, keeping it from the market may deprive individual patients of important therapeutic benefits. As Wardell and Lasagna put the argument, ". . . this type of risk-benefit decision should ultimately be made by single physicians for individual patients, rather than by a regulatory agency for society as a whole" (1975, p. 63). Making decisions for society as a whole does not necessarily maximize the expected benefit for particular individuals, even if the conclusion of Wardell and Lasagna is not accepted.

The present structure of regulation of the safety and efficacy of new drugs, then, entails certain costs in terms of precisely those values that it is the purpose of regulation to advance—that is, in terms of the well-being of the patient. The more exacting the requirements of regulation are, the higher these

---

*There is one major exception. FDA controls apply to each use of drug claimed by the manufacturer. A drug approved for sale for one purpose may be used for another purpose by doctors even though the manufacturer neither claims this as a use nor provides suitable directions, cautions, and the like. Of course, the fact that the manufacturer does not claim a new use and does not provide directions may discourage doctors from using the drug in this way. The evidence on this point is, however, unclear.

costs are likely to be. An absolute standard of safety would prevent all drugs from being marketed. On the other hand, eliminating the regulatory structure—allowing anything and everything on the market—might recreate the conditions that led to the regulatory structure in the first place. The ideal, then, is presumably somewhere between the extremes of no drugs and no regulation, a point where the benefits of regulation in terms of consumer protection still outweigh the costs.

At least since the implementation of the 1962 amendments, there has been a lively debate over where this point of bliss is located. That there has been such a debate is not surprising. Therapeutic accidents are highly dramatic. The amendments strikingly altered the operating conditions of a major industry. They impinge upon the status of doctors as well. The amendments are a central element in the emerging consumer movement (Nadel 1971). Congress has long had a significant interest in the drug industry. And finally, there has been in recent years a noticeable resurgence of academic interest in the nature and consequences of government regulation.

The debate, then, has concerned whether we are protecting the drug consumer insufficiently, enough, or too much. In other words, did the 1962 amendments (and FDA actions) go too far or not far enough, or are they just right?

There are no simple answers to these questions. In the rest of this chapter, I will examine the ways in which some of the interested actors have approached the problem of providing answers and the ways in which they have reacted to the answers proposed by others.

FOUR ALTERNATIVE APPROACHES

Economics

As presented in the preceding section, evaluation of the 1962 amendments is a relatively straightforward question of costs and benefits. It is not surprising that a Chicago school economist, Sam Peltzman (1973a, 1973b, 1974a), has produced such an evaluation. It is a highly technical work of empirical analysis, relying upon both the economic theory of consumer surplus and data analysis linked to a long chain of assumptions. I will attempt here only a very crude sketch of Peltzman's analysis.

Let us consider first efficacy. The amendments appear to assume that, at least initially, consumers' (doctors') demand curves for new drugs before 1962 were "too high" because they were acting upon exaggerated claims of efficacy. Because of this, demand should fall over time as consumers learn that the claims are exaggerated. Using data on market shares and prices for new and old drugs within therapeutic categories, Peltzman estimates pre-1962 demand curves for new drugs shortly after introduction and four years later. He finds little difference, and therefore concludes that there was in fact little waste due to ineffective drugs that the Amendments could eliminate: the gain in consumer surplus is therefore small. (The same analysis in the post-1962 period produces similar results, which implies the same conclusion.) (This analysis is based on overall consumer behavior. Peltzman checks it against the behavior of presumed experts. The results do not overturn the conclusion.)

This conclusion implies that the initial demand for new drugs in the pre-1962 period is close to the "true demand." Peltzman then compares this with the post-1962 demand for new drugs and finds that the new demand curve is lower. He attributes this decline to the reduction in information provided to the consumer. This reduction has occurred because claims that do not meet FDA standards can no longer be made by the manufacturers; consumers, it is implied, would demand more of these new drugs if the amendments allowed more information. Since additional consumer surplus would be generated through the additional demand, the effect of the amendments is a loss of consumer surplus.

Consumers also lose, Peltzman argues, because the amendments retard innovation in drugs, with the result that some drugs that would appear on the market were it not for the amendments do not appear. Since consumers would benefit from these as well, there is additional loss of consumer surplus. To establish that this decline in innovation has in fact occurred, Peltzman performs a kind of interrupted time-series analysis on the annual number of new chemical entities (a smaller category than new drugs) introduced, and concludes that there has in fact been a substantial decline attributable to the amendments. (For related analyses see Clymer 1975; Wardell and Lasagna 1975a, 1975b; Grabowski, Vernon, and Thomas 1976.)

Peltzman also analyzes the effects of the amendments on drug prices, and concludes that there has been a rise in the price of existing drugs due to a reduction in competition produced by the effective entry barriers raised by the amendments.

Peltzman then finds both benefits and costs to the consumer. However, the benefit from decreased spending on ineffective drugs is estimated to be on the order of $100 million annually, while the costs from "a reduced flow of new drugs and information about them" (1974a, p. 49) are on the order of $300 to $400 million annually and those resulting from decreased competition are $50 million annually. Overall, there is a substantial net loss to the consumer.

Safety is more difficult to address, but Peltzman bravely makes the attempt. The strategy is to compare the cost of an occasional thalidomide tragedy with the costs of delay in introduction of major therapeutic advances. The analysis is necessarily highly speculative because no one knows what the incidence of major therapeutic disasters would be with or without the amendments, what major therapeutic advances are likely, how much they would be delayed, or how to put dollar values on death and disease (Mishan 1971; Zeckhauser 1975). Peltzman notes that the "safest conclusion that can be drawn is that the amendments have not produced significant safety benefits so far, nor have they foreclosed or delayed extraordinary therapeutic advance" (1974a, p. 71). On the other hand, he suggests that his analysis indicates that the amendments go too far in avoiding risk, that we would probably be better off if we accepted a higher likelihood of thalidomide tragedies in return for speedier introduction of major therapeutic advances. Once again, the 1962 amendments are seen as a net loss to society.

In the subsequent discussion of Peltzman's analysis, two points in particular should be kept in mind. First, the analysis is focused entirely upon results; the process through which the FDA reaches its decisions is ignored. Second, Peltzman uses aggregate data almost entirely. He does not, except in the tentative discussions of safety, point to any single drug as exemplifying his points. He has chosen to "avoid pharmacological issues . . ." (Peltzman 1974b).

Medicine and the Drug Lag

Not surprisingly, those with somewhat different professional training take a different approach. A major line of criticism concentrates on particular drugs. While this approach has been used by others (U.S. Congress 1974, pp. 511-12), it is most closely associated with the name of William M. Wardell (1975, 1974, 1973a, 1973b; Wardell and Lasagna 1975a), a professor of pharmacology, toxicology, and medicine at the University of Rochester. Wardell's strategy is to compare the availability of drugs in the United States with availability in Great Britain in the post-1962 period. The assumption is that the patterns of regulation in Great Britain (Dunlop 1973) and the United States were far more similar before the 1962 amendments than after.

Wardell tabulates drugs introduced into the two countries during the period in question according to whether they are exclusively available in the United States, exclusively available in Great Britain, or available in both. For those drugs available in both countries, he checks whether there was a period of exclusive availability. He concludes that "at least in numerical terms, the United States has lagged considerably behind Britain in the introduction of new drugs" (Wardell 1973b, p. 786). This, of course, may be good or bad for the United States, depending upon the value of the drugs in question. Wardell approaches this problem in three ways. First, he examines the medical evidence concerning the uses, effectiveness, and safety of most of the drugs in question, generally concluding that the evidence indicates the drugs not available in the United States should be (Wardell 1973b). Second, he surveys British and U.S. doctors and discovers that British doctors consider these drugs important, while U.S. doctors are generally unaware of them. In those cases where the U.S. doctors are aware of the drugs or of unapproved uses of available drugs, they generally think that the drugs should be available or the uses approved (Wardell 1973a). Finally, he attempts an analysis similar to Peltzman's of the safety question but he considers the impact of particular drugs actually available in Britain. He concludes that "it is difficult to argue that the United States has escaped an inordinate amount of new-drug toxicity by its conservative approach; it has gained little else in return. On the contrary, it is relatively easy to show that Britain has gained by having effective drugs available sooner." Furthermore, the costs to Britain of higher levels of adverse drug reactions have been small. "In view of the clear benefits demonstrable from some of the drugs introduced into Britain, it appears that the United States has, on balance, lost more than it has gained from adopting a more conservative approach than did Britain in the post-thalidomide era" (Wardell 1974, p. 90).

While Peltzman concludes that the 1962 amendments (and perhaps even the pre-1962 structure) ought to be repealed (1973a, pp. 207-08), Wardell's conclusion is not so simple. He advocates a rather different approach to the entire question of drug regulation, an approach relying less upon the all-or-none marketing decision and more upon release subject to postmarketing surveillance and new controls (or at least influences) upon actual use of the drugs by doctors (Wardell and Lasagna 1975a, p. 154).

While Wardell does speak to the mechanism of regulation, his analysis is primarily in terms of results, not process. In this it is similar to Peltzman's. It parts company with Peltzman in that it does not "avoid pharmacological issues" and does not provide an overall measure of the impact of the 1962 amendments, as Peltzman's measure of consumer surplus does.

Pressures and Disasters

Detailed evaluation of results is not the only route to a judgment of the impact of regulation. Process is another. Process-based evaluations are rarely made in as explicit a form as the results-based evaluations already discussed, but they can be pieced together from interviews, hearing transcripts, and similar materials.

A process approach commonly found on Capitol Hill is based on the standard political science model of interest groups (or pressures). FDA decisions are seen as heavily influenced by the pressures of the drug industry, by constant contact between regulators and the regulated in which the regulated seek to have drugs approved, by what Landis calls "the daily machine-gun-like impact on both agency and its staff of industry representation that makes for industry orientation on the part of many honest and capable agency members as well as agency staffs" (1960, p. 71). This perspective may be clearly seen in Mintz (1967). It is also nicely captured by the following exchange between Senator Edward Kennedy and Ralph Nader:

SENATOR KENNEDY: . . . Commissioner Schmidt of the FDA has put the question . . . that the agency is caught between the devil and the deep blue sea. On the one hand the pressures of the various drug industries, and on the other hand, the harrassment by active consumer groups, such as you that are after them criticizing them. . . . Do you think this is a fair contrast or comparison really, the type of influence or pressure that they are under? I mean, is it a fair description of the dilemma?
MR. NADER: Not at all.
SENATOR KENNEDY: Are the two forces equal?
MR. NADER: They are basically magnified 1,000 times greater on the part of industry. [U.S. Congress 1974a, p. 466]

This model of the process leads many to view the 1962 amendments as not providing sufficient protection for the public. While this view may not require analysis of results, some analysis of results supports the view and validates the model: it is possible to take almost any FDA decision approving a drug for marketing and demonstrate both that the evidence upon which the desicison was based does not meet the rigorous standards supposedly required and that injury or death will result in at least instances from use of the released drug. If the benefits resulting from the decision are ignored, any FDA drug approval will therefore appear to be a disaster. It is easy to ignore the benefits: they are rarely so colorful or identifiable as the injuries that may be directly traced to the drug. Public display of these disasters has become a major congressional activity. As FDA Commissioner Schmidt has said, "The occasions on which hearings have been held to criticize approval of a new drug have been so frequent in the past ten years that we have not even attempted to count them" (U.S. Congress 1974a, p. 207). These hearings serve two purposes, one within the context of the model and one outside it. First, they serve to provide a counterweight to industry pressures. Second, they serve the publicity needs of the congressional actors (Mayhew 1974). For both purposes, press coverage is essential. As one congressional staffer deeply involved in drug hearings told me, there is "no sense in having hearings unless you are going to get coverage." As the hearings usually deal with dramatic subjects, that coverage is generally forthcoming (perhaps particularly in Washington, where Morton Mintz, himself a leading exponent of this pressure-model interpretation of FDA decisions, covers them for the Washington *Post*).

There is a variant of the pressure model that leads in a very different direction. It sees the balance of pressure as leading to overprotection. Central to this view are precisely these "counterbalancing" congressional hearings. As one drug industry official stated,

> The most important influence on the actions of the regulatory agency is the political pressure exerted upon it. In concert with the

> mass media, the regulatory agency is continuously badgered for not fulfilling adequately its role as adversary. It is almost never criticized for failing to make any decisions—particularly where any negative information at all is in hand—and indeed the history of the handling of thalidomide in the United States is a classic example of the rewards of procrastination. The continuing tendency in the United States to imply conspiracy between government and industry against the interest of the general welfare finds particular emphasis in the case of the regulatory agency. The result is inevitably to complicate and delay the decision-making process. [Hubbard 1973, p. 49]

Bureaucratic self-interest may then lead to overcautious treatment of NDAs. The same view is taken by the FDA itself. As Commissioner Schmidt has said,

> By far the greatest pressure that the Bureau of Drugs or the Food and Drug Administration receives with respect to the new drug approval process is brought to bear through Congressional hearings. In all our history, we are unable to find one instance where a Congressional hearing investigated the failure of FDA to approve a new drug. . . . the message conveyed by this situation could not be clearer. . . . Until perspective is brought to the legislative oversight function, the pressure from Congress for FDA to disapprove new drugs will continue to be felt, and could be a major factor in health care in this country. [U.S. Congress 1974a, p. 207]*

The pressure model, then, leads in two directions and implies two different answers to the evaluation problem.

Structure

There is another view of process that can provide the basis for evaluation. In this view, there is not much to be gained by looking at the results of decisions. Rather, what is important is the structure that leads to the decisions. As Peter Hutt, until recently FDA's general counsel, said in another context, "procedure determines substance" (Culliton 1976). While this perspective might be expected of lawyers, I found it in interviews not merely with FDA legal staff, but also with other FDA officials. The director of FDA's Bureau of Drugs has

---

*In fact, there is reason to think that at least one drug, levodopa, was approved for marketing in part because of congressional interest (Cooper 1972, p. 180).

written that "[t]o be credible, regulatory decisions must not only be scientifically sound and legally correct. They must be made for the right reasons and result from a valid, open decision-making process administered by persons of integrity" (Crout 1976, p. 243).

The essence of the FDA's decision is a judgment of costs (or risks) and benefits. The problem is that, as one official put it, benefit-risk is a "correct, useful way of thinking and a goal—but it is not quantifiable with current technology." Consequently, "The only thing you can do is set up the best procedure possible." In recent years, the FDA has attempted to structure the process so as to assure that "a lot of reasonable people have input." In practice, this has meant the multiplication of advisory committees (U.S. Congress 1976). It is through the use of these committees that the best available judgment is to be brought to bear on regulatory decisions. Of course, even if the result is a set of good decisions, these are good decisions within the statutory framework. If, as Peltzman and Wardell suggest, there are serious shortcomings in the statutory framework, FDA's reliance upon advisory committees for its decisions will not address the major questions. From this evaluative perspective, however, these major questions are matters for societal decision through the political process, not matters for agency determination.

The use of outside advice by the FDA can be put in other perspectives as well. The reliance upon others can be seen as a means of diffusing responsibility for decisions. One FDA official has said as much: ". . . the responsibility that is imposed on us by law is too heavy for a government agency to bear alone. When we speak of outside advice . . . what we are actually seeking is a means of widening the base of decision-making, and thus, broadening responsibility" (Cooper 1971, pp. 8-9). Congressional reaction has stressed this perspective (U.S. Congress 1976). But even so, the view from the standpoint of evaluation is that "procedure determines substance."

REACTIONS AND INTERACTIONS

Two of the approaches described above led to sharp critiques of the status quo in drug regulation. Major policy actors in Washington—Congress and the FDA—had their own perspectives on the situation, perspectives that did not predispose them toward a favorable reaction to these critiques. The ensuing reactions may provide a useful picture of the impact of policy evaluation.

The Nelson Hearings

The first major public response to Peltzman and the drug lag theorists (other than Wardell, whose work had not yet been published) came in the form of five days of hearings before Senator Gaylord Nelson's Subcommittee on Monopoly of the Senate's Select Committee on Small Business (U.S. Congress 1973). This subcommittee had long been interested in the pharmaceutical industry and pharmaceutical regulation, and these hearings fit into an ongoing program of investigatory hearings. Committee staff explicitly saw the hearings as a response to criticism of the 1962 amendments, and a response in particular to Milton Friedman, who had publicized Peltzman's work in a *Newsweek* column (1973). In the view of staff members, Chicago-school economics is a closed deductive system at odds with the scientific method, so that Peltzman's findings were not merely without value. They were also "dangerous," particularly when publicized by someone as influential as Friedman. Hearings would be an opportunity for a publicized discrediting of unpalatable views. Senator Nelson's opening statement makes clear the purpose of the hearings: "Since these are serious charges, the subcommittee would be happy to have Dr. Dripps [who had charged the FDA with creating a "drug lag"], Mr. Peltzman, and Mr. Friedman come to document them or withdraw them" (U.S. Congress 1973, p. 9107).

The major burden of discrediting the "charges" fell to the FDA itself, which provided the first witnesses. FDA's defense of U.S. drug regulation had five major points.

(1) There has been no decline in innovation attributable to regulatory practices. Peltzman had relied here on a decline in the development of new drugs. The FDA noted that the decline began before 1962 (U.S. Congress 1973, p. 9386). (Peltzman had realized this. He modeled innovation as a response to growth in the market for drugs and showed that the relationship changed with the amendments. FDA did not comment on this.) Then FDA argued that Peltzman (and others) were looking at the wrong data: "The relevant question is not now and never has been how many new drugs are marketed each year, but rather how many significant, useful and unique therapeutic entities are developed. . . . the rate of development and marketing of truly important, significant, and unique therapeutic entities in this country has remained relatively stable for the past 22 years . . ." (U.S. Congress 1973, p. 9386). (In response, Peltzman points to the highly subjective character of the criteria, and notes that "an unpublished version of the same FDA listing" shows a statistically significant shift [1974a, p. 86].)

(2) In any case, if there is a "drug lag," it comes about because the 1962 amendments require decent testing of drugs, rather than "subjective impression." No alternative to controlled clinical trials is "scientifically as reliable," and the law requires them (U.S. Congress 1973, p. 9373). The fault, if there is one, does not lie with the FDA. (While Peltzman had never suggested it did, some of the drug lag theorists had.)

(3) In any case, comparison with other countries does not show that the United States has been hurt by the amendments. Exchanges between Senator

Nelson and Dr. Henry Simmons, then director of FDA's Bureau of Drugs, illustrate the argument:

> SENATOR NELSON: Are you aware of any significant drug entity marketed in any foreign country that is not available here and for which there is no viable alternative available here?
> DR. SIMMONS: I do not. I do not know of such a drug and the phrase there, Mr. Chairman, that is known to be safe and effective. ... [U.S. Congress 1973, p. 9377]
> In our judgment, there is no condition amenable to drug therapy that cannot be treated as safely and effectively in this country as any place in the world. The American public is not deprived of significant therapeutic drugs whose safety and effectiveness have been adequately substantiated. [U.S. Congress 1973, p. 9382]

The "key phrase" is indeed "known to be safe and effective," for it comes close to reducing the FDA's position to a tautology. In order for the FDA to consider a drug as "known to be safe and effective," it must consider the evidence of safety and effectiveness to be sufficient to justify approval of the drug for the U.S. market. (In theory FDA could be aware of such evidence even though no NDA had been submitted, but this is a rare situation.) The more important question is whether there are drugs available in other countries that ought to be on the market in the United States even though they are not, by the FDA's standards, "known to be safe and effective."

"Viable alternative" is also a key phrase. Two drugs marketed in Great Britain but not in the United States at the time were practolol and oxprenolol, both "beta-blockers," a type of cardiovascular drug. An alternative to these drugs is propranolol, another beta-blocker that was available in the United States. Is propranolol a "viable alternative," as Senator Nelson and the FDA suggest (U.S. Congress 1973, p. 9107)? Perhaps, but "both practolol and oxprenolol have less cardiac and bronchial side effects than propanolol [sic]. They can therefore be used in some of these patients with asthma or heart failure who do not tolerate propranolol and for whom in the United States propranolol is specifically contraindicated" (Wardell and Lasagna 1975a, p. 62, citations omitted). (These two drugs may actually be available for use in emergencies, but the point remains.) Some patients might be better served by the unavailable drugs than by the available ones.

(4) The attempt to judge the overall impact of tighter safety regulations is simply unacceptable: "the difficulty we have [with Peltzman's analysis] is that we do not know how to put a dollar value on a human life. . . . I do not know what dollar value to put on a child born without arms or legs. . . . That is why it is so difficult to argue with economists . . ." (U.S. Congress 1973, p. 9383). As the FDA rejects the suggestions that there might be valuable drugs not available in the United States as a result of the regulatory scheme, it is not necessary to

balance these lives and children against the lives lost and limbless children born as a result of the regulatory scheme.

(5) Though the preceding argument seems to imply the impossibility of cost/benefit analysis, the FDA reaches the conclusion of one anyway: "The allegation has been made that the cost to our society to prevent a thalidomide-type tragedy far exceeds the benefits of a regulatory system developed to prevent such a tragedy. We disagree. We believe the benefits that accrue to society because of our regulatory system are worth the cost and far outweigh any risks" (U.S. Congress 1973, p. 9367). But the FDA does not attempt to measure the costs and benefits.

The FDA, then, used the hearings to enter a sweeping defense of both the regulatory structure and the agency's practices, paying scant attention to the details of Peltzman's analysis and not much more to questions of pharmacology (since the then-existing statements of the drug-lag argument did not themselves present much pharmacological argument). If Peltzman's critique raised important questions, they were left unresolved at the conclusion of the FDA testimony.

Somewhat greater attention was given to Peltzman's critique on the final day of the hearings, when Peltzman himself appeared as a witness. Prior to Peltzman's presentation of an abbreviated version of his then-unpublished research (the full version does not appear in the hearing record), two other economists presented technical critiques of his work. Points covered included Peltzman's estimates of the proportion of drugs marketed before 1962 that were ineffective, the appropriateness of his model of the flow of innovation, his evidence concerning increased length of the developmental period for drugs, and some questions of statistical procedure (U.S. Congress 1973, pp. 9766-801). Understandably, the two economists did not present alternative analyses, but merely raised questions. As these questions were not central to the discussion that day, I will ignore them here.

What was central was the confrontation between Peltzman and Senator Nelson and the subcommittee staff. Two points in particular were returned to time and time again. Peltzman's analysis depends upon estimates of the demand for various drugs. The contention of his congressional antagonists was that all such reliance upon a "marketplace test" is inappropriate: what counts is expert judgment. One exchange captures some of the flavor of the dispute:

> SENATOR NELSON: Well, do I understand correctly, what you are saying is that the marketplace demand determines the scientific value of a product?
> MR. PELTZMAN: No, but turn that around, Senator. If the drug has scientific merit, if it is truly a significant advance as some of these statements say, somebody ought to be buying it. They ought to be buying it more than the average drug. They are not. [U.S. Congress 1973, p. 9820]

Senator Nelson then cited one drug that, it is generally thought by experts, is prescribed quite frequently when it should hardly be used at all (U.S. Congress 1973, p. 9821), implying that the therapeutic choices of the typical doctor should not be taken as indicating the worth of drugs.

This view of the average quality of prescribing decisions in the United States may well be central to evaluation of the 1962 amendments. If doctors generally prescribe poorly, it may be that the appropriate governmental response is a great hesitancy to approve drugs, not because they are unsafe or ineffective when used properly, but rather because they are likely to be used improperly. One congressional staff assistant told me that "Putting a new drug on the market is putting another weapon in their hands, another killer drug in the hands of doctors who will misuse it." This is a peculiar defense of the 1962 amendments and the FDA, for it implies that the need is less to control drugs and drug companies than to control the practice of medicine, which the present regulatory structure is not well designed to do. As one observer has written, "Substantial improvement in the quality of drug utilization, if it is to occur, is more likely to come from the subjection of doctors to direct bureaucratic control than from anything that can be accomplished by the FDA" (Quirk 1973, p. 2).

The other central point in the rather hostile subcommittee interrogation of Peltzman was his failure to cite specific drugs available in other countries but not in the United States. To no avail Peltzman pointed out first that he was not a pharmacologist and second that his analysis did not require this, as he depended as much upon drugs that were never developed because of the amendments. Though he mentioned practolol and oxprenolol and cited Wardell's unpublished work, Peltzman was repeatedly attacked:

> SENATOR NELSON: I say to you name one, just one, significant drug entity [available in Great Britain but not in the United States].
> MR. PELTZMAN: Now, Senator, you know I am not going to do that. I told you—
> SENATOR NELSON: Well, then you have no case at all, do you? . . . So what I am saying is that your whole case just collapses unless you can prove that we are being deprived of valuable drugs. And if we are not being deprived of valuable drugs, I must say with all due respect, your study is totally useless.
> MR. PELTZMAN: Well, I appreciate your opinion, Senator. [U.S. Congress 1973, pp. 9834-35]

The rejection of Peltzman's analysis of the safety question once again follows from a rejection of the view that the U.S. public is being deprived of anything of value.

The entire Nelson hearings, then, can be seen as a hard-line defense of the FDA and of a policy in which significant congressional actors had much invested. The only thing missing from the hearings was a serious attempt to come to terms with the critiques of agency and policy. The critiques were not so much refuted as dismissed out of hand.

Reactions to Wardell

Wardell added something new to the debate, an answer to the pharmacological and therapeutic questions that had been used to discredit Peltzman. Peltzman could be dismissed as irrelevant because his intellectual framework was foreign to the policy community—as one high FDA official said, "An economic analysis is kind of ridiculous." Previous drug-lag arguments lacked detailed specifications. Wardell provided evidence within a framework the FDA could accept. (The same FDA official who dismissed Peltzman so easily said that Wardell's work was important.) I have not pieced together a full account of the FDA's reaction to Wardell (and in particular I cannot separate a possible reaction to Wardell from a reaction to the same set of facts that may have been independently considered by the FDA), but there is reason to think that arguments of the kind Wardell advanced have had an impact at FDA.

While the structure of FDA decision making may call for bringing the judgments of many individuals to bear on decisions concerning new drugs, there are points in the process where single individuals can block approval of new drugs. Several members of the FDA staff told me that there had been one individual with such power over cardiovascular drugs, and he was very suspicious of anything he was told by the drug companies. Furthermore, he believed that in general there were already enough drugs on the market. ("Both are sound attitudes, but he carried them to extremes.") As a result, between 1968 and 1972, no new cardiovascular drugs were approved (U.S. Congress 1974a, p. 491). (Practolol and oxprenolol, discussed above, are cardiovascular drugs, as is propranolol, the "viable alternative.") Higher officials at FDA became convinced that there was in fact a lag at least in cardiovascular drugs and perhaps elsewhere as well.

Between 1972 and 1974, the administration of the FDA stepped in, reorganizing and taking other actions to remove what it saw as bottlenecks in the drug-approval process. In September 1974, Wardell testified that the situation had improved: "I have been critical of the FDA in the past but I must acknowledge that in the last 2½ years the FDA has improved markedly. Large anachronisms still remain, which I pointed out 2 or 3 years ago, but I have found they are decreasing in most areas and in some cases have vanished . . ." (U.S. Congress 1974a, p. 490).

Dr. Richard Crout, director of the FDA's Bureau of Drugs, appeared with Wardell and retracted previous FDA statements on the drug lag. Senator Kennedy reminded the witnesses of an FDA statement at the Nelson hearings to the effect that, "there is no condition amenable to drug therapy which cannot be treated as effectively in the United States as anywhere in the world and that the American public is not being deprived of safe and efficacious drugs." Dr. Crout replied that, "we would modify that statement today...." He explained that in the list of drugs available elsewhere but not in the United States, "you can pick out drugs in there that we recognize are potential gains from the standpoint of somewhat improved effectiveness, improved safety and convenience gains" (U.S. Congress 1974a, p. 477). He later pointed directly to the cause of the drug lag: "It is evident that regulatory requirements are an important influence on the availability of new drugs in this or any other country, and any drug lag that exists in this country regarding important drugs is an inevitable result of the standards set by our laws on safety and effectiveness." He rejected, however, suggestions that the 1962 amendments be repealed (U.S. Congress 1974a, p. 505).

It is difficult, obviously, to reconcile such statements with earlier FDA statements. Presumably what happened is that sufficient dissatisfaction with the results of the new drug-approval process emerged for the FDA to recognize that there was a structural problem. They altered the structure somewhat, improved the process, and continued to support the basic outlines of the policy, if not the details that had accompanied implementation of the policy for a number of years. The grounds upon which the policy itself is to be supported remain obscure.

Wardell's analysis, or something similar to it, therefore appears to have had at least some effect upon the FDA. The reception in Congress and elsewhere was less warm. What from one perspective looks like a reorganization of the agency for the purpose of better serving the public interest, from another perspective may appear to be a purge of those who would protect the public against the machinations of the drug industry. That some of the individuals purged had built substantial reputations as defenders of the public interest further helped confirm the positions of those who see the new drug-approval process as a case study in the politics of pressure. Associates of Ralph Nader quickly suggested this view:

> In the past three weeks, an acute and deepening crisis has developed at the Food and Drug Administration which seriously threatened the health of American citizens. Two medical doctors, John Nestor and John Winkler, both specialists in cardiovascular disease with unassailable records of protecting the public from harmful drugs, have been removed from their positions and assigned new tasks.... By these adverse actions against two doctors who have served the public in an exemplary way, FDA officials are supporting fears that they are more responsive to complaints from industry than to their responsibility to protect the public health. [Wolfe and Johnson 1972, pp. 242, 251]

Hearings in the House (U.S. Congress 1974b, 1976) attacked the procedures used by the FDA to get certain new drugs approved. The purges themselves were aired in the Senate (U.S. Congress 1973-74, part 7; 1974a). Morton Mintz's coverage (1974) captures the sense of the Senate hearings: "Eleven Food and Drug Administration scientists charged yesterday that the FDA's top echelon always supports them when they recommend approval of new medicines for the market but commonly harasses and intimidates them when they question the safety or effectiveness of new drugs." The FDA responded with a report of more than 900 pages that, not surprisingly, concluded that on the whole the charges were without foundation and that the agency was neither improperly subject to industry influences nor biased toward approval of drugs (Schmidt 1975, pp. 895-96). The Secretary of the Department of Health, Education and Welfare appointed a review panel to investigate the charges and the FDA's investigation. That group's first report (Review Panel 1976), only 524 pages, concludes that the FDA's investigation of the charges against it was inadequate and that some of them should be reinvestigated. The validity of the charges, still undetermined after the expenditure of more than a quarter of a million dollars, is a matter separate from whether the FDA actions that led to the charges also led to wise or unwise drug approvals. The panel intends to consider the substance of drug approval decisions in its later work. Additional reports will no doubt follow.

In summary, then, Wardell's approach to evaluation was received far more sympathetically at FDA than was Peltzman's, but pressure models of the regulatory process treated actions to shorten the drug lag as caving in to industry pressure. There is no evidence, for example, that Congress was moved greatly by Wardell's arguments. Indeed, in a strict sense there is little evidence that Wardell influenced the FDA either. It is possible that industry pressures concerning the drugs Wardell considered important were all that interested FDA officials. I cannot resolve this question, except by saying that Wardell's critique was treated by the FDA as if it were important.

CONCLUSIONS

A single case study does not provide a good basis for generalizations. Those I offer here should be considered as speculations that, while perhaps not entirely derived from the material presented here, are at least not inconsistent with it.

On Congress and Policy Analysis

Congress appears to be almost totally impervious to systematic policy analysis. The Wardell and Peltzman analyses were not considered and rejected by

Congress; they were simply rejected. No single reason fully explains this rejection, but several taken together may provide an adequate explanation.

(1) Relevant congressional actors have substantial investments in at least the general outlines of current regulatory policy and practice. They have clearly staked out positions and roles as defenders of the "public interest" against the drug manufacturers. These positions and roles are useful in generating political support and perhaps even more useful in generating publicity. (Attacks on FDA drug approvals are an almost inexhaustible source of favorable publicity.) Accepting the results of policy analysis might require reversing positions and liquidating investments, not a politically attractive step. There is, then, little to be gained by taking policy analysis seriously, and possibly much to be lost. As Weiss (1976, p. 225) notes, "Research can be more of a threat than a help. Evaluative research is apt to uncover shortcomings of favored programs; policy research may recommend actions unpalatable to significant constituencies." Therefore, the logical approach to a policy analysis with unpalatable conclusions is to ignore it as long as is feasible and then to seek to discredit it. This was particularly the fate of Peltzman's analysis and that of the early drug-lag theorists. Once FDA came to agree with Wardell, a new strategy was required, and the congressional focus shifted to administrative matters, the FDA "purge." The publicity again was good, and the analysis could be forgotten.

(2) The mode of analysis that seems pervasive on Capitol Hill (a pressure-group model) is uncongenial to policy analysis based on other models. Seemingly locked into their own mode of analysis, the relevant congressional actors respond to evaluations in other modes by placing them within the pressure model. As Lindblom says, "policy analysis is incorporated as an instrument or weapon into the play of power . . ." (1968, p. 30). The important question about any given policy analysis is not whether it is technically competent, or even correct. What counts is which side it supports. Again, Weiss (1976, p. 227) is to the point: "The most common use of research in government policy-making is probably as support and ammunition for a predetermined position." To accept the conclusions of Wardell or Peltzman is to cave in under pressure from the drug manufacturers, and therefore these conclusions are unacceptable. The analysis can be judged without examination of its details, and such examination of details as occurs—as in the testimony of other economists concerning Peltzman's work—is a sideshow. Senator Nelson gave Peltzman's testimony roughly the same reception that F. Lee Bailey gave that of Dr. Joel Fort in the Patty Hearst trial, and for much the same reason: it was testimony for the wrong side. Actions taken by the FDA that produced results suggested by Wardell's analysis were viewed by Congress entirely in pressure terms. (As noted above, the pressure model can lead in a rather different direction. But supporters of that side of the model do not surface prominently in Congress.)

(3) Two risks are inherent in drug regulation, the risk of harm from approved drugs and the risk of the consequences of delay and failure to develop

drugs. In some sense these risks are symmetrical. Stanley Lebergott, an economist who testified before the Nelson subcommittee, put this nicely: "The central point is, you are choosing one set of deaths and suffering and illness and cost against another. That is the only choice open to us" (U.S. Congress 1973a, p. 9859).

In another sense, however, the risks are not symmetrical. Therapeutic accidents often produce identifiable victims. Horrible pictures can be shown. Grieving families can testify. Particular decisions can be identified as unfortunate. The victims on the other side are not so easily identified. Their injuries cannot be traced so easily to particular decisions and causes. There is a diffuseness on one side of the balance that is not found on the other. While policy analysis may weight the two sides of the balance equally, they appear to be treated differently in Congress. Congress appears to be biased toward concrete, visible victims, and against unknown, unidentifiable (and perhaps even hypothetical) ones.

This kind of bias is surely not limited to Congress. There is a parallel in the peculiarities and complexities that arise in the consideration of "statistical lives" and the lives of identifiable individuals (Calabresi 1969): we spend vast amounts to rescue trapped miners, but relatively little for potentially more important improvements in mine safety. But Congress, oriented toward distributive benefits, may be peculiarly troubled by the bias: diffuse benefits have something of the character of public goods, for which it is hard to claim credit (Mayhew 1974).

This bias implies that the political system—and Congress in particular—will be inefficient in the saving of lives. (Medicare funding of renal dialysis comes to mind; see Lyons 1973.) In some situations, this will lead to overprotection in consumer-protection legislation. (This is not to say that current pharmaceutical regulation generates overprotection, or that Peltzman is right. It may be that the bias provides a useful counterbalance to other factors in the political system that lead in other directions, or that visible victims of preventable therapeutic accidents are relatively rare.)

On FDA and Policy Analysis

The FDA reacted to Peltzman in much the same way as did Congress: his entire approach was rejected without consideration of the details. The economic framework was foreign to its standard modes of analysis, and FDA did not feel obliged to take it seriously. Wardell, however, approached the problem in precisely the terms normally used by FDA in deciding on drugs: what is the evidence of effectiveness, and how safe is the drug? To read Wardell as questioning only particular decisions is to miss much, but not all, of the point. FDA appears to have accepted much of what Wardell said about particular decisions, but to have translated his critique of the regulatory structure into more congenial terms, a critique of process within that structure. In a sense, then, FDA reacted to Wardell just as Congress did: it placed his analysis within its own frameworks of analysis, its own models, and treated it only in those terms. If FDA is less impervious to systematic policy analysis than is Congress, it may well be because its models and frameworks are more congenial to analysis than is the congressional model of pressures.

On the Potential Impact of Policy Analysis

The potential impact of comprehensive, systematic analysis of the effects of policy appears to be limited. Analyses infrequently change minds. If these analyses do not produce results consistent with the needs, preconceptions, and perspectives of policymakers, they are likely to be ignored—or attacked. And the analyses are likely to be vulnerable to such treatment. As Lindblom says, analysis "will always fail to prove that the right policy has been found and will always be subject to challenge" (1968, p. 14). No analysis is perfect and complete. Consequently, "even those who would like to see more analysis in policymaking will not wholly endorse it, will never wholly accept its results, and will obviously want some kind of political machinery to make policy decisions . . ." (Lindblom 1968, p. 20). This limited role for analysis may be entirely appropriate. As Lowrance (1976, p. 99) says of risk-benefit analysis, the "art is . . . primitive." Peltzman's work is interesting, but his framework of analysis is open to question, and even within it the results may not be correct. Criticism was presented at the Nelson hearings, and both critiques (McGuire, Nelson, and Spavins 1975) and alternative analyses (Grabowski, Vernon, and Thomas 1976) have appeared in print. The disputation is highly technical, and a congressional committee could hardly hope to resolve the issues in the terms used in the technical literature. If it could, the resolution might not be the correct one. Under the circumstances, what can the policymaker do? In the case of the congressman, he can take the side of his traditional allies, which is precisely what Senators Nelson and Kennedy did. The Bureaucrat can say he is just doing his job, which is what the FDA did. Politics is one mechanism for evaluating evidence. It may even be an adequate one.

On Pharmaceutical Regulation

The current system of pharmaceutical regulation in the United States is far from ideal. Both those who attack it and those who defend it, both those who think drugs are too freely approved and those who think more drugs should be approved, agree that a substantial part of the problem lies in the prescribing habits of physicians. Because the present system is a blunt instrument, either blocking a drug from almost all use or else making it available to doctors to use as they please, it will always be possible to show both that useful drugs are not available (when they presumably should be) and that patients are being injured in appalling numbers by the drugs already approved. The present system, however, does not address the question of how drugs are used. It is limited instead to whether they are used at all. Suggestions for alternatives to the current system have been made by many (Merrill 1973; Quirk 1973; Wardell and Lasagna 1975a). These suggestions should be taken seriously.

REFERENCES

Adams, Samuel Hopkins. 1905. "The Great American Fraud," *Colliers*, October 28. In *The Muckrakers*, ed. Arthur and Lila Weinberg, pp. 195-201. New York: Simon and Schuster, 1961.

Applied Management Sciences. 1974. "Final Report: Survey of Drug Information Needs and Problems Associated with Communications Directed to Practicing Physicians (Part I: Physician Information Survey)." Prepared for Food and Drug Administration, Bureau of Drugs. In U.S. Congress, Senate, Committee on Labor Hearings. 1974. *Examination of the Pharmaceutical Industry, 1973-74*, 93d Cong., 2d sess., pt. 5: 1548-859.

Calabresi, Guido. 1969. "Reflections on Medical Experimentation in Humans." *Daedalus* 98 (Spring): 387-405.

Clymer, Harold A. 1975. "The Economic and Regulatory Climate: U.S. and Overseas Trends." In *Drug Development and Marketing*, ed. Robert B. Helms, pp. 137-54. Washington, D.C.: American Enterprise Institute for Public Policy Research, 1975.

Cooper, Joseph D. 1973. "Purpose, Technique, and Strategy in the Regulation of New Drugs." In *Regulating New Drugs*, ed. Richard L. Landau, pp. 21-32. Chicago: University of Chicago, Center for Policy Study, 1973.

―――, ed. 1972. *Philosophy and Technology of Drug Assessment*, Volume 3, *The Philosophy of Evidence*. Washington, D.C.: Interdisciplinary Communications Associates.

―――. ed. 1971. *Philosophy and Technology of Drug Assessment*, Volume 2, *The Quality of Advice*. Washington, D.C.: Interdisciplinary Communications Associates.

[Culliton, Barbara J.] B.J.C. 1976. "Handler Defends Academy Elitism." *Science* 191 (February 13): 543.

Crout, J. Richard. 1976. "New Drug Regulation and Its Impact on Innovation." In *Impact of Public Policy on Drug Innovation and Pricing*, ed. Samuel A. Mitchell and Emery A. Link, pp. 241-60. Washington, D.C.: American University, 1976.

Dunlop, Sir Derrick. 1973. "The British System of Drug Regulation." In *Regulating New Drugs*, ed. Richard L. Landau, pp. 229-37. Chicago: University of Chicago, Center for Policy Study, 1973.

Friedman, Milton. 1973. "Frustrating Drug Advancement." *Newsweek*, January 8, p. 49.

Grabowski, Henry G.; John M. Vernon; and Lacy Glenn Thomas. 1976. "The Effects of Regulatory Policy on the Incentives to Innovate: An International Comparative Analysis." In *Impact of Public Policy on Drug Innovation and Pricing*, ed. Samuel A. Mitchell and Emery A. Link, pp. 47-82. Washington, D.C.: American University, 1976.

Harris, Richard. 1964. *The Real Voice*. New York: Macmillan.
Hubbard, William N., Jr. 1973. "Preclinical Problems of New Drug Development." In *Regulating New Drugs*, ed. Richard L. Landau, pp. 35-51. Chicago: University of Chicago, Center for Policy Study, 1973.
Ingelfinger, F. J. 1974. "The Side Effects of Aspirin." *New England Journal of Medicine* 290: 1197.
Landis, James M. 1960. "Report on Regulatory Agencies to the President-Elect."
Lindblom, Charles E. 1968. *The Policy-Making Process*. Englewood Cliffs, N.J.: Prentice-Hall.
Lowrance, William W. 1976. *Of Acceptable Risk: Science and the Determination of Safety*. Los Altos, Calif.: William Kaufman.
Lyons, Richard D. 1973. "Program to Aid Kidney Victims Faces Millions in Excess Costs." New York *Times*, January 11. In *Congressional Record* (daily ed.), February 26, 1973, pp. S3218-19.
Mayhew, David R. 1974. *Congress: The Electoral Connection*. New Haven and London: Yale University Press.
McGuire, Thomas, Richard Nelson, and Thomas Spavins. 1975. "An Evaluation of Consumer Protection Legislation: the 1962 Drug Amendments: A Comment." *Journal of Political Economy* 83 (June): 655-61.
Merrill, Richard A. 1973. "Compensation for Prescription Drug Injuries." *Virginia Law Review* 59: 1-120.
Mintz, Morton. 1974. "FDA Harassment Alleged." Washington *Post*, August 16, P. A1.
———. 1967. *By Prescription Only*. Boston: Beacon Press.
Mishan, E. J. 1971. "Evaluation of Life and Limb: A Theoretical Approach." *Journal of Political Economy* 79: 687-705.
Nadel, Mark V. 1971. *The Politics of Consumer Protection*. Indianapolis and New York: Bobbs-Merrill.
Peltzman, Sam. 1974a. *Regulation of Pharmaceutical Innovation*, AEI Evaluative Studies 15. Washington, D.C.: American Enterprise Institute for Public Policy Research.
———. 1974b. Personal communication, November 11.
———. 1973a. "The Benefits and Costs of New Drug Regulation." In *Regulating New Drugs*, ed. Richard L. Landau, pp. 113-211. Chicago: University of Chicago, Center for Policy Study, 1973.
———. 1973b. "An Evaluation of Consumer Protection Legislation: The 1962 Drug Amendments." *Journal of Political Economy* 81 (September/October): 1049-91.
Quirk, Paul. 1973. "Politics and Prescribing: The FDA, the Medical Profession, and Prescription Drug Utilization." Unpublished manuscript, Harvard University.
Review Panel on New Drug Regulation. 1976. *Assessment of the Commissioner's Report of October 1975*. Washington, D.C.: U.S. Department of Health, Education and Welfare.
Sandusk, Joseph F., Jr. 1974. "The Impact of Drug Legislation on Clinical Evaluation of Drugs." Paper presented at a symposium at the Gottlieb Duttweiler Institute, Ruschlikon-Zurich, August 28-29.
Schmidt, Alexander M. 1975. *The Commissioner's Report of Investigation of Charges*. Washington, D.C.: Food and Drug Administration.
Sellers, Ashley, and Nathan D. Grundstein. 1940. "Administrative Procedure and Practice in the Department under the Federal Food, Drug, and Cosmetic Act of 1938, Prepared under the Direction of Mastin G. White, Solicitor." In *A Treatise on the Law of Foods, Drugs, and Cosmetics*, 2nd ed., Harry Aubrey Toulmin, Jr. Cincinnati: W.H. Anderson, 1963.
Silverman, Milton. 1976. Prepared testimony before U.S. Senate, Select Committee on Small Business, Subcommittee on Monopoly. May 26.

Silverman, Milton, and Philip R. Lee. 1974. *Pills, Profits, and Politics*. Berkeley: University of California Press.
Toulmin, Harry Aubrey, Jr. 1963. *A Treatise on the Law of Foods, Drugs and Cosmetics*. 2d ed. Cincinnati: W.H. Anderson.
U.S. Congress, House. 1976. Committee on Government Operations. *Use of Advisory Committees by the Food and Drug Administration*. 94th Cong., 2d sess., H. Rept 94-787, January 26.
——, Senate. 1974a. Committee on Labor and Public Welfare and Committee on the Judiciary. Hearings. *Regulation of New Drug R. and D. by the Food and Drug Administration*. 93d Cong., 2d sess.
——, House. 1974b. Committee on Government Operations. Hearings. *Use of Advisory Committees by the Food and Drug Administration*. 93d Cong., 2d sess.
——, Senate. 1973-74. Committee on Labor. Hearings. *Examination of the Pharmaceutical Industry, 1973-74*. 93d Cong., 1st and 2d sess., pts. 1-8.
——, Senate. 1973. Select Committee on Small Business. Hearings. *Competitive Problems in the Drug Industry*. 93d Cong., 1st sess., pt. 23, *Development and Marketing of Prescription Drugs*.
——, Senate. 1972. Select Committee on Small Business. *Competitive Problems in the Drug Industry: Summary and Analysis*. 92d Cong., 2d sess. November 2. Prepared by the Congressional Research Service, Library of Congress. Committee Print.
——, House. 1964-66. Committee on Government Operations. Hearings. *Drug Safety*. 88th Cong., 2d sess.–89th Cong., 2d sess., pts. 1-5.
Wardell, William M. 1975. "Developments in the Introduction of New Drugs in the United States and Britain, 1971-74." In *Drug Development and Marketing*, ed. Robert B. Helms, pp. 165-81. Washington, D.C.: American Enterprise Institute for Public Policy Research, 1975.
——. 1974. "Therapeutic Implications of the Drug Lag." *Clinical Pharmacology and Therapeutics* 15 (January): 73-96.
——. 1973a. "British and American Awareness of Some New Therapeutic Drugs." *Clinical Pharmacology and Therapeutics* 14 (November-December): 1022-34.
——. 1973b. "Introduction of New Therapeutic Drugs in the United States and Great Britain: An International Comparison." *Clinical Pharmacology and Therapeutics* 14 (September-October): 773-90.
Wardell, William M., and Louis Lasagna. 1975a. *Regulation and Drug Development*, AEI Evaluative Studies 21. Washington, D.C.: American Enterprise Institute for Public Policy Research.
——. 1975b. "The Rate of New Drug Discovery." In *Drug Development and Marketing*, ed. Robert B. Helms, pp. 155-63. Washington, D.C.: American Enterprise Institute for Public Policy Research, 1975.
Weiss, Carol H. 1976. "Policy Research in the University: Practical Aid or Academic Exercise?" *Policy Studies Journal* 4 (Spring): 224-28.
Wolfe, Sidney, and Anita Johnson. 1972. "Conflict against the Public Interest at the Bureau of Drugs." In *The Commissioner's Report of Investigation of Charges*, Alexander M. Schmidt, pp. 242-59. Washington, D.C.: Food and Drug Administration, 1975.
Zeckhauser, Richard. 1975. "Procedures for Valuing Lives." *Public Policy* 23 (Fall): 419-64.

CHAPTER 11

THE ROLE OF STATE PLANNING IN THE DEVELOPMENT OF CRIMINAL-JUSTICE FEDERALISM

Malcolm M. Feeley
Austin Sarat
Susan O. White

Crime, criminality, and what to do about both have proven to be major problems for the American people and for government officials since the founding of the republic. Crime has been traditionally perceived as a threat not only to individual well-being but also to the maintenance of social trust and community solidarity (Wilson 1975). Yet concern about the problem of crime and attempts to deal with it have been episodic. Periodic crime waves have met with—or perhaps been caused by—marked increases in citizen concern and generally futile efforts to "stamp out" crime. The crime problem and efforts to control crime have been traditionally regarded as the responsibility of state and local government. Federal criminal law and federal efforts have never been a major means of crime control in the United States; the national police force—the FBI—has continued to be legally restricted in its mission, and until the late 1960s little federal money was spent on crime control.*

The mid-1960s saw a dramatic change in the attitude of the federal government. Crime, while a problem with localized origins and impacts, appeared to be, when considered in the aggregate, a problem that was national in scope. Furthermore, the issue of crime and what to do about it became an important national political issue largely as a result of the presidential campaign of 1964. At about the same time, the national government was caught up in a "war mentality;" domestic and social ills, as well as foreign enemies, were dealt with through a massive mobilization of resources and the development of a coherent national

---

*The one major effort at developing a policy on crime has been a clearinghouse function in the FBI's collection, compilation, and distribution of its semiannual Uniform Crime Reports.

strategy. The response to the problem of crime and the application and elaboration of the war metaphor in this area occurred with the passage of the Omnibus Crime Control and Safe Streets Act of 1968 (P.L. 90-351). This act was the master plan for the national government's war on crime.*

Yet the Safe Streets Act represented a major departure from the strategy of reform and intervention embodied in other government programs like the war on poverty. Instead of direct national intervention, the act provided for a blockgrant approach in which the national government's role was to be primarily that of a provider of revenue and ideas to state and local governments, which would, in turn, develop programs for their own use. Fighting crime, although an effort requiring new and expanded sources of funds, was to continue to be left to state and local control. Emerging at the time that it did, the Safe Streets Act antedated general revenue sharing and thus became the first major expression of the New Federalism.

Our purpose in this chapter is to analyze the implementation of federal crime-fighting efforts under the Safe Streets Act. Ideally, we would like to be able to evaluate the success or failure of those efforts; however, the analysis of important public policies, especially in the area of crime and law enforcement, does not lend itself to conventional impact analysis; it does not lend itself to even the most hard-fought conclusions about what works in reducing crime. Crime is, and should be acknowledged to be, an intractable social problem. There is no technology for nor very many convincing ideas about how to go about reducing crime. To measure the success of any single public policy against that standard is to measure it against an impossible and unrealistic standard. Policies, like the Safe Streets Act, are usually aimed at affecting continuing and complex social processes rather than specific and soluble social problems; they have multifaceted and ambiguous goals rather than precise and definite objectives, and they are often designed to foster new structures and processes to cope with continuing problems rather than to tackle social problems directly. As a consequence, their impact is long in coming, indirect and intertwined with a host of other disparate efforts.

Because the reduction of crime is so remote from the actions of any government agency, and because the measurement of crime is itself problematic, we think it important to focus instead on the implementation rather than the

---

*The 1968 Act was preceded by the Law Enforcement Assistance Act of 1965 (P.L. 89-197), which created an Office of Law Enforcement Assistance (OLEA) within the Department of Justice; this was a much smaller scale effort than LEAA, and allocated funds on a categorical grant basis. Also in 1965, President Johnson created, by executive order, the President's Commission on Law Enforcement and Administration of Justice, which in 1967 produced voluminous reports, including *The Challenge of Crime in a Free Society*.

impact of the Safe Streets Act. In contrast to a study of the consequences of a policy decision like the Safe Streets Act, our study of implementation examines factors that contribute to the realization or nonrealization of the more proximate policy objectives of this act. (See Van Meter and Van Horn 1975, and Hargrove 1975). Those objectives involve an attempt to foster a new and efficient organizational capability at the state level, a capability to strengthen and improve local law enforcement and criminal-justice agencies and thereby combat crime.

The implementation of the Safe Streets Act lies with the organizations created under its mandate. At the national level, the most important of these organizations is the Law Enforcement Assistance Administration (LEAA); at the state level the most important are what are generically called State Planning Agencies (SPAs). The success or failure of the act is to an extent likely to be determined by the ability of these organizations to cope with and reconcile the obligations of the act and the conceptual, technical, and political constraints under which any policy delivery system must work. Thus, in this chapter we focus primarily on SPAs and on the ways in which they have dealt with the problems of planning, "innovation," and evaluation, for these are the problems that lie at the heart of the Safe Streets approach to crime and to reform in the administration of criminal justice.

To this end we conducted lengthy interviews with SPA staff members in 11 states, talked informally to officials in several other states, and held formal and informal discussions with national LEAA officials and state and local criminal-justice officials. Our purpose in these interviews and conversations was to gather information about the operations, functions, and problems of the Safe Streets Act and the criminal-justice federalism that it fostered.*

THE PROVISIONS OF THE SAFE STREETS ACT

Any attempt to understand the implementation of legislation must begin with the legislation itself. Its specific goals and requirements as well as the "intention of the framers" provide the broad parameters within which the process of implementation is carried out. Repeatedly during our interviews,

---

*This chapter does not seek to rank individual SPAs or to make predictions about their futures. Because SPAs are still relatively new and unknown in state governmental structure, they remain unstable, vulnerable to abrupt changes in direction and in leadership. Consequently, a precise description or placement of any single SPA in light of its larger state context is at present less important than an exploration of the major common problems and tensions with which all SPAs must cope.

reference was made to the language of the Safe Streets Act and to the tasks that it imposes on the LEAA and SPAs. The most general and ambitious of these tasks were to "fight crime" and, simultaneously, to improve and upgrade the capacities of state and local law-enforcement agencies. (For a complete account of congressional thinking and debate over the goals of the Safe Streets Act, see *Legislative History* (U.S. Congress, 1973.)

State Planning Agencies were charged, under the terms of the act, with the task of working with state and local criminal-justice agencies in developing and implementing the specific programs through which federal financial assistance was to be channeled. This programmatic role at the state level was itself a major reform. The Safe Streets Act mandated the creation of new state agencies and charged them with three general functions. First, these agencies were directed to engage in "comprehensive planning" for the entire criminal-justice system, unconstrained by the rather rigid and narrow boundaries* that characterize most existing criminal-justice agencies and officials. The act speaks in broad language about encouraging, through the State Planning Agencies, the "states and units of general local government to prepare and adopt comprehensive law enforcement plans based on their evaluation of state and local problems of law enforcement." The Safe Streets Act thus mandated a new way of thinking about the administration of criminal justice, a way of thinking that took seriously the metaphorical use of the word "system" (See Freed 1967). One of the most important parallel responsibilities of LEAA is to supervise the implementation of this new way of thinking and its specific manifestation in statewide criminal-justice planning. The act attempts to improve the capacity of individual states for defining the nature of their particular crime problems and to provide them resources for pursuing their own distinctive solutions.

In addition to their planning function, State Planning Agencies were to be the primary funding agencies for Safe Streets money; they were charged with the responsibility of deciding which specific programs and projects were to be funded and which problemss tackled with federal money. Yet the language of the act imposes on SPAs the general requirement that federal funds be used for "the improvement of law enforcement throughout the state." Subsequent interpretations of the act and the guidelines developed by LEAA to implement it have linked the term "improvement" closely with the term "innovation." SPAs

---

*What we characterize as "narrow and rigid boundaries" are both jurisdictional and functional. In most states, law-enforcement agencies are fragmented into state, county, and local jurisdictions; criminal-court jurisdictions often include town, city, and county courts, and even special state prosecution offices; correctional institutions range from city jails and lockups to county jails to state prisons. Furthermore, the functional differences among law-enforcement agencies, courts, and correctional institutions are significant, and territorial prerogatives are jealously guarded.

are expected to plan for and fund something other than incremental expansions of existing and traditional criminal-justice functions or displacing local sources of funding (which is, by way of contrast, permitted under general revenue sharing). The language of the act and its common-law development provides SPAs a role in developing, encouraging, and supporting new and different approaches to the crime problem, approaches that state and local agencies could not have developed or supported themselves.

A third function of SPAs was not directly mentioned in the 1968 Safe Streets Act, yet it has in recent years—through amendments to the act and guidelines—become an important part of what they are required to do,* namely to evaluate their own efforts at improving the administration of criminal justice by evaluating projects and programs funded with Safe Streets money. Here again, as in the area of comprehensive planning, the Safe Streets Act and LEAA have tried to promote a new way of thinking about law enforcement, a greater interest in efficiency and a curiosity about finding out what works. SPAs are not only expected to plan and develop new and different projects, they are also expected to document what works, what does not, and why.

UNDERSTANDING THE ACT

The rather broad and general language of the act and the requirements and tasks that it imposes on those charged with carrying it out poses the first and perhaps most important problem of implementation. It is a problem generic to any important public policy; it is, however, complicated when the policy is as ambitious as is the Safe Streets Act. The problem to which we refer is a conceptual one. In order for any policy to be effectively implemented it must be possible for those charged with the task to understand what is required and intended under the terms of the original policy. To the extent that the requirements or intent are either ambiguous or are the subject of continuing political contention, the process of implementation becomes complicated and difficult (Pressman and Wildavsky 1973). The problem of deriving clear and relatively unambiguous understandings of the purpose, objectives, and intent of a public

---

*Although LEAA guidelines have emphasized evaluation from the beginning, it was not until 1971-72 after the Monagan hearings, which publicized waste and mismanagement within LEAA and which resulted in LEAA's interest in insuring accountability, that the commitment to evaluation became a condition of the acceptance of SPA plans and a condition of SPAs awarding of grants. This interest in accountability was translated into an LEAA guideline that required a percentage of state action-grant funds be earmarked for evaluation purposes.

policy is particularly acute in the case of the Safe Streets Act. It is acute because of the difficulties of defining the proper boundaries of federal and state action under a block-grant program and because the specific policy objectives of the act are so complex. These difficulties hinder the process of implementation and pose problems that structure the way in which federal funds are spent in each state.

The first problem involves the range of permissible federal involvement that the Safe Streets Act envisions and allows, especially involvement in substantive decisions as to what SPAs are to do and how they are to do it. Some of the sponsors of the act, particularly its conservative congressional supporters, viewed the act as little more than a means of getting federal money to the states without "strings" attached. The few strings that were attached, for example, the requirement for comprehensive planning, were kept rather general so as to allow for some diversity in the way states would respond. Furthermore, some supporters, including some SPA officials, believe that the combination of responsibilities assigned to SPAs—grants management; developing, reviewing, and funding grant proposals from state and local agencies; planning, surveying state needs, and developing a coherent strategy for dealing with them, was designed to insure that the responsibilities would overwhelm the SPAs and leave them with little more to do than pass out federal money. In any case, the block-grant approach, which is the basis of the federal government's war on crime, can be interpreted as a way of giving maximum flexibility to state and local officials. The Safe Streets Act and its block-grant philosophy is interpreted by proponents of this "local" view as a political compromise in which the goal of minimum federal involvement was achieved by placing primary responsibility for administering that effort in the hands of state government. (For several case studies and other materials illustrating the local perspective see *Columbia Human Rights Law Review* 1973.)

The local perspective has also informed and influenced many criminal-justice practitioners in state and local agencies—the police, corrections, and courts. As seen from their perspective, LEAA is simply a source of additional, "free" funds. (For an extended discussion of an SPA-funded project and the local perspective see Feeley 1976.) The conditions placed on them by LEAA and the SPAs are requirements to be minimally complied with, simply part of the bureaucratic costs of obtaining "federal grants." If there are requirements to be innovative, project proposals will be described as innovative; if there are requirements to be "crime specific," project proposals will be so characterized. These agencies feel hard-pressed for funds and are willing to accommodate to SPAs in order to get support from them. They do not, however, view SPAs as a source of ideas, or programs, only of extra money. The recession has only served to reinforce this perspective as local agencies have sought the "federal" money in order to prevent cutbacks in regular program areas.

The block-grant approach permits other interpretations of the varying roles of federal, state, and local governments. Some would argue, for example, that the block-grant approach means more than revenue sharing; it is designed to insure a cooperative federal-state relationship in which both sides have important functions. (See U.S. Advisory Commission of Intergovernmental Relations 1970.) The Safe Streets Act, according to this "national" perspective, gives the federal government the responsibility for guiding and supervising the way federal funds are spent. Thus, for example, LEAA through its ten regional offices, is given the responsibility to review and approve state plans. If LEAA is dissatisfied, it may attach "special conditions" to the receipt of Safe Streets money. Furthermore, since the act does not define what it means when it charges SPAs to plan comprehensively so as to improve law enforcement, it requires interpretation. Unlike the local view, which would leave the responsibility for doing so to state and local officials, the national perspective believes that the development of the act's "common law" ought to be done by LEAA.* Since LEAA officials are accountable to Congress for how federal money is spent and for its impact or lack of impact, they have an easily understandable incentive to take an expansionist (or at least protectionist) view of the federal government's role.

Shaping the meaning of the requirements for "comprehensive plans" and for "improvement" provided one important opportunity for these federal officials to try to work their wills on the states. This was done by developing guidelines that provide content and specific meaning to the ambiguous terms and conditions of the act. The initial guidelines for comprehensive planning—a hefty document running over a hundred pages, and since then altered and expanded many times—clearly announced the intention of LEAA to affect not only the procedure by which federal funds would be spent, but how and for what purposes. The annual guidelines contain, in essence, a theory of the problems of local criminal-justice agencies, and propose a solution through greater statewide centralization, a solution in which Safe Streets money would be used to induce change in the administration of criminal justice rather than to support its ongoing operations.

Subsequent interpretations of the act and provisions in the guidelines have attempted to further direct the efforts and orientations of the SPAs in accordance with this vision. The act's requirement for "improvement of law enforcement and criminal justice" has come to mean "innovation." The term is understood to require the adoption of new and different techniques and approaches. Likewise, the amorphous notion of comprehensive planning has been carefully detailed by national LEAA. The 1976 *Guidelines Manual*, for instance, includes a two-page definition and enumeration of the components of

---

*This debate between a national perspective and a local perspective is clearly a contemporary example of the classic debate of American federalism, going back at least as far as the landmark Constitutional case of *McCulloch v. Maryland*, 17 U.S. (Wheat.) 316 (1819).

"comprehensiveness," a list that insists on a provision for evaluation of SPA efforts and the use of the results in subsequent planning efforts. (See 1976 *Manual*, pp. 62-64.)

Above all, the guidelines and direction from national LEAA officials have emphasized a desire to foster and sustain a systemwide perspective in thinking about concerns of criminal justice, one that will contribute to an ability to coordinate the traditionally fragmented and often antagonistic parts of the existing system. This perspective, stated and restated in numerous ways in the *Guidelines* and by all of LEAA's administrators identifies fragmentation of the criminal-justice system itself as one factor contributing to the ineffective crime-control policies. The analysis contains its own prescription, which is found in the language of the guidelines: "coordinate," "integrate," "consolidate," "cooperate," and "combine" hitherto fragmented, disparate, and inefficient efforts. The national perspective accords the SPAs the task of beginning this effort.

The national perspective envisions the emergence of SPAs as important state institutions whose potential far exceeds merely the allocation of federal funds. SPAs are, in this view, the forerunners of strong, centralized statewide efforts in organizing and administering the "nonsystem" of criminal justice. As a result, it is important to require the SPAs to aggressively pursue the tasks of planning—not simply to provide a program for spending federal funds—but to engage in long-range, comprehensive planning for the entire criminal-justice system. Likewise it is important to get them to assume an active leadership role among state criminal-justice agencies. Because each SPA has a supervisory board composed of representatives of various criminal-justice agencies and the public, the SPA is in a prime position to locate and identify common interests, act as a spokesman for the entire law-enforcement and criminal-justice community and foster coordinated policies. But the national perspective sees the expenditure of federal money as a means through which these ends might be accomplished rather than as the end for which the Safe Streets Act was enacted.

The block-grant strategy, because it permits these competing interpretations, provides one of the major factors influencing the implementation of the Safe Streets Act. The different interpretations of the act and its block-grant approach establish an important source of tension that shapes the way state SPAs function. On one side is LEAA, insisting that its guidelines be met and exhorting SPA planning staffs to be professionals, to think in systemwide terms, and to develop plans and projects that make a difference. On the other side are the criminal-justice agencies, which want as much money as possible and tend to view any requirements on applications or restrictions on the use of funds—let alone any requirements for a demonstration of need and an evaluation of results—as hindrances to be avoided, evaded, or ignored.

Another problem in understanding the act arises from the ambiguity of the functions assigned to SPAs under its terms. It is safe to assume that this ambiguity has not been eliminated; some would argue it has been compounded by the development of the minutely detailed, frequently changed, common law embodied in LEAA guidelines. Put quite simply, what we have found is that SPA officials have no common set of concrete ideas about what it means to plan comprehensively, or to improve the criminal-justice system, or to evaluate criminal-justice programs. This means that the first task in the implementation of the Safe Streets Act, and its most important continuing problem, is conceptual. SPA officials are called upon to perform tasks for which they perceive no available technology and for which many feel uniquely ill-equipped. Furthermore, the difficulty of developing an understanding of the functions assigned to SPAs allows for so many competing interpretations that the "healthy pluralism" envisioned in the block-grant strategy has, we think, become little more than each state taking its own "shot in the dark" or complying with the letter of LEAA guidelines in ways that often undermine or ignore their spirit and intent.

The difficulty of comprehending and therefore implementing the mandates of the Safe Streets Act was revealed repeatedly in our conversations with SPA staff members. For example, when we asked one planner to explain what "comprehensive planning" meant, she laughed and responded that no one knew and no one would be able to tell us. Other planners were willing to attempt a definition, but they gave a variety of meanings to the concepts. To some it is an ideal, a long range goal toward which the SPA ought to be reaching. When queried as to what made a plan comprehensive, one staff member replied:

> I would very much like to be involved in the overall criminal justice plan and budget determination. When all the money on criminal justice is being considered, I'd like to see how LEAA money could become the strategic dollar. I'd like to see a central planning and coordinating unit and become part of it.

This respondent echoed the views and desires of many SPA members, to whom the goal of comprehensive planning was a coordination of the system's entire efforts "with an eye toward using the LEAA funds for strategic purposes." No one, however, argued that this was the effort they, themselves, were currently engaged in. It was, at best, the eventual goal, a goal many felt was supported by national LEAA officials.

In contrast, the staff of most SPAs who were familiar with their agency's planning functions agreed that planning consisted of little more than arranging the applications before them, and presenting them as a package—a description of what they were going to do.

Rarely did we encounter a planner who had an understanding of planning in any traditional sense. Even those who had elaborated views of planning—saying that it involved surveying the domain under their jurisdiction, identifying problems, comparing their magnitude, mobilizing "hard evidence," establishing priorities and goals, and organizing a coherent strategy for dealing with them—felt that SPAs were ill-equipped to plan in anything close to that way.

Many SPA planners view questions about planning and the "philosophical" perspectives held by the national LEAA with a great deal of amusement. They argue that not only are they constrained by the realities of their relatively weak position vis-à-vis the older, established criminal-justice agencies, but also that their days are literally taken up by pushing paper, by responding to the multitude of grant applications that are submitted to them (they do not control who can submit proposals, and guidelines require that all applications must be reviewed and responded to), and by meeting the detailed requirements of the national guidelines. Their jobs as planners, they continue, consist of little more than being reactive to the claims of others. It is a process of responding to others, and reacting to how they—not the planners—define the problems.

Aside from the requirements that funds must be spent in accordance with a comprehensive plan—which at a minimum means that all major segments of the criminal-justice system must receive some financial support*—the SPAs are required under LEAA guidelines to concentrate their support on innovative solutions to persistent problems and to improve criminal-justice agencies. Innovation is a term used frequently by SPA staff planners and heard even more frequently from national LEAA officials, who regularly exhort the SPAs to be more creative, and develop and apply new ideas and methods in combating crime and increasing the system's efficiency. The purpose of LEAA, as many SPA planners and almost all national officials indicate, is not to provide open-ended subsidies for existing criminal-justice agencies or to supplant existing funds, but rather to develop programs that are experimental, are new and different, and which would not otherwise be funded from existing sources of support.†

---

*It is interesting to note that various segments of the criminal-justice system have claimed that they are excluded from their fair share of the LEAA pie. Such complaints have led Congress to provide special categorical allocations: so-called Part E funds for corrections and proposed Part F funds for the courts. Ironically, these moves not only run counter to the revenue-sharing basis of block-grant funding, but they are also the antithesis of the mandated function of comprehensive planning.

†Our review of the literature on innovation was a distressing experience. The best work in the area seemed to be limited to discussions of the adoption rates of unambiguous technologies, for example, more productive strains of grain or improved vaccines. Although this innovation—adoption approach has been applied to state adoptions of new types of legislation, we are not impressed. Innovation implies a high consensus on values, and while there may be a high consensus among those directly affected on the relative merits of a new type of corn—although even here we are prepared to acknowledge the problematic nature of the assertion—it is difficult to see the same consensus in such government provision as compulsory education, child labor laws, and income taxation. It is difficult to see what understanding results in an examination of adoption rates of these types of government programs that rely on an epidemiological model. Thus whose understanding of innovation prevails becomes the central problem for study. Because of the lack of advanced technologies in criminal justice and because of the widely varying perspectives held and types of functions pursued by criminal-justice agencies, the positing of a single notion of innovation—as a goal to be pursued and as a benchmark against which state activities can be judged—would be meaningless. The meaning of the concept itself must be the primary focus of attention.

Most SPA planners agreed in essence that the call for innovation by the national LEAA is little more than an attempt to convince Congress that it is doing something distinctive. By its very nature, SPA staff planners seemed to be saying, the National LEAA is an agency without a great deal of distinctiveness and the challenge to "be innovative" and the admonition to "discover the undiscovered" was a way of coping and perhaps trying to protect themselves from an increasingly restive Congress. Trying to respond to the often abstract admonitions, however, proves to be a difficult and frustrating task for SPA planners.

Although committed to the idea that action-grant funds should be used to support new and distinctive projects, many planners understood new to be something new in reference to a particular agency, while others view it as new for the state. Thus, for example, some might encourage police departments to apply for funds to support police advisors because they have been judged to work in an initial few departments, while others would take a perspective that the SPA-funding effort should be completed once its projects have been judged as successes after the initial effort. Since it was judged a success, they argue, there is no need for continued SPA support. It is a tried and tested project, ready to sink or swim on its own.

The third component of the SPA mandate is to evaluate. This requirement is, in theory, integrally linked with the planning and innovation functions of SPAs. Not only are they expected to plan and develop new and different projects, they are also expected to document what works, what does not, and why. However, as with the other two functions, there is nothing approaching a consensus as to what evaluation is or should be (see O'Connell and White 1974). Evaluation research to some is an experiment, a test of hypotheses that requires measurements of change in experimental and control groups. Evaluation to others is the production of progress reports on projects by means of periodic memos from project staff to SPA monitors. Some evaluation staffs were found preparing auditing and monitoring reports on their projects, while others appeared to be administrative assistants to SPA directors. Still others take an even more minimalist view of evaluation, viewing it as whatever is required to satisfy the LEAA guidelines and requirements.

LEAA officials and guidelines, on the other hand, make a distinction between project monitoring and evaluation, the former being a continuous social and financial auditing of the projects to see that "things are moving along on pace," that people are doing what they were hired to do, that proper equipment is purchased, and that no one has flown the coop with the money. Essentially, monitoring is to determine if the project is doing what it was intended to do, and if job descriptions square with job performance. Whether what is being done makes any difference is the function of evaluation, according to LEAA. Despite this difference, SPA evaluators almost invariably gravitate toward the monitoring function, in part because they are one of the few groups within the SPA who remain in continuing communication with the myriad of SPA-funded projects.

Before SPA directors are likely to ask "Does it make any difference?" they want to know: "How many projects are we funding?" "How large are they?" "Where are they?" "Are there any problems with them?" It is supplying answers to these latter questions that tends to eat up the time of the evaluation staffs.

The variations in how the SPA evaluation units are organized are in part a function of what they perceive their function to be. Some see themselves as experimenters, people who test particular ideas—projects—to see what works, what does not work, and why. Their goal is to focus on new, particularly innovative ideas and see how effective they are. If the project proves successful, it should be continued and expanded. If not, it should be terminated. This view embodies a more generalized "social-engineering" view of public policymaking.

At the other extreme is a belief that evaluation provides little useful information. Proponents of this view appear willing to see the evaluation requirement abandoned by LEAA, although some acknowledge that ideally it could be put to good use. Ironically, proponents of this view held that the better the evaluation, by academic-research standards, the less likely it is to be useful. As one planner stated:

> The evaluations come in too late and their impact is minimal. . . . Another problem is that evaluators tend to be equivocal, so they are not useful in making a yes/no decision . . . they keep wanting better data and more detailed information.

Evaluations, especially the more "professional" ones, tend to be hedged with qualifications, and filled with complaints about the limitations of imperfect research designs and sloppy data, and as a consequence are so equivocal as to be of little or no use to planners who want categorical answers. Another problem with "good" evaluation studies is that they take a long time, and as a consequence are received too late to be helpful in the annual planning and budgetary cycle of the agency. Many planners express scorn at evaluators who submit reports hedged with qualifications, obtuse prose, and recommending "continued study," all submitted months after the refunding decision on the project has had to be made and thus too late to be of use to them.

There are other dilemmas for the SPA evaluation staff. Many projects, they feel, fall into two categories for which the value of evaluation is questionable. On one hand many projects are one-shot affairs—training programs for police, prosecutors, or judges, or equipment purchases—efforts that are not likely to be repeated within the state. Others are contributions to long and complex effort at institutional change (for example, consolidation of smaller police departments or changes in treatment of juveniles), in which the federal money constitutes only an initial and probably small portion of the total in the continuing effort. In the former, SPA planners and evaluators argue, there is little need to evaluate, while in the latter, evaluation is rendered difficult because the SPA funding is only a portion of a large and long-term effort.

Ambiguity, uncertainty, and frustration are characteristic of the way in which SPA officials think about the mandates and intentions of the Safe Streets Act. These problems, all of which involve the problem of understanding the act, complicate the process of implementation and insure that the operations of SPA will be highly unstable and variable from state to state. Ambiguity, uncertainty and frustration prevent the development of an institutionalized formula through which SPAs might operate. As people come and go in SPAs, new interpretations—interpretations often radically difference from those that have previously guided a SPA—may take hold. Furthermore, ambiguity, uncertainty, and frustration contribute to the vulnerability of SPAs as organizations. Without a clear idea of their mandate, SPAs are caught up in tensions of the block-grant approach and are caught between the frequently competing demands of LEAA and their constituents in the criminal-justice system. How they adapt to and cope with uncertainty and the pressures it generates goes far in determining how the Safe Streets Act is implemented.

STRATEGIES OF IMPLEMENTATION

The process of implementing any public policy is inevitably a process of adaptation, a process through which the objects and goals of legislation are shaped by and fit into a context of resources, conditions, and pressures operative in the policy environment. This is certainly true of the Safe Streets Act. Among the major pressures and conditions affecting the implementation of that act, perhaps none is more important than the competition between the national and local interpretations that we have discussed. This competition means that SPAs have had to adjust to and deal with various and frequently contradictory demands. The process of implementation has been further confused by the unique character of the administration of criminal justice and of crime as a social problem. Introducing new ways of thinking into established legal institutions is a very difficult task that SPAs, equipped as they are with funds generally totaling no more than 2 or 3 percent of a state's total criminal-justice expenditures, may not be in a position to do. Yet the Safe Streets Act's greatest long-run contribution may result from its requirement that states develop such a new and comprehensive way of thinking about crime. The act has created new structures, structures that may develop the capacity for continuous innovation and reform. It is the way these structures develop and cope with their problems that is crucial to the effort of building at a new "criminal-justice federalism."

It is, however, premature to assess the impact this act has had in achieving this procedural or structural goal. LEAA has been run almost entirely by a Republican administration, and has not yet weathered sustained attack by an incumbent administration or an antagonistic Congress. Nor have SPAs come to be regarded as permanent fixtures in the state house* Nevertheless it is possible to suggest some alternative ways in which SPAs are coping with problems of implementing the Safe Streets Act and some strategies through which the process of implementation is being carried out. In our research we uncovered three kinds of strategies. They are ideal types rather than actual examples, and while individual SPAs tend more toward one than the others, these tendencies may be more in the ideals and goals of the staff rather than any concrete and measurable differences of practice, and they are subject to abrupt shifts as SPA directors and state governors change.

Revenue-Sharing Strategy

One strategy of implementation begins by rejecting the metaphor of the criminal-justice system. SPAs that pursue a revenue-sharing strategy reject the national interpretation of the act according to which SPAs are supposed to plan for the rational development of a system of criminal justice. From the point of view of the revenue-sharing strategy, SPAs are not and cannot be in a position to plan for or even coordinate a state's criminal-justice agencies. They handle only about 2 or 3 percent of the total criminal-justice budget and have no voice in the expenditure of the other 97 to 98 percent. Furthermore, they are organized as a state agency while most crime-control agencies are local. In fact, no single office or agency has a voice in the total criminal-justice budget because there is no single crime budget. The notion of a unified budget and planning effort is much like the notion of a criminal-justice system itself, a fiction of idealists' imaginations. (For a discussion of this general problem see Reich 1973.)

The revenue-sharing strategy assumes that efforts at comprehensive planning are fictions, little more than exercises to assure that all segments get some portion of the LEAA pie. It dismisses efforts at identifying program areas and establishing priorities for funding, arguing that when such priorities are established, they are so broadly construed that they do little to restrict the types of projects that can be funded.

---

*Most of the SPAs remain creatures of the governor, established under executive order, not statute. None of the SPA staff, when queried, could foresee the continuation of their SPA in the event of congressional deauthorization of LEAA. Only one of the SPAs we visited, Kentucky, has been legislatively established and delegated planning duties beyond the preparation of the annual plan for LEAA. All this is not unexpected. Major alterations in state governments emerge slowly. It is, therefore, somewhat premature to assess the impact of the Safe Streets Act on the structure of state government.

As for innovation, this strategy holds that the SPAs are not in a position to make substantial changes in the operations of criminal-justice agencies. Although they may have some marginal effect in suggesting new or additional projects, these are only a drop in the bucket and are probably the result not of organized comprehensive planning but of the creativity of a few individuals in the SPAs and their informal contacts in the agencies. If major changes are required to improve existing agencies, the SPAs are not in a position to bring them about.

Under the revenue-sharing strategy, the SPA staff is little more than the agent of its supervisory board, which in turn represents and speaks for traditional criminal-justice interests. Furthermore, in many states the substate regional planning units (RPUs) are closely connected to local governments and therefore to local law enforcement. In a revenue-sharing strategy, the RPUs can exercise considerable influence over funding decisions in terms of traditional criminal-justice interests. Nor is the organizations of the SPAs and their planning boards such that it is likely to foster innovation. Innovation, one planning director argued, is likely to come about through the quiet and concerted efforts of a small number of people, not public meetings at which vested interests are represented.

As for evaluation, it is of little use. This strategy assumes that change is incremental. Dramatic new projects do not emerge overnight to be tested and pronounced good or bad, they emerge slowly and from within established institutions. New institutions emerge not so much in response to clear goals or objectives, but rather emerge in response to what is not wanted, a movement away from bad practices. Evaluation research, in a classic sense, plays little if any part in this type of change. In any event, most SPAs are not in a good position to oversee any serious type of evaluation effort because they do not control the projects they fund in such a way as to assure adequate controls and a disinterested evaluation. Furthermore, evaluation results are not easily coordinated with budgeting and planning cycles, so they are not particularly useful even when they are produced.

This strategy holds that these inherent limitations on SPAs should be recognized and squarely faced, and that the job of a SPA is only to disperse funds according to a relatively stable formula for distribution. SPA functions are, thus, restricted to the minimal, but nevertheless important, tasks of project auditing and administration, seeing that federal fiscal and other requirements are complied with by the grantees.

The Cutting-Edge Strategy

A second way in which some SPA staff envision implementation of the Safe Streets Act is by adopting a "cutting-edge" strategy. This strategy is based on the view that the influx of federal funds and the establishment of a statewide planning agency provides a unique opportunity for the hitherto fragmented criminal-justice system to develop its own research and development (R and D) capacity. The SPAs and the action grants are conceived of as R and D efforts designed to stimulate new ideas. Control of the action grants means that the SPA is in a position to encourage experimentation by trying out new and different ideas that the already hard-pressed criminal-justice agencies are not likely to try with their own limited resources.

The cutting-edge strategy would like to use comprehensive planning to review existing functions and programs for the purpose of identifying shortcomings and pointing out needs. Planning is intertwined with innovation since its purpose is to identify continuing problems and propose new and different solutions to overcome them.

Although a small fraction of the total criminal-justice budget, LEAA funds are considered the cutting edge for innovation. They should be used exclusively for R and D purposes, and the SPA staff seeks to approximate a think tank, working in close cooperation with existing criminal-justice officials to experiment with projects and forms of operation. Although small in proportion to R&D resources in private industry (which can run as high as 15 to 20 percent of the total budget), SPAs are an important first step in developing the system's capacity to engage in this type of creative activity.

A major problem for a cutting-edge strategy involves the way projects are funded. Although projects are funded on an annual basis, most of the planners we talked to argued for the necessity of providing project support for several years. They argued that it takes a minimum of two years for a complex project to become properly staffed and be operating in a way that its effectiveness can reasonably be judged. Many, they claim, take even longer.*

The cumulative effect of multiyear funding commitments has substantially affected the ability of SPAs to do anything at all. Planners acknowledged that in any given year upward of 60 to 75 percent of their funds are tied up in carry-over commitments from previous years. Given the faddishness of so much of the discussion of innovation within LEAA, the high turnover, and the attendant changes of emphasis of the new staff members, many planners—recruited with the expectation of designing new and innovative programs—find themselves caught up in the frustrating process of having to honor and administer the commitments of their predecessors. During the first few years of operation, most planners indicated, they operated under the conditions of rapid growth and

---

*It appears that on the average SPAs fund projects for three years, although a number of substantial projects (for example, experiments in restructuring the nature of incarceration) are funded for as long as six or seven years, and many others are one-shot equipment purchases or training programs.

expansion. Receiving large sums of money to dispense even before they themselves were fully staffed, the SPAs gave little heed to the eventual implications of multiyear commitments. As appropriations have leveled off, this problem now looms larger in the minds of the SPA staffs.

The response of the cutting-edge SPAs is to tighten up requirements for multiyear funding. While previous self-imposed restrictions limiting project funding to two or three years were often honored in the breach, they are now being more carefully enforced, and in those states with no formal rules on refunding, time limits are now being introduced.

Reducing long-term commitments, however, is not without its drawbacks. Major and substantial changes are not likely to be forthcoming overnight, and many acknowledge that their most successful projects are those that have been nurtured over extended periods. Thus ironically the interest of cutting-edge agencies in flexibility and creativity seems to be, at least in part, pursued at the expense of their ability to make large and long-term commitments that may eventually produce substantial changes.

Evaluation is, at least in theory, very important in cutting-edge agencies. Their major thrust is to find out whether a new idea works and then to disseminate that information. They assume that if an idea works, criminal-justice agencies will be able to find other sources of funds to sustain them. Once an idea has proved itself, the cutting-edge strategy is to abandon it and try something else. At the same time, this strategy requires a high tolerance for failure. Those who subscribe to it are interested in knowing what does not work as well as what does. The experiments that the cutting-edge agency seeks to fund thus must be closely watched, sometimes replicated, and carefully assessed before they can be approved and marketed for wider distribution.

The likelihood of the cutting-edge strategy sustaining itself is never very great. However, it is the strategy that many believe is favored by the national LEAA administrators. This strategy assumes that local criminal-justice claims for money can be held in abeyance, so that the funds can be used for timely experimental projects. Thus, those adhering to the cutting-edge strategy are sympathetic to the LEAA guidelines insisting on innovative projects, excluding the expenditure of funds for personnel and buildings, and requiring evaluations. Although at times some criticize the LEAA guidelines as placing unnecessary restrictions on them, they generally appreciate the intent of these guidlines and would, in fact, appreciate additional requirements that would further insulate them from the politics of the process of allocating action-grant funds and would free an even larger portion of the funds for innovative projects.

Centralized-Planning Strategy

A third strategy of implementation differs from the second in its emphasis on coordination rather than experimentation. This strategy emphasizes the role or opportunity of SPAs to foster the systemwide approach to the problem of crime and to oversee the operations of the criminal-justice agencies. The emphasis is on dealing with what is already going on in the criminal-justice agencies and on the development of an integrated system rather than on specific program ideas.

Although most SPAs are restricted to planning and administering projects supported by LEAA money, the comprehensive-planning strategy requires a SPA to develop a total-system perspective and involves it in virtually every facet of law enforcement and criminal-justice administration. Its perspective is unique and its information valuable. As state governments grow in size and as efforts to adopt more rational management and budget techniques continue, the SPA is in a natural position to begin to assume expanded planning and oversight functions.

The view of comprehensive planning implied in this model is that the SPA should not only develop plans for spending its funds, but that it should, in light of the whole, use these funds strategically, as an incentive to get the existing criminal-justice agencies to change. If the cutting-edge strategy views planning primarily as an isolated R and D effort to develop innovative ideas, the centralized-planning strategy views planning not only as a means for coming up with new ideas, but also as a means for securing implementation of new ideas and redirecting the allocation of existing resources. Its initial means of doing this is the strategic use of action-grant funds, in the classic matching-grant tradition. In the long run, it may assume independent powers to review budgets and plan for criminal-justice programs. Its goal, as one SPA planner put it, is to be in the position—for the first time—to be able to ask the question: "Where is it more efficient to invest an additional dollar, in judges or police officers?"

This strategy emphasizes managerial development, and it views innovation primarily in terms of increased management capabilities. In many respects it talks past, not in opposition to, the other models of SPAs. For instance, while the cutting-edge strategy emphasizes development of new and different techniques to be used in combatting and controlling crime and in processing arrestees, this strategy emphasizes the rationalization of the management of the system as itself the most important innovation. This does not preclude the possibility of the adoption of new crime-fighting techniques; it simply puts a premium on increased efficiency and redeployment.

Evaluation plays an important role in this strategy, although not necessarily of the experimental-research variety. Here SPAs are interested in cost-effectiveness studies, projects that might lead to the consolidation of small police forces, the closing of prisons, the development of cheaper alternatives to incarceration, and the development of local coordinating councils. Following its emphasis on innovation as efficiency, evaluation would also focus on measuring efficiency.

We have discussed three strategies by which SPAs have sought to cope with the major functions mandated by the Safe Streets Act. In each case the functions are viewed differently, and dealt with in ways that fit an overall strategy of implementation rather than a standard conception of what that function is or should be. Even though they are ideal types rather than descriptions of individual SPAs, it is these strategies—revenue sharing, cutting edge, and centralized planning—that most accurately characterize the variation in SPA implementation of the Safe Streets Act.

CONCLUSIONS

The problem of crime is a longstanding and difficult social problem. Yet direct federal involvement with local law enforcement is relatively new. In this paper we have attempted to analyze patterns of implementation of this policy change. We have tried to identify the problems and pressures inherent in the Safe Streets Act's block-grant approach and to suggest that these problems and pressures have resulted in substantial confusion and variation in the way in which the Safe Streets Act has been implemented. We have focused on the way these problems and pressures are dealt with at the state level and on the way they have caused SPAs to develop a wide range of strategies to cope and adapt and, in the process, have led to a variety of definitions of the role and function of SPAs. We have identified three different strategies that SPAs use in coming to grips with their primary functions, strategies that embody different responses to the difficulties of implementing the Safe Streets Act.

One of these strategies, the revenue-sharing strategy, is clearly the one most responsive to local criminal-justice interests, while the other two—the cutting-edge and the centralized-planning strategies—are variations on the national perspective. In our research we found that the impulse toward all three of these strategies existed in each of the SPAs although they varied in balance and intensity in each of the states. Because LEAA is such a new entity and the SPAs are still in their infancies, it is difficult and of questionable value to try to categorize or rank individual SPAs in terms of these strategies.

We can, however, suggest that when SPAs move in any one of these directions, powerful forces will rise to "correct." The block-grant approach seems to cause tensions which require that the agencies it creates become preoccupied with the nature of their mission, to an extent we think is not likely under either grants-in-aid or general revenue-sharing programs.

Furthermore, if we begin to look at the implications for the SPAs as they attempt to define more precise roles for themselves (or have them defined for them), we can anticipate several possible consequences. If the local perspective prevails and they employ a revenue-sharing strategy, then they are likely to be ineffective and unnecessary, not because additional funds for criminal-justice systems might not be useful, but because other, more efficient means of getting funds to local justice agencies are available, and the expenses attached to creating a planning, evaluation, and innovation function are likely to be unnecessary and unproductive. To the extent that SPAs and their supporters employ either of the other two strategies, they are likely to be ineffective because SPAs at present exert virtually no control over the primary resources of the criminal-justice agencies. Furthermore, it is not reasonable to expect the SPAs to gain such natural authority over existing agencies through the slow but continued performance of their currently limited functions of comprehensive planning, innovation, and evaluation. In many respects these activities seem to be counterproductive. For to the extent that they are vigorously pursued, they insulate the SPAs from the real politics of the allocation process in criminal justice, and force nuisances and unwelcome functions on existing criminal-justice interests, something that will gain them neither respect nor authority. This we see as the continuing dilemma facing the Law Enforcement Assistance Administration and the derivative State Planning Agencies. To the extent that they try to work closely with the existing and more powerful criminal-justice agencies, they become unnecessary. And to the extent they try to exercise a strong leadership role in planning and innovation, they become isolated and hence ineffectual.

REFERENCES

Columbia Human Rights Law Review. 1973. "The Law Enforcement Assistance Administration: A Symposium On Its Operation and Impact," 5: 1.
Feeley, Malcolm. 1976. "Innovation and Implementation of a Public Agency: The Case of the New Haven Redirection Center." In *Innovation and Implementation in Public Agencies*, eds. Douglas Yates and Richard Nelson. Boston: D. C. Heath, 1976).
Freed, D. J. 1967. "The Non-System of Criminal Justice." In *Report to the Task Force on Law and Law Enforcement*, pp. 265-84. Washington, D.C.: Government Printing Office, 1967.
Hargrove, Edwin. 1975. *The Missing Link: The Study of the Implementation of Social Policy*. Washington, D.C.: Urban Institute.
Law Enforcement Assistance Administration. Guidelines Manual: *State Planning Agency Grants*, January 16, 1976.
Legislative History of the Omnibus Crime Control and Safe Streets Act of 1968. 1973. Washington, D.C.: Goverment Printing Office.
O'Connell, Lawrence W., and White, Susan O. 1975. "Politics and Evaluation in LEAA: the New England States." In *Management and Policy Science in American Government*, eds. Michael J. White, Michael Radnor, and David A. Tansik. Lexington, Mass.: D.C. Heath, 1975.
Pressman, Jeffrey, and Wildavsky, Aaron. 1973. *Implementation*. Berkeley: University of California Press.
Reich, Robert E. 1973. "Operations Research and Criminal Justice," 22 *Journal of Public Law*: 357-87.
U.S. Advisory Commission on Intergovernmental Relations, 1970. *Making the Safe Streets Act Work: An Intergovernmental Challenge*. Washington, D.C.: U.S. Advisory Commission on Intergovernmental Relations. 1970.

———. 1976. *Safe Streets Reconsidered: The Block Grant Experience, 1968-1975.* Washington, D.C.: U.S. Advisory Commission on Intergovernmental Relations.

Van Meter, Donald, and Van Horn, Carl. 1975. "The Policy Implementation Process: A Conceptual Framework," *Administration and Society* 6: 445-88.

CHAPTER 12

THE POLICY IMPACT OF POLICY EVALUATION: SOME IMPLICATIONS OF THE KANSAS CITY PATROL EXPERIMENT

Jeffrey Henig
Robert L. Lineberry
Neal A. Milner

Experimentation is knowledge production. The experimental model is presumably the strongest mode of policy analysis, just as the natural sciences, from which that model is drawn, are presumably the most "scientific" branches. The promise of an experimenting society holds great appeal for some social scientists.[1] And applying the exactitude and control associated with post-Newtonian science bears an attraction that is also felt beyond those whose own stature rises and falls with that of the university.

But while the virtue of a policy-relevant social science has long been touted, there is emerging a sense of confusion and disappointment over the apparent failure of policy evaluations and experiments to have their expected impact. Rossi and Williams construct their edited volume on social-policy analysis around the question of why the quality and quantity of social-program evaluation are both so low.[2] But even more disturbing is the nonutilization by policymakers of those studies that have been done, even those that have been done fairly well. Francis G. Caro notes that:

This chapter represents a very preliminary effort to assess the consequences of the Kansas City experiment for long-run changes in police departments. Supporting this was Grant Number 75NI-99-0130 awarded by the National Institute of Law Enforcement and Criminal Justice, Law Enforcement Assistance Administration, U.S. Department of Justice, under the Omnibus Crime Control and Safe Streets Act of 1968, as amended. Points of view or opinions stated herein are those of the authors and do not necessarily represent the official positions or policies of the U.S. Department of Justice.

> Since the ultimate purpose of evaluation is to contribute to the effectiveness of action programs, implementation of research results is a critical phase in the process. Yet numerous writers have warned that even the most carefully designed and executed evaluative research does not automatically lead to meaningful action.[3]

Caro and others speculate about the skimpy utilization payoff of policy research, but there has been little empirical research on the matter.

We hope to begin to redress that lack by investigating the process of diffusion, communication and impact of one specific policy evaluation. The focus is on the Kansas City patrol experiment, conducted through the auspices of the Police Foundation under perhaps the most rigorous methodological constraints available in policy experimentation. We shall be asking what factors are likely to affect whether knowledge produced by policy evaluations will have any impact on organizations and policymaking institutions, and what factors mitigate this impact. In doing so, we shall borrow freely from the literatures of judicial impact, policy implementation, and policy-evaluation research, each of which offers a compatible perspective on what happened to a policy (and, by analogy, to a policy experiment) once the shouting and cursing have died down.

First, a word on the centerpiece of our inquiry. The Kansas City Police Department, with guidance and financial assistance from the Police Foundation, conducted from October 1, 1972 to September 31, 1973 an experiment, the results of which called into serious question the traditional assumptions of the routine patrol function.[4] Essentially, following the canons of experimental design, the department divided certain of its beats into three types. In one area, no routine patrol functions whatsoever were performed, and police units responded only on call; in a second, patrol functions were beefed up considerably to the point of being doubled or trebled; and in the third, the control group, patrol functions were maintained at previous levels. The results suggested that there had been no statistically significant differences in crime rates among the three types of beats. Nor were there appreciable differences in citizen attitudes, reported criminal victimization, citizen behavior, police behavior, or even in traffic accidents.

The reactions to the experiment in Kansas City were varied. The assistant chief of the police department was initially quoted as remarking that, "we went out and proved that the liberal cliche is correct: crime is caused by social conditions which very frequently are beyond the control of the police."[5] Much later, in the introduction to the report of the experiment, Chief of Police Joseph McNamara remarked more circumspectly that, "a great deal of caution must be used to avoid the error of believing that the experiment proved more than it did. One thing the experiment did not show is that a visible police presence can have no impact on crime in selected circumstances."[6]

As a superior example of a policy experiment, the Kansas City study provides an ideal focus for an investigation of the factors that intervene between the completion of such a study and the incorporation of its findings in public policy. So far, few scholars have paid much attention to the policy impact of policy experimentation. We propose to do that by emphasizing the diffusion and legitimation of experimental results and processes. The three sets of literature on which we draw in interpreting this case have apparently evolved independently, yet each is concerned with the process by which some policy-related information (a court ruling, a policy decision, a research finding) is translated into action. While there are shortcomings of the existing studies in each of these areas, we have found that there are commonalities, emergent themes, upon which we can build with our own research. Specifically we ask what orientation to the study of impact they commonly suggest, and what impact-mitigating variables they commonly find.

NOTES TOWARD A THEORY OF EXPERIMENTAL IMPACT

Social scientists have long been deluded by the belief that their impact on policy will be automatically strengthened by better methodologies, stronger measures, and better theories. From this belief comes the "if only" perspective on social science and policymaking: if only we had better crime data; if only we had more controls; if only the sample size permitted more sophisticated statistical analysis; if only we had had a hand in designing the policy to be evaluated; and so forth. Happily, the Kansas City patrol experiment minimized the "if only" complaint, being the culmination of a slow but certain accretion of research in policing. Though hardly above methodological criticism, the study is regarded as perhaps the soundest policy experiment ever undertaken. Judith Dahmann, after reviewing five previous efforts to apply experimental techniques to the relationship of police patrol and crime, suggests that the Kansas City study provides the "first reliable information on the effectiveness of preventive patrol."[7]

We suggest that the policy impact of policy experimentation is a political, not a methodological, phenomenon. Walter Williams emphasizes:

> No evaluation can be expected to be unassailable in terms of its methodological and field development. And these deficiencies open up the debate so that ideological or political concerns can be pursued in a methodological framework.[8]

Whether experimentation ultimately implies impact depends far less on methodological rigor than upon the simultaneous processes of diffusion and legitimation. We put the matter in rough diagrammatic form in Figure 12.1. Whatever the content and methodology of a particular policy evaluation, unless the knowledge of the evaluation is somehow transmitted from the conductors of the research to those with responsibility for policymaking, no impact can be expected. An evaluation that goes unheard of is like the tree that falls in the forest with no one to hear it.

The process of legitimation occurs within a policy community, which we conceptualize as the network of officials, researchers, private- and public-sector spokesmen, and national, state, and local law-enforcement practitioners. A policy community is a producer and a consumer of research, a creator of paradigms defining conventional wisdom in a policy area, and a powerful source of professional reward and deprivation.

No organization—not even local police departments, which are probably the most autonomous policymaking in the political system—is an island.[9] Organizations are imbedded in larger networks of organizations, through which information flows, innovations diffuse, personnel are transplanted, and professional paradigms are both nurtured and sustained. Jack Walker has coined the term "policy communities," an amorphous but suggestive concept for describing the gatekeeper function. Policy communities, he suggests,

> include those primarily engaged in studying the policies and procedures being employed in an area, as well as administrators of the major agencies with operating programs. The communities involve bureau chiefs and officials in operating agencies, academics and consultants employed by research and development firms, publishers or editors of professional journals and magazines, representatives from business firms that are major suppliers of goods and services employed in the area, members of legislative staffs and legislators themselves who specialize in the subject, and other elected officials and lobbyists with interest in the policies. Beyond the assumption that people with such diverse backgrounds constitute a form of community, we make three further assumptions, all of which are plausible but as yet unsubstantiated: (1) members of communities of this kind constantly exchange information about their activities and ideas; (2) they do this, at least in part, to receive approval or recognition from other members of the community; and (3) ideas and information that conform to the currently established professional consensus will most likely be rewarded with esteem and recognition.[10]

The following issues emerge from this brief discussion of the impact of policy evaluation that uses the experimental method: there are important differences between what the study says and its ultimate results; direct, formal sanctions play a limited role in getting these studies implemented;

FIGURE 12.1

A Rough Diagrammatic Scheme of the Process of Experimental Impact

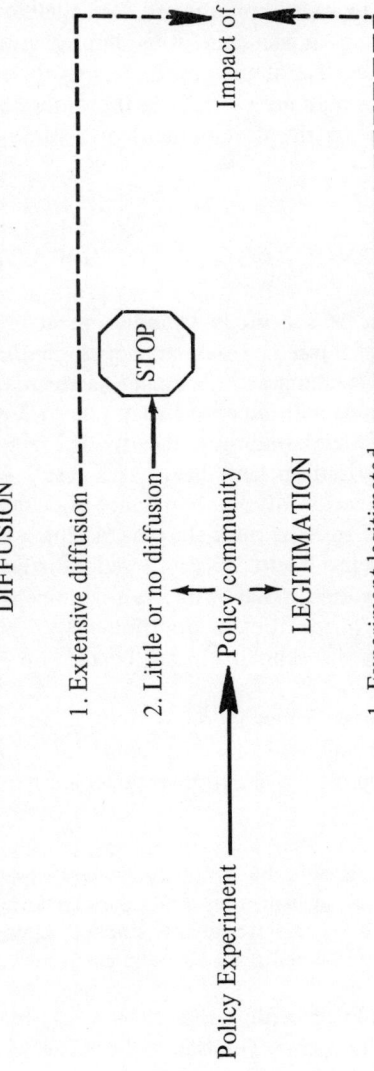

Source: Compiled by the author.

communication and legitimation strategies are crucial in mitigating impact; and, finally but not surprisingly, organizational goals and behavior have a great deal to do with this process. The literature that we shall subsequently review considers all of these points. There is, consequently, a symbiotic relationship between the study of evaluation impact and other impact studies. The other studies give some important clues about the approaches to the study of evaluation impact and the results one may anticipate. On the other hand, evaluation-impact studies can contribute to the development of a more general policy-impact theory.

ON THE IMPONDERABILITY OF IMPACT

One common theme can be succinctly stated: Impact tends to be problematical and indirect. Critics of Supreme Court impact studies have increasingly emphasized this point. Legal scholars are no longer as surprised at finding a disparity between court decisions and impact as they once were. It may be, as some have argued, that this general finding is due to the fact that the court decisions receiving the most attention have been, as a result of their controversial nature, biased in the direction of noncompliance and impact mitigation. In his study of police reactions to legal rules, Jerome Skolnick argues that both defenders and critics of Supreme Court decisions tend to overestimate their likely impact. Rather, decisions tend to have "differential impact" in a stratified society.[11] In short, our standard operating assumption should be that impact is indirect and problematical. Current scholarship has been more cautious in estimating impact.[12]

Jeffrey Pressman and Aaron Wildavsky show quite convincingly how this skeptical orientation applies to policies other than courts'. On the basis of their analysis of an economic-development and antipoverty program in Oakland, they conclude:

> Our normal expectations should be that new programs will fail to get off the ground and that, at best, they will take considerable time to get started. The cards in this world are stacked against things happening, as so much effort is required to make them move.[13]

What makes their argument more forceful is that there was a high level of consensus and support by all relevant actors. The Oakland policies were not *Miranda v. Arizona* or *Brown v. Board of Education* or the federal antipoverty program. Quite the contrary. None of the groups, organizations, or individuals that were involved opposed the substantive goals of the program.

The literature on policy evaluation has recently begun to sound a similar note. For many evaluators, however, this has not progressed beyond a naive bewilderment that others could consistently fail to consider their findings. Often this bewilderment is coupled with a broad attribution of blame to policy administrators, who are portrayed as belligerent, recalcitrant, narrow-minded, or hopelessly outdated. Even the more sophisticated analyses are uncertain about the implications of these disappointing conclusions. To some of the contributors to the Rossi and Williams volume, for example, the utility of the experimental model itself is opened up to question; to others a reaffirmation of experimental principles and a call for their more rigorous application are the more reasonable responses. In spite of their lack of definitiveness, these analyses are useful for two reasons. First, although the writers seldom explicitly draw a conclusion, the lack of impact is readily apparent.[14] Second, some of these writers have argued that the problems of limited impact are endemic.[15]

WHY IMPACT IS IMPONDERABLE

Policy Content and Communication

Scholars working in all three bodies of literature agree that the less ambiguous a policy, the less problematical is its impact. According to the policy-evaluation literature, for an evaluation to have a relatively direct impact it must be specific and concrete enough to operationalize easily. Carol Weiss, for example, suggests that when evaluators fail to probe the accepted description of the policies they are examining, it becomes more difficult for administrators to interpret exactly what was tested and how.[16] On the basis of his review of court impact studies, Stephen Wasby hypothesizes that, "information about the specifics of how to comply with a decision will bring greater impact than [will] a general discussion of the case."[17] A little guidance, it seems, may be the best cure for a case of bureaucratic inertia. But the problem is not simply one of linguistic clarity. Policies, as Pressman and Wildavsky suggest, can incorporate conflicting goals, mask potential conflicts, or reflect uncertainties as to how to proceed.

A related proposition is that impact is mitigated by endemic, structural characteristics of the policy itself. Certain policies require yes or no answers, while others are more flexible. A community, for example, either fluoridates its water, or it does not. The range of feasible sex education policies on the other hand makes it less likely that the impact will be direct.[18] By their very nature, some policies can inform implementers explicitly what actions are called for; others are necessarily more vague.

The characteristics of the policy-issuing institutions can also affect impact. Each organization or institution may exhibit different strengths and weaknesses in implementation. The Supreme Court, for instance, exercises a great deal of moral suasion as a result of historical and cultural reservoirs of support. But the range of cases in which it may bring these strengths to bear is limited. As Kenneth Dolbeare and Phillip Hammond argue:

> Courts must await the initiation of cases by parties with the psychic and financial capacity to challenge authoritative decision makers, and then they must work within the narrow confines of the law and its application in the particular relationships of the existing parties.[19]

Because the range of the application of court decisions, even those of the U.S. Supreme Court, is frequently uncertain, there is often ample opportunity for someone to argue or to believe that the decision is not applicable here. It is inherently very difficult for evaluators to argue that an evaluation of specific Program A also applies to Program B. Program B administrators can argue that "our program is different and that evaluation does not apply to us." The problem here is not simply ambiguity. Rather the question is the degree to which one jurisdiction is persuaded of the analogousness of another's circumstances. Being an outsider hurts the evaluator by making the message less relevant.

Though court impact analysts have argued the need for better understanding of the relationship between policy content and policy impact, such links have not been sufficiently developed. The evaluation literature makes some link between content and process by stressing the need to develop simultaneously a policy evaluation and a concrete strategy for getting the evaluation implemented.[20] Evaluation is presumably more effective if it is clear how each component part of the program is affected and how it must be changed. Again, however, this link between policy content and implementation is more suggestive than precise.

Pressman and Wildavsky offer another insight. Implementation, they suggest, is frustrated by the fragmentation of the communication process and by the autonomy that implementers have from policymakers as well as from each other. The greater the number of parties that must be involved with implementation, the more problematical the impact. Pluralism lessens the probability of impact.

Court impact studies reinforce this generalization. The number of community elites that a school superintendent has to placate affects his ability to act consistently with U.S. Supreme Court school prayer decisions. Decentralized police force and a tradition of local control over law enforcement affect the impact of police interrogation decisions.

As a whole, these studies suggest that though clarity is an important factor, other characteristics of the communication process may be more important. Typically, impact and implementation do not involve a straightforward diffusion of innovation, nor does the lack of impact evolve solely from refusal to listen. Coercion, Rodgers and Bullock demonstrate, is undeniably an important factor,[21] but other, more reciprocal interactions deserve serious attention. Implicit in this notion is the need to pay greater attention to the tactics used by policymakers and implementers to bring about behavior change in the absence of automatic acceptance and outright rejection.

We might refine our previous proposition somewhat and state it as: Impact is mitigated by the number of parties that must be involved and the strategies available to get the parties to behave in a way that maximizes impact.

The Organizational Context

All three bodies of literature support the proposition that the more a policy is either consistent or inconsistent with the goals of an organization, the more predictable the implementation of that policy. A policy congruent with organizational goals will be straightforwardly implemented, ceteris paribus. One that requires fundamental definition of an organization's goals, or threatens them, is also predictable, but the prediction is that the policy will not be implemented. Those policies in between are most problematic. This is well established in the court impact literature. Several scholars have emphasized that organizational priorities and costs are important determinants of rule-compliance.[22]

A recent study of the impact of the Supreme Court's abortion decisions shows how direct the relationship between costs and impact can be. Hospitals with the most free beds were the most likely to increase their abortion offerings. The empty beds were slack resources that the hospitals could afford to use to bring about this innovation in their service delivery. Similarly, the diffusion of innovation literature shows that organizations with slack resources are more likely to innovate.[23]

Evaluation literature discusses this proposition in terms of the instability that evaluation creates for an organization. The more alterations that are implied by an evaluation's implementation, the less likely it is that the organization will accept it.[24] Indeed, evaluation and organizational goals may be naturally in tension. Wildavsky stated it this way:

> "Move over," says evaluative man to his forebearers, "you boys have got it all wrong." The organization doesn't matter unless it meets social needs. Procedures don't matter unless they facilitate the accomplishment of objectives encompassing these needs. Objectives are not properly specified unless they can be achieved at reasonable cost compared to alternative possibilities. Efficiency is beside the point if the objective being achieved at lowest cost is inappropriate. Getting political support doesn't mean that the programs devised to fulfill objectives are good; it just means they had more votes than the others. Both objectives and resources, says evaluative man, must

be continuously modified to achieve optimal response to social need.[25]

Administrators may see evaluations as challenges to organizational goals. Workers may see them as threats to their jobs. These threats are compounded when the source of the evaluation comes from outside the organization or agency.

The review of the literature suggests another proposition about the effect of organization priorities: Under some circumstances, organizational priorities may mitigate policy impact even when the policymakers and those being impacted upon display great consensus over implementing the policy. Dolbeare and Hammond illustrate this nicely when they show that the impact of school prayer decisions was limited by the simple fact that school superintendents and their bureaucracies had many other important things to do and other goals to accomplish. The adoption of other policies was more important, and the educational policymakers were not willing to risk the conflict that might have evolved. This conflict, after all, could adversely affect other, more important issues.

Again, Pressman and Wildavsky are especially useful. They deal with a policy for which consensus is high and present a list of circumstances where organizational priorities mitigate impact even when the organization believes in and accepts the substantial ends of the program. These are the circumstances that lead to opposition or failure to facilitate even when consensus is high:[26]
1. When there is direct incompatibility with other goals.
2. When there is no direct incompatibility but there is a view that other goals are more important.
3. When there is simultaneous commitment to other programs.
4. When there is a difference of opinion over proper leadership and organizational roles, or over legal and procedural matters.

The Political and Structural Context

Curiously, all of these studies lack a sense of the political context. In the case of evaluation literature, it is perhaps not so surprising because the task of the evaluation researcher, who is sometimes a paid consultant, is typically to focus on organizational response.

Other reviews of the court impact literature advocate the importance of the political context, but perhaps because the empirical studies give them little to work with, the hypotheses are not very precise. For example, Wasby's five-page list of hypotheses listed under the category "political environment" says virtually nothing about the structure of local government or of general patterns of political participation in policymaking.[27] Likewise, though Pressman and

Wildavsky's study purports to be about the very guts of politics—and in many ways it is—it is too situational to offer much help here.

There are so few studies that consider these structural factors that we cannot build propositions on the basis of the literature we have heretofore discussed. Studies of local policy adoption have stressed the importance of structural factors like bureaucratization, reformism, and participation.[28] If we assume that, (a) policy impact is part of this policy process, (b) some of the same strategies and organization may come into play in trying to implement policy, and (c) comparative analysis is called for, then our view is that political context deserves more careful attention.

Generalizations, such as those set forth above, provide us with some guidance toward understanding the policy impact of policy evaluation. But they are not sufficient as an end in themselves. They must be anchored in the texture of actual cases. We must continually translate our discrete, abstract categories—impact, ambiguity, structure—into the real world. And so we turn our attention to a specific case—the impact of the Kansas City Preventive Patrol Experiment upon the police community. Although our findings are preliminary, they serve to provide some flesh to the skeleton.

AFTER THE EXPERIMENT: THE CASE OF KANSAS CITY

Before policy impact can be observed, the diffusion and legitimation processes must occur. An experiment that does not travel through the communication networks of the policy community will make few waves; one that travels fast but is constantly challenged will also have little impact.

We had initially suspected that the policy community in law enforcement was too fragmented, decentralized, and localistic to diffuse information very rapidly, even about a blockbuster bit of news like Kansas City. One way in which members of a policy community communicate with each other is through professional periodicals, and our content analysis of a sample of professional journals revealed little attention paid to Kansas City from the first leaks to the summer of 1975. Of the handful of professional journal articles even to mention the experiment, few paid attention to the policy significance of the results. The most common source of information was Burnham's New York *Times* article in November 1973, which spilled the beans.

We suggest, however, that bad news travels fast. Among some policy communities, news travels via the written word. In policing, communications networks are more commonly face-to-face. In some preliminary conversations we had with local police officials in the summer of 1975, we found near-unanimous recognition of the report, and several raised the issue spontaneously. Much of the communications process was serendipitous—through a sergeant who had attended a training session with a Kansas City officer, by word of mouth from other local chiefs, and the like.

But much of the credit for the diffusion belongs to the accident of the Burnham article, which came out well in advance of the official conclusion and publication of experimental results. And the rest of the credit belongs to the Foundation itself. The Kansas City results were not merely disseminated; they were orchestrated. Mailing lists of mayors, managers, police chiefs, sheriffs, leaders of the policy community, and academics were compiled and used to send out an initial mailing of 7,000 copies of the summary report. By the end of 1975, about 6,000 additional copies had been dispersed. In contrast to typical policy evaluations that get buried in academic journals or a bureaucrat's filing cabinets, the Kansas City researchers combined policy analysis with public relations.

The process of legitimation is just as critical as the process of diffusion. The most widely publicized experiment may still face a hostile reception. Policy research that contravenes a century and a half of conventional wisdom will not automatically be received favorably. Conventional wisdom dies hard. How policy analysis gets legitimated is a process about which little is known. Nor is much known about the role that policy communities play in this process. All appearances suggest that, in law enforcement, the policy community is highly decentralized, but remarkably consensual. There is probably more dissensus at the top than at the bottom. The particular position of the Police Foundation itself, and its controversial president, Patrick Murphy, was not incidentally related to the difficulty of legitimation. In the national law-enforcement policy community, Murphy and the Foundation are identified with a relatively more liberal police policy. One of Murphy's longtime antagonists within the law-enforcement community, Chief Edward Davis of Los Angeles, took it upon himself to author one of the most systematic critiques of the Kansas City experiment yet published.[29] How the process of legitimation proceeds, then, is critical in determining the ultimate policy impact of policy experimentation.

AVOIDING THE CONFRONTATION OF UNPLEASANT FINDINGS

There are as many ways to avoid confronting unpleasant experimental evidence as there are ways to avoid changing one's opinion. The cognitive dissonance literature suggests a multiplicity of ways in which individuals can avoid unpleasant threats to long-held opinions.[30] Organizations can also find numerous ways of avoiding unpleasant threats to their organizational performance. Fortunately, we can assess the policy impact of policy experimentation by drawing upon the three bodies of literature—compliance, implementation, and impact analyses—which we addressed earlier. Our examination supports the general conclusion from these literatures that impact is problematical and indirect.

In spite of our expectations derived from the literature on cognitive dissonance, we found little in the way of flat denial as a way of avoiding confrontation. We were frankly surprised, in our conversations with police officials, that they accepted the possible conclusions of Kansas City with equanimity. One captain "drastically disagreed" that more police-patrol resources could reduce crime and held that preventive patrol "doesn't deter anything." Most agreed with the observation of one chief that "it's hard to tell" whether police patrol has much impact on crime. Preventive patrol may be an example of conventional behavior rather than of conventional wisdom.

Organizations, though, have a multiplicity of goals. Policies that impinge upon one goal, without regard to the others, may receive little organizational attention. Routine patrol is rationalized in the textbooks because it prevents crime, and makes the city safer. Police chiefs are also convinced that patrol makes people feel safer, whether it actually makes them safer or not. Organizations satisfy political demands upon them for allocation of resources. Neighborhood groups that believe—rightly or wrongly—that more police resources will make them safer can hardly be ignored. The overwhelming evidence of Kansas City demonstrated that the fear of crime was not altered in the three experimental neighborhoods. But departments elsewhere can hardly placate their citizens with consolations like that. As we emphasized, few investigators of the politics of evaluation pay attention to the expressly political dimensions of the impact process. Thus they have overlooked the fact that even when the relevant policymakers are sympathetic to experimental findings, the relevant constituencies may not be.

The basic structure of an experiment often provides little positive direction even to the most favorably disposed administrator. Knowing that one should do something—or perhaps even stop doing something—is different from knowing what exactly must be done. The Kansas City experiment was one of that class of policy experiments which essentially failed to disprove the null hypothesis of "no effect." The finding that the introduction of a new policy produces no effect (as in the educational performance contracting experiments) cues a policymaker not to implement. But the finding that an on-going policy, one that lies at the core of organizational responsibilities, has no effect, does not suggest new policies to implement. Even if resistance to old policies does not die hard, rebutting a null hypothesis does not insure change. One needs to know what does work, not only what does not.

One of the most common difficulties in implementing compliance with court decisions is the argument that "it doesn't apply here." This is a problem in the transferability of evaluative research. The policy-implementation literature emphasizes that the multiplicity of actors reduces the probability of implementation. And more than 20,000 local jurisdictions constitute indeed a multiplicity of actors. In perhaps the cleverest broadside against the Kansas City experiment, Davis and Knowles emphasize that "before a law enforcement administrator attempts to identify his situation or jurisdiction with the Kansas City finding, it is imperative that he ask himself the following set of questions..."[31] and proceed to identify (exactly) twenty questions designed to differentiate departments from Kansas City's. The scientific model emphasizes adherence to controlled experimental conditions, which permits, in turn, generalization to wider categories of cases. The experiential model of most police officials tends to emphasize the idiosyncratic, the localized factors, and the uniqueness of "our town." To the degree that the experiential model prevails within a policy community, the cards are always stacked against the policy impact of policy experimentation.

Our initial assessment suggests that the greatest difficulty in securing attention to policy experimentation may well not be flat denial or initial rejection of unpleasant findings. As both the court impact research and Pressman and Wildavsky demonstrate, policy implementation is problematic even with high consensus. We detect a similar phenomenon. While an articulate and hard-core wing of the police policy community rejects flatly the validity of the experiment, the larger police policy community is more sanguine. The more appropriate questions, therefore, are often not those of why people disagree with experimenting findings, but why, even with an umbrella of neutrality or acceptance, impact remains problematical.

CONCLUSION: ON EVALUATING EVALUATIONS

Dentler has drawn attention to certain parallels between the role of the policy evaluator and that of a mendicant friar. Rossi, in outlining Dentler's discussion, notes of the evaluator that:

> Like the friar, he is produced by an institution, in this case a university graduate social science department, which is not oriented toward the "real world." The evaluator is also at the mercy of his clients, just as the friar is dependent on the strength and distribution of Christian charity. But most important, the evaluator judges his own activities in terms of the standards set by his academic mentors and peers in the same way as the mendicant friar retains the otherworldliness of the monastery in which he served his novitiate.[32]

Whereas the friar exercises his principles safely tucked away in the monastery on the hill, however, the evaluator wields his "scientific" standards like a broadsword, hacking away uncompromisedly at the standard beliefs and assumptions that the policy administrator relies upon in his day-to-day battles. As in all holy wars, the cause is righteous and the promises are great. But one of the intentions of this chapter has been to raise as issues some of the reasons why these promises have not been swiftly fulfilled. To note this is also to raise the question of whether policy experimentation is the most effective, most efficient instrument for achieving the knowledge-guided policy that is its professed goal.

The cost of social experimentation is not trivial. The New Jersey Negative Income Tax experiment, which was designed to test the effect of various negative tax structures on recipients' motivation to work, cost more than 10 million dollars. Added to these budgeted expenses must be such indirect costs as those incurred by the disruption of the organization or program under investigation, and the constraints imposed upon the administration while the experimental conditions are being maintained.

But the fact that the impact of policy experimentation is problematic and indirect, and the costs high and clear, does not suggest that no impact has occurred. We are far from declaring that the "experimenting society" is a clearly undesirable or infeasible goal. Rather, we suggest that the implementation and impact literature has proved that the policy process does not stop with the enunciation of dicta and policies. What we have argued here is that the "experimenting society" poses equivalent problems in implementation. Evaluation and experimentation are political processes, directly touching organizations, their goals, and their constituents. What happens after the experiment is concluded may be more important than experimental findings in determining its ultimate impact.

NOTES

1. Donald Campbell is the most noted articulator of the benefits of this experimental approach. See also Henry W. Riecken and Robert F. Boruch, *Social Experimentation: A Method for Planning and Evaluating Social Intervention* (New York: Academic Press, 1974).

2. Peter H. Rossi and Walter Williams, eds., *Evaluating Social Programs* (New York: Seminar Press, 1972).

3. Francis G. Caro, "Evaluation Research: An Overview," in *Readings in Evaluation Research*, ed. Francis G. Caro (New York: Russell Sage Foundation, 1971), p. 12.

4. George Kelling et al., *The Kansas City Preventive Patrol Experiment: Summary Report* (Washington, D.C.: Police Foundation, 1974).

5. Quoted by David Burnham, New York *Times*, November 19, 1973, p. 1.

6. Kelling, op. cit., Preface, pp. v-vi.

7. Judith S. Dahmann, *A Review of Six Research Studies on the Relationship Between Police Patrol Activity and Crime* (Washington, D.C.: The Mitre Corporation, 1974).

8. Walter Williams, *Social Policy Research and Analysis* (New York: American Elsevier, 1971), pp. 103-04.

9. On the autonomy and variety of local departments, see John A. Gardiner, *Traffic and the Police: Variations in Law Enforcement* (Cambridge, Mass.: Harvard University Press, 1969).

10. Jack L. Walker, "The Diffusion of Knowledge and Policy Change: Toward a Theory of Agenda Setting," paper prepared for delivery at the 1974 annual meeting of the American Political Science Association, August 29-September 2, 1974, pp. 4-5.

11. Jerome Skolnick, *Justice Without Trial* (New York: Wiley, 1966), p. 219.

12. James Levine, "Methodological Concerns in Studying Supreme Court Efficacy," *Law and Society Review* 4 (1970): 583; Stephen L. Wasby, "The Supreme Court's Impact," *Law and Society Review* 5 (1970): 49; and Neal Milner, "Supreme Court Effectiveness and the Police Organization," *Law and Contemporary Problems* 36 (1971): 485.

13. Jeffrey L. Pressman and Aaron B. Wildavsky, *Implementation* (Berkeley: University of California Press, 1973), p. 109.

14. See the Rossi and Williams, op. cit.

15. Martin Trow, "Methodological Problems in Evaluation of Innovation," in Caro, op. cit., pp. 81-94; Aaron Wildavsky, *Evaluation as an Organizational Problem* (London: Center for Environmental Studies, 1972).

16. Carol H. Weiss, "Utilization of Evaluation: Toward Comparative Study," in Caro, op. cit., pp. 136-42.

17. Stephen L. Wasby, *The Impact of the U.S. Supreme Court: Some Perspectives* (Homewood, Ill.: Dorsey Press, 1970), p. 252. Wasby argues that more information about specifics leads to greater compliance. It could also have the opposite effect. For example, if one is more certain that the policy is contrary to one's values, then one might be less willing to comply. For that reason we stated our proposition to suggest that clarity is more likely to encourage more direct responses without specifying whether the response is pro or con.

18. James Hottois and Neal Milner, *The Sex Education Controversy* (Lexington, Mass.: D.C. Heath, 1975).

19. Kenneth Dolbeare and Phillip Hammond, *The School Prayer Decision* (Chicago: University of Chicago Press, 1971), pp. 135-36.

20. Wildavsky, op. cit.; Weiss, op. cit.

21. See Chapter 9 of this volume.

22. Harrell R. Rodgers, Jr., and Charles S. Bullock, III, *Law and Social Change: Civil Rights Laws and Their Consequences* (New York: McGraw-Hill, 1972); Levine, op. cit.; Samuel Krislov, "The Perimeters of Power," in *Compliance and the Law*, ed. Krislov et al. (Beverly Hills: Sage Publications, 1972), pp. 333-50.

23. D. W. Brady and K. A. Kemp, "The Supreme Court's Abortion Rulings and Social Change," *Social Science Quarterly* (forthcoming). This study adds a further dimension by considering court impact as a form of innovation. Hospitals that were less well off were more likely to expand the facilities available for abortion. On the surface, their findings are paradoxical; innovation is typically related to high levels of resources. In this case, the paradox is explained by the measures that Brady and Kemp used to measure resource strength. Poorer hospitals were those with more empty beds. Thus, these hospitals in effect had a greater amount of slack resources.

24. Caro, op. cit., p. 7.

25. Wildavsky, op. cit., pp. 13-14.

26. Pressman and Wildavsky, op. cit., pp. 99-102.

27. Wasby, *The Impact of the U.S. Supreme Court*, pp. 252-57.

28. Robert Alford and Harry Scoble, *Bureaucracy and Participation* (Chicago: Rand McNally, 1970); Robert L. Lineberry and Edmund P. Fowler, "Reformism and Public Policies in American Cities," in *City Politics and Public Policy*, ed. James Q. Wilson (New York: Wiley, 1968), pp. 127-48.

29. Edward M. Davis and Lyle Knowles, "An Evaluation of the Kansas City Patrol Experiment," *The Police Chief*, June 1975, pp. 22-27. See also Richard C. Larson, "What

Happened to Patrol Operations in Kansas City? A Review of the Kansas City Preventive Patrol Experiment," *Journal of Criminal Justice* 3 (1975): 267-97.

30. See Roger Brown, *Social Psychology* (New York: Free Press, 1965), Chapter 11.

31. Davis and Knowles, op. cit., p. 27.

32. Peter H. Rossi, "Testing for Success and Failure in Social Action," in Rossi and Williams, op. cit., p. 37. Robert Dentler's paper, "The Phenomenology of the Evaluative Researcher," was presented at a conference on evaluation research sponsored by the American Academy of Arts and Sciences, May 2-5, 1969.

ABOUT THE EDITOR AND THE CONTRIBUTORS

LAWRENCE BAUM is Assistant Professor of Political Science at Ohio State University, specializing in the fields of judicial politics and public policy analysis. He has written on the implementation of judicial decisions, judicial regulation of access to litigants, and federal policymaking on patents.

CHARLES S. BULLOCK, III is Professor of Political Science at the University of Houston. His primary areas of teaching and research are policy analysis and legislative politics. In addition to writing a number of articles, he is coauthor with Harrell R. Rodgers, Jr., of *Coercion to Compliance* (forthcoming), *Racial Equality in America*, and *Law and Social Change*. He is coeditor of *Black Political Attitudes* and *The New Politics*.

LIEF H. CARTER teaches Political Science at the University of Georgia. His doctoral dissertation, "The Limits of Order," won the 1973 Edward Corwin Award of the American Political Science Association and has since been published by D.C. Heath.

NICHOLAS ELLIOTT is Assistant Professor of Political Science and Director of Metropolitan Region Studies at the University of Wisconsin-River Falls. Among his publications are "Attitudinal Change Associated with the Introduction of a Municipal Information System" (with Sherman Wyman), and "Receptivity of Local Elites Toward Planning" (with Russell W. Getter), in *Journal of the American Institute of Planners*.

MALCOLM M. FEELEY is Assistant Professor of Political Science at the University of Wisconsin-Madison, and formerly a Guggenheim Criminal Justice Fellow at the Yale Law School and Research Associate at the Institution for Social and Policy Studies at Yale, pursuing research on the administration of criminal justice. He is currently engaged in a study of the process of adjudication in lower criminal courts and an examination of reform in criminal-justice systems. His articles have appeared in such journals as *Law and Society Review*, *Polity*, and *Ethics*, and he has contributed chapters to several books.

JOHN A. GARDINER is Professor of Political Science at the University of Illinois at Chicago Circle. Among his publications are *Traffic and the Police*, *The Politics of Corruption*, *Theft of the City* (edited with David J. Olson), and *Crime and Criminal Justice* (edited with Michael Mulkey). He formerly taught at the University of Wisconsin and the State University of New York at Stony Brook, and was on the staff of the National Institute of Law Enforcement and Criminal Justice.

JEFFREY HENIG is a graduate student in Political Science at Northwestern University. His fields of interest include urban politics, public policy, and collective action.

CHARLES A. JOHNSON is Assistant Professor at Texas Tech University, having completed his Ph.D. at the University of Kentucky. His field of specialization is judicial process and judicial behavior.

ROBERT L. LINEBERRY is Associate Professor of Political Science and Urban Affairs at Northwestern University. He is coauthor of *Urban Politics and Public Policy* and coeditor of *The New Urban Politics*. His principal research interests concern public policy and the problem of inequality in the city.

LYNN M. MATHER is Assistant Professor of Government at Dartmouth College, specializing in the field of administration of justice. Among her publications are "Some Determinants of the Method of Case Disposition: Decision-Making by Public Defenders in Los Angeles" (in *Law and Society Review*) and an article in *The Potential for Reform of Criminal Justice* (edited by Herbert Jacob).

NEAL A. MILNER is Associate Professor of Political Science at the University of Hawaii. From 1974-76, he was a Visiting Associate Professor in the Department of Political Science and the Center for Urban Affairs at Northwestern University. He is the author of *The Court and Local Law Enforcement* and *The Sex Education Controversy* (with James Hottois). He is currently conducting research on the impact of police reform, and on community crime-prevention programs.

STUART NAGEL is Professor of Political Science at the University of Illinois at Champaign-Urbana and a member of the Illinois Bar. He is the coauthor with Marian Neef of the forthcoming book *Policy Optimizing Models and the Legal Process* (Lexington, Mass.: D.C. Heath, 1977) and editor of *Modeling the Criminal Justice System* (Sage Criminal Justice Annuals, 1977). He was recently a visiting fellow at the National Institute of Law Enforcement and Criminal Justice.

MARIAN NEEF is a Ph.D. candidate in political science at the University of Illinois at Champaign-Urbana. She has published criminal-justice articles in such periodicals as the *Journal of Urban Law, New York Law Forum*, and *Et Al*. She has a number of forthcoming articles in press dealing with criminal justice decision-making models.

HARRELL R. RODGERS, JR., is Professor of Political Science at the University of Houston. His latest book is *Coercion to Compliance* (forthcoming), with Charles S. Bullock, III.

AUSTIN SARAT is Assistant Professor of Political Science at Yale University and at Amherst College, specializing in public law. He has published articles in the *American Political Science Review, American Politics Quarterly, American Journal of Political Science*, and *Law and Society Review*, and has authored a book entitled *The Rule of Law and the American Legal System*.

DAVID SEIDMAN is a Staff Associate at the Social Science Research Council's Center for Coordination of Research on Social Indicators in Washington, D.C. Among his publications are articles on crime statistics, administrative structure, and statistical methodology.

WESLEY G. SKOGAN is Associate Professor of Political Science and Urban Affairs at Northwestern University, specializing in crime policy. During 1974-76 he was a Visiting Fellow at the National Institute of Law Enforcement and Criminal Justice of the Law Enforcement Assistance Administration, where he worked on an analysis of the victimization survey data being collected by the Bureau of the Census.

THOMAS M. UHLMAN is Assistant Professor of Political Science at the University of Missouri-St. Louis, specializing in the fields of public law and ethnic politics. His recent professional activities include papers presented at the American, Southern and Midwest Political Science Association meetings and an article, "Black Populations and School Integration—A Research Note," in the March 1973 issue of *Phylon*. His dissertation, "Racial Justice: Black Judges and Defendants in the Metro City Criminal Court, 1968-74," was awarded the 1976 Edwin S. Corwin Award of the American Political Science Association for the best Ph.D. dissertation in public law.

SUSAN O. WHITE is Associate Professor of Political Science at the University of New Hampshire, specializing in public law and criminal justice. She is presently on leave at the National Academy of Sciences as Study Director for an NAS evaluation of the research program of the National Institute of Law Enforcement and Criminal Justice. Among her publications are "A Perspective on Police Professionalism," in *Law and Society Review*; "Controlling Police Behavior," in *Police: Perspectives, Problems and Prospects*, edited by Donald E. J. MacNamara and Marc Riedel; and "Politics and Evaluation in LEAA," in *Management and Policy Science in American Government*, edited by Michael White.

RELATED TITLES
Published by
Praeger Special Studies

*COST-BENEFIT ANALYSIS
         E. J. Mishan

ISSUES IN CRIMINAL JUSTICE: Planning and Evaluation
         edited by Marc Riedel
         and Duncan Chappell

*SOCIAL SCIENCE AND PUBLIC POLICY IN THE UNITED STATES
         Irving Louis Horowitz and
         James Everett Katz

TOWARD A JUST AND EFFECTIVE SENTENCING SYSTEM:
Agenda for Legislative Reform
         Pierce O'Donnell, Michael J.
         Churgin, and Dennis E. Curtis

URBAN PROBLEMS AND PUBLIC POLICY CHOICES
         edited by Joel Bergsman
         and Howard L. Wiener

*Also available in paperback as a Praeger Special Studies Student Edition.